HAMLET

The RSC Shakespeare

Edited by Jonathan Bate and Eric Rasmussen

Chief Associate Editor: Héloïse Sénéchal

Associate Editors: Trey Jansen, Eleanor Lowe, Lucy Munro, Dee Anna Phares, Jan Sewell

Hamlet

Textual editing: Eric Rasmussen

Introduction and Shakespeare's Career in the Theatre: Jonathan Bate

Commentary: Héloïse Sénéchal

Scene-by-Scene Analysis: Esme Miskimmin

In Performance: Karin Brown (RSC stagings), Jan Sewell (overview), Jonathan Bate (captions)

The Director's Cut (interviews by Jonathan Bate and Kevin Wright): Ron Daniels, John Caird, Michael Boyd

Editorial Advisory Board

Gregory Doran, Chief Associate Director, Royal Shakespeare Company

Jim Davis, Professor of Theatre Studies, University of Warwick, UK

Charles Edelman, Senior Lecturer, Edith Cowan University, Western Australia

Lukas Erne, Professor of Modern English Literature, Université de Genève, Switzerland

Maria Evans, Director of Education, Royal Shakespeare Company

Akiko Kusunoki, Tokyo Woman's Christian University, Japan

Ron Rosenbaum, author and journalist, New York, USA

James Shapiro, Professor of English and Comparative Literature, Columbia University, USA

Tiffany Stern, Fellow and Tutor in English, University of Oxford, UK

The RSC Shakespeare

WILLIAM SHAKESPEARE

HAMLET

Edited by
Jonathan Bate and Eric Rasmussen

Introduced by Jonathan Bate

Macmillan

Published by arrangement with Modern Library, an imprint of The Random House Publishing Group, a division of Random House, Inc.

Published 2008 by
MACMILLAN PUBLISHERS LTD
Houndmills, Basingstoke, Hampshire RG21 6XS
Companies and representatives throughout the world

ISBN-13   978–0–230–21786–7 hardback
ISBN-13   978–0–230–21787–4 paperback

This book is printed on paper suitable for recycling and made from fully managed and sustained forest sources. Logging, pulping and manufacturing processes are expected to conform to the environmental regulations of the country of origin.

A catalogue record for this book is available from the British Library.

10   9   8   7   6   5   4
17   16   15   14   13

Printed in China

CONTENTS

INTRODUCTION

HAMLET'S QUESTIONS

The mood of *Hamlet* is set by its opening exchange: 'Who's there?' 'Nay, answer me . . . .' The play creates the illusion of asking as many questions of its audience and interpreters as we may ask of it. Shakespeare won't tell us who he is or where he stands. Instead, he makes us – and our culture – reveal ourselves. That is the source of his endurance and one of the reasons why *Hamlet* has long been regarded as his greatest, or at least his most characteristic, play.

The Prince of Denmark himself is the most famously inter-rogative of all dramatic characters. He is Shakespeare's ultimate man of words. The actor who plays him has to learn over 340 speeches; the role has a higher proportion of its play's words (nearly forty per cent) than any other in Shakespeare. Hamlet's favourite intellectual move is to make an action that he witnesses – a player weeping, a skull tossed from an old grave – into the occasion for speculation: 'What's Hecuba to him, or he to Hecuba, / That he should weep for her?', 'Where be your gibes now, your gambols, your songs, your flashes of merriment that were wont to set the table on a roar?' In watching or reading the play, we are moved, like Hamlet, to ask the big questions: What should we believe? How should we act? What happens after death? In whose version of the truth should we have faith?

Horatio, the commentator who comes closest to being the voice of the audience, says that he 'in part' believes stories about ghosts and portents. His qualifier is a watchword for the whole play. Humankind is *in part* a god-like creature, full of mental and verbal powers, 'The beauty of the world, the paragon of animals'. But, to take the other part, we are also 'quintessence of dust' – the

1

politician, the lawyer, the heroic man of action (Alexander the Great) and the humble clown (Yorick) all end up in the same place.

Like the wood in *A Midsummer Night's Dream*, but with tragic as opposed to comic consequences, Elsinore is a place where 'everything seems double'. Rosencrantz and Guildenstern are a double act engaged to spy on Hamlet, with the result that he has 'at each ear a hearer'. Hardly anyone in the play seems able to speak without producing a double epithet: 'the sensible and true avouch / Of mine own eyes', 'the gross and scope of my opinion', 'post-haste and rummage in the land', 'the grace and blush of modesty', and so on. Stage props also come in pairs: two contrasting portraits of two brothers, a pair of rapiers (one of which is sharpened and anointed for the kill), two skulls. Entrances seem to repeat themselves: the appearances of the Ghost; Hamlet overheard in meditation, first with a book, later with his reflections on being and not being; the king and Gertrude in their respective private rooms after the trauma of the *Mousetrap* play; Ophelia's two mad scenes.

The story of a son seeking vengeance for his father's death is doubled after Hamlet kills Polonius: 'by the image of my cause I see / The portraiture of his', remarks Hamlet of Laertes. The motif is redoubled in the figure of Young Fortinbras out to avenge the defeat of Old Fortinbras. A further commentary is provided by the Player's speech about Pyrrhus, son of Achilles, furiously seeking atonement for his father's loss by slaughtering old King Priam. But this might be construed as a negative example: Priam himself is an 'unnervèd father' and his slaughter moves a wife and mother, Hecuba, to distraction. If Hamlet were to become a killing machine like Pyrrhus, he would be diminishing himself to the inhumanity of his adversary, besides emotionally destroying his mother: that is his dilemma 'bounded in a nutshell'.

Hamlet is a student, a model for the perpetual students and idealists who populate later literature, especially in Germany and Russia. Like Shakespeare's other highly intellectual drama, *Troilus and Cressida*, this is a play that debates the great questions of epistemology, ethics and metaphysics. 'Humanism', the dominant educational theory of the sixteenth century, proposed that wisdom was to be derived from book learning. The student developed the arts of language through his rhetorical training, while collecting the wisdom of the ancients in the form of citations and *sententiae* copied into a commonplace book. Polonius' maxims on how Laertes should behave when away from home, climaxing in the cliché 'to thine own self be true', are classic examples. The art of 'reason' was refined through the study of 'common themes', one of which was 'death of fathers'. Reason and judgement were supposed to prevail over will and passion. The Stoicism of Seneca provided a model for the use of 'philosophy' as protection against the fickleness of fortune and the vicissitudes of court politics.

Hamlet's uncle must once have been a good student. He is a master of balanced rhetoric, the measure and decorum of his verse belying his crime against the order of nature and state:

... as 'twere with a defeated joy,
With one auspicious and one dropping eye,
With mirth in funeral and with dirge in marriage,
In equal scale weighing delight and dole.

He thinks he knows, and that everyone in the court will accept, what is the appropriate length of time to mourn the death of a brother, husband, father.

Hamlet despises such propriety. He is not interested in the 'common' way of behaving. He speaks for the 'particular', the individual. 'Mourning duties', maintained for a set period, are to him mere outward show, the signs of a 'seeming' with which he refuses to play along. He has 'that within which passeth show': the solitary self is set against social custom. He has returned from university determined to 'wipe away' all the customary wisdom of Stoic decorum, all that 'discourse of reason' which humanist theorists regarded as the gift that set men above the beasts. He will have nothing to do with 'saws of books' or the codes of behaviour that 'youth and observation' are supposed to copy from their humanist texts. After encountering the Ghost, he vows to fill his commonplace book ('my tables') from experience instead of books.

This new way of seeing is initially regarded by his fellow-students Horatio and Marcellus as no more than 'wild and whirling words', madness brought on by an encounter with an evil spirit. But Hamlet knows what he is doing. He tries on his 'antic disposition' as a way of testing the limits of the rational 'philosophy' embodied by Horatio. Ophelia tells of how she witnessed Hamlet utter a sigh that seemed to 'end his being'. That end is also a beginning: the birth of a new man dedicated to the proposition that the opposite of reason is not madness, but true feeling. Later, when Ophelia is mad, she is described as 'Divided from herself and her fair judgement, / Without the which we are pictures or mere beasts'. When Hamlet feigns madness, by contrast, he speaks with true judgement, as even Polonius half-recognizes: 'A happiness that often madness hits on, which reason and sanity could not so prosperously be delivered of.'

REVENGE

Hamlet is a political drama as well as a play about the journey of an individual self. It begins with portents betokening 'some strange eruption to our state'. It holds up a mirror to a world of royalty, courtiers, politicians and ambassadors, but also ordinary people: students, actors, gravediggers, even (on the margins) an underclass of 'lawless resolutes' following Fortinbras and a 'rabble' who want Laertes to be king.

'Denmark's a prison': Hamlet is cabined, cribbed and confined by his princely birth, by the machinations of statecraft, and by the limitations of the material world. In his melancholy, when he complains that he has lost interest in all gentlemanly pursuits ('custom of exercise'), he points to the 'canopy' over the stage. The self-conscious allusion to the architecture of the Globe Theatre hints at how he finds his freedom: in play, first by pretending to be mad, then through theatre. It is the arrival of the actors that reinvigorates him. Hamlet loves plays and the players because he recognizes the power of acting to expose the feigning of public life, the fact that courtiership and rhetorical decorum are themselves but perfor-mances. He comes to the truth through 'a fiction' and 'a dream of passion'. In this he can only be regarded as an apologist for the art of his creator.

The play was registered in 1602 'as it was lately acted by the Lord Chamberlain his servants' (Shakespeare's theatre company), but a book published in 1596 refers to a ghost in a play crying 'Hamlet, revenge!', and as early as 1589 Thomas Nashe mentioned 'whole *Hamlets* – I should say handfuls – of tragical speeches'. Scholars therefore suppose that Shakespeare's play was written in about 1600, but that it was a reworking of an older, now lost play, just as *King Lear* was a reworking of the anonymous *History of King Leir*, which does survive. The old *Hamlet* is sometimes speculatively attributed to Thomas Kyd, whose *Spanish Tragedy* established the late-Elizabethan vogue for blood-and-guts revenge drama. A few scholars suppose that Shakespeare himself wrote the early version and a tiny minority that the poorly printed First Quarto text of 1603 may in some way derive from it. Though there is no firm evidence as to authorship or content, we may safely assume that the old Hamlet play (sometimes known as the *Ur-Hamlet*) was broadly similar to *The Spanish Tragedy* and Shakespeare's early assay in this genre, *Titus Andronicus*, both of which achieved immense popularity with their plotting of revenge by means of feigned madness, their spectacular multiple murders and the revenger's elaborately rhetorical outbursts of tragic passion. Hamlet's shortest soliloquy, after he has been fired up by the play-within-the-play, is very much in this style: 'now could I drink hot blood / And do such bitter business as the day / Would quake to look on.'

Hamlet is as capable of violent action as any other revenger – witness his cruel rejection of Ophelia and his casual lugging of Polonius' guts into the neighbouring room. Nor does he delay nearly so much as he tells us he is delaying: he has to establish the authenticity of the Ghost, to ensure that it is not a devil sent to tempt him into evil action, and as soon as he has done this by watching Claudius' reaction to the play he goes off to kill him. He doesn't kill him at prayer because that would be 'hire and salary, not revenge', would send him to heaven not to hell. He then thinks that he has killed him in Gertrude's closet, though it turns out that he has killed

Polonius instead and as a result he is packed off to England. As soon as he has tricked and dispatched Rosencrantz and Guildenstern, effected his daring escape via the pirate ship and returned to Denmark, he is in a state of 'readiness' and the revenge then takes place during the duel. Looked at this way, where is the delay?

But the style of the 'hot blood' soliloquy is completely unlike that of the other solo speeches, which are all much longer and more introspective. It is from them that we derive our image of the character of Hamlet. In the first act, he is so disgusted by his mother's hasty remarriage that he wishes he were dead. In the second, he is moved to self-disgust by the way in which the player can work himself into a frenzy for the fictional sorrows of Hecuba, while he himself has not yet done anything about his father's murder. In the third, he meditates on the pros and cons of suicide, and in the Quarto text of the fourth he is still chiding himself when he compares his own inaction with the military activity of Fortinbras and his army ('How all occasions do inform against me / And spur my dull revenge'). Hamlet's self-analysis has led some commentators to wonder whether his failure to kill the praying usurper might be the result of procrastination, not calculation about whether he would be sending him to heaven or hell. The soliloquies present such a convincing picture of irresolution and inaction that even when it comes to the final scene it may occur to us that the killing of the king seems to be not so much the climax of Hamlet's plans as an incidental consequence of Laertes' quest for revenge for the deaths of his father and sister.

For the Romantics such as Goethe and Coleridge, Hamlet was the archetype of the sensitive man paralysed into inaction by his sheer capacity for thought – which is to say an image of themselves as poets uneasily inhabiting the public sphere. Debatable as this reading is, there can be little doubt that Shakespeare's innovation in *Hamlet* was to take the figure of the revenger from the old play and turn him into an intellectual, so making revenge into a moral dilemma as opposed to a practical task to be carried out through effective plotting. Hamlet's problem is that his intelligence makes him see both sides of every question, whereas in the drama of revenge there is no place for debate and half-measure. The lesson from both the Old Testament and Greek tragedy, which was mediated to Shakespeare via Seneca's Latin plays, was that action requires reactions: a crime in one generation demands the meting out of punishment in the next, an eye for an eye. Requital must be exact and complete. The code of revenge requires Hamlet not to kill the king while he is praying because that would send him straight to heaven, which does not correspond to the fate of Old Hamlet, who was murdered 'grossly, full of bread, / With all his crimes broad blown'. It is one of the play's many ironies that, immediately on Hamlet's departure, the king acknowledges that his prayer for forgiveness is not working – if Hamlet had struck, he would have damned his enemy.

CONSCIENCE AND RESOLUTION

One of the paradoxes of the play is that the Ghost of Old Hamlet comes from Purgatory, where he is confined in fire 'Till the foul crimes done in [his] days of nature / Are burnt and purged away', while Hamlet's speech giving his reasons for not plunging his sword into his praying uncle implies that the act of penitence can instantly purge sin away and allow even a man who has committed the most terrible crime immediate access to heaven on his death. Purgatory is a Roman Catholic doctrine, the leap to grace supposed by Hamlet a Protestant one. At several points, the play engages with the great doctrinal disputes of the Reformation and counter-Reformation. There appear, for instance, to be passing allusions to the nature of the sacrament of Holy Communion, the question of whether the bread and wine at the altar is literally or only symbolically transubstantiated into the body and blood of Christ.

Hamlet longs to be back at Wittenberg, the university of Martin · Luther, architect of the Reformation. Wittenberg was the intellectual home of the Protestant revolution, in which the individual's relationship with God matters more than the intercession of priests, saints and the Church. In Protestantism, authenticity of feeling is paramount and a key term is 'conscience'. As Hamlet says at the end of 'To be, or not to be':

> Thus conscience does make cowards of us all:
> And thus the native hue of resolution
> Is sicklied o'er with the pale cast of thought,
> And enterprises of great pith and moment
> With this regard their currents turn away,
> And lose the name of action . . . .

In Elizabethan English, 'conscience' meant not only moral scruple but also 'consciousness'. A polyglot dictionary of the period glossed the word as 'witness of one's own mind, knowledge, remorse'. It is Hamlet's extreme self-consciousness that sets him apart from the traditional revenger. When alone on stage, reflecting on his own situation, he seems to embody the very nature of human *being*. It is 'conscience' in its multiple senses that forms his self-image, his 'character', and in so doing makes it agonizingly difficult for him to perform the action that is demanded of him. Yet when he does come to act, he is decisive and ruthless. He reaches the point of 'readiness' when he accepts – never easy for an intellectual – that what will be will be. Thereafter, he considers it 'perfect conscience' to kill the king and has no compunction about his treatment of the former schoolfellows who have betrayed not only him but the precious virtue of friendship: Rosencrantz and Guildenstern, he says, 'are not near my conscience'.

It is sometimes said that chance, not Hamlet, brings the plot to a resolution. Hamlet certainly believes that Providence is operating on his behalf, as witnessed by the good fortune of his having the means to seal Rosencrantz and Guildenstern's fate. But the exchange of rapiers during the fencing match with Laertes is not a matter of chance, as is sometimes suggested. Many modern productions use the épée that had not been invented in Shakespeare's time – a flexible foil that may be knocked from the hand, leading to the possibility of an accidental exchange of weapons. But Hamlet and Laertes would originally have duelled with 'rapier and dagger', the commonest weapons for such an encounter, as illustrated in

1. 'Rapier and dagger': on-guard position, as illustrated in Vincentio Saviolo's English fencing treatise of 1595. There were strong links between the actors and Saviolo's fencing school in Ludgate.

Vincentio Saviola's treatise on fencing skills, *The Art of Practice* (1595).

The grip used for the rapier meant that it was very hard to remove it from the opponent's hand save by an advanced manoeuvre known as the 'left-hand seizure'. Hamlet would have dropped his dagger to the ground and grabbed the hilt of Laertes' rapier with his left hand, twisting it out of his grip. Laertes would have responded with the same action, resulting in the switch of weapons.

The move, which is illustrated in continental fencing handbooks of the period, is so skilful that Hamlet's action must have been purposeful. He would not initially have seen that Laertes' rapier was 'unbated' (not blunted in the way that was customary to prevent the injury of gentlemen participating in sporting fights), but on receiving a 'hit' his skin would have been pierced by the point. Realizing that

2. *'They change rapiers'*: disarm and exchange by left-hand seizure, as illustrated in Henri de Saint-Didier's French fencing treatise of 1573.

Laertes is in earnest, not play, he instantly responds with the manoeuvre that makes the switch. Now he is in deadly earnest himself. Deeds take over from words, revenge is performed without further compunctious visitings of nature, and 'the rest is silence'.

HOW MANY *HAMLETS*?

Shakespeare couldn't decide what to do with his most famous speech. The earliest surviving text of *Hamlet** is highly inaccurate in many of its particulars, but there is little doubt that its shape reflects that of the play as performed early in its stage history. In that text (known as the 'First Quarto'), Hamlet enters 'reading on a book' and launches into his soliloquy 'To be or not to be there, ay, there's the

---

* For further discussion of the play's complicated textual history, see 'Text' in 'Key Facts', pp. 25–6.

point.' His famous question is asked as if in response to something in the book he is reading. The soliloquy is followed by the 'get thee to a nunnery' dialogue with Ophelia and then the 'Fishmonger' sequence with her father.

But in the Second Quarto and First Folio texts – published later, but considerably longer and more accurately printed than the First Quarto – Hamlet's entrance with the book leads straight to the 'Fishmonger' dialogue (2.2.177–230 in our text). 'To be, or not to be, that is the question' and the 'nunnery' scene are held back until after the arrival of the players (3.1.62–159 in our text). This is only the most striking of the many textual variants between the early versions of *Hamlet*. Is the flesh that Hamlet wishes would melt too 'sullied' or too 'solid'? Did Old Hamlet smite a leaded or a steeled poleaxe on the ice or did he smite the Polack from a sledge on the ice? So much depends on whether you favour Quarto or Folio.

Scholars traditionally prefer the Second Quarto because it is the fullest text and apparently the one closest to Shakespeare's original manuscript. But it may represent a 'reading text' as opposed to a 'performance' one. Coming in at around four thousand lines, Second Quarto *Hamlet* could never have been played in full within the 160 or so minutes that was the legal maximum for an Elizabethan play (shows began at 2 p.m., there was always a closing comedy and dance routine known as a jig, and then the theatre had to be cleared by 5 p.m.). The full flow of Shakespeare's tragic vein must be reined in and cut for performance, and with a play as long as *Hamlet* he must have known that this would be the case.

Every modern production makes its own choice of cuts, of textual variants and of innovative business. In working on his text for the Royal Shakespeare Company production of 2004, director Michael Boyd* considered not only the three versions that emerged from Shakespeare's own acting company but also the so-called 'Players' Quarto' that was handed down – with cuts marked up – to their Restoration successors, the acting company of Shakespeare's godson

---

* See further the interview with Michael Boyd about his production in 'The Director's Cut', pp. 198–217.

William Davenant. Both the First Quarto and the Players' Quarto offer striking suggestions as to how the play may have been cut in Shakespeare's own time. The cuts are not always the most obvious ones: Reynaldo, whom Polonius commissions to spy on Laertes in Paris, might seem an obvious candidate for the axe, but in the Players' Quarto he remains, probably in order to highlight the way in which the world of Elsinore – like that of Elizabethan England – was one of pervasive spying.

Like most modern directors, Boyd was eclectic in his choices, weighing each textual variant according to its merits, moving freely between the early texts and opting for rigorous pruning rather than reckless lopping. So, for instance, the First Folio cuts the whole of Hamlet's last soliloquy, 'How all occasions do inform against me', delivered after witnessing the army of Fortinbras on the march, whereas Boyd retained an abbreviated version of it that makes the key distinction between acting upon 'great argument' and finding 'quarrel in a straw'.

The Reynaldo role was also retained, but the character was merged with Osric. Since one of them only appears near the beginning of the play and the other only near the end, the roles may well have been doubled in the original production. To make them into the same character is both an elegant economy and a device to highlight the role of Polonius as spymaster-general. Most boldly, the nunnery scene was placed early, as in the First Quarto, while – as Boyd explains in his interview about the production – a radical new position for 'To be, or not to be' was seriously considered, but ultimately rejected. The process of thinking through production choices of this sort is what enables directors and actors to defamiliarize and remint the language and action of the best known play in the history of world drama, and so to keep it alive. The progressive alterations through the early texts are of a piece with the process of remaking in the play's subsequent theatrical life.

TALKING ABOUT HAMLET

Hamlet is not only the pre-eminent talker in Shakespeare. He is also the most talked-about character in western literature. Because he is both poet and philosopher himself, poets and philosophers have been particular enamoured of him. Hamlet-mania reached its zenith with the self-consciously troubled musings on art and life of the nineteenth-century Romantics. One of their favoured literary devices was the 'imaginary conversation', in which their cultural heroes gathered round a table and talked about a topic of absorbing interest. It was in Samuel Taylor Coleridge's *Table Talk* that he said 'I have a smack of Hamlet myself, if I may say so.' *Hamlet* is a play that provokes so many opinions, animates so many energetic voices, that the best way to conclude an introduction to it is simply to bring together some of the play's most impassioned readers in an 'imaginary conversation'.

Let them begin from that key moment when Hamlet decides not to kill King Claudius while he is praying, since that would be to send him to heaven, not hell:

Up, sword, and know thou a more horrid hent:
When he is drunk asleep, or in his rage,
Or in th'incestuous pleasure of his bed,
At gaming, swearing, or about some act
That has no relish of salvation in't,
Then trip him, that his heels may kick at heaven,
And that his soul may be as damned and black
As hell, whereto it goes . . . .

Dr Samuel Johnson, eighteenth-century Christian of high moral sensitivity: 'This speech, in which Hamlet, represented as a virtuous character, is not content with taking blood for blood, but contrives damnation for the man that he would punish, is too horrible to be read or to be uttered.'

Samuel Taylor Coleridge, Romantic poet with a smack of Hamlet himself, if he may say so: 'Dr Johnson's mistaking of the marks of reluctance and procrastination for impetuous, horror-striking fiendishness! – Of such importance is it to understand the *germ* of a character.'

Johann Wolfgang von Goethe, in the voice of Wilhelm Meister, hero of the archetypal Romantic *Bildungsroman*, the novel in which a young man or woman grows to emotional maturity (a genre for which *Hamlet* itself was a key model): '"The time is out of joint: O, cursèd spite / That ever I was born to set it right!" In these words, I imagine, will be found the key to Hamlet's whole procedure. To me it is clear that Shakespeare meant, in the present case, to represent the effects of a great action laid upon a soul unfit for the performance of it. In this view the whole piece seems to me to be composed.'

August Wilhelm von Schlegel, Romantic critic: '*Hamlet* is singular in its kind: a tragedy of thought inspired by continual and never-satisfied meditation on human destiny and the dark perplexity of the events of this world, and calculated to call forth the very same meditation in the minds of the spectators.'

Lord Byron, always glad to play the devil's advocate:

Who can read this wonderful play without the profoundest emotion? And yet what is it but a colossal enigma? We love Hamlet even as we love ourselves. Yet consider his character, and where is either goodness or greatness? He betrays Ophelia's gentlest love; he repulses her in a cruel manner; and when in the most touching way, she speaks to him, and returns his presents, he laughs her off like a man of the town. At her grave, at the new-made grave of Ophelia his first love, whom his unkindness had blasted in the very bud of her beauty, in the morn and liquid dew of youth, what is the behaviour of Hamlet? A blank – worse than a blank; a few ranting lines, instead of true feeling, that prove him perfectly heartless. Then his behaviour in the grave, and his insult to Laertes, why the gentlest verdict one can give is insanity. But he seems by nature, and in his soberest moods, fiend-like in cruelty. His old companions, Rosencrantz and Guildenstern, he murders without the least compunction; he desires them to be put to sudden death, 'not shriving-time allowed'... Polonius, father of Ophelia, he does actually kill; and for this does he lament or atone for what he has done, by any regret or remorse? 'I'll lug the guts into the neighbour room' – 'You nose him as you go up the stairs into the lobby!' But suppose him heartless, though he is for ever lamenting, and complaining, and declaiming about the false-heartedness of every one else; Richard III is heartless – Iago – Edmund. The tragic poet of course deals not in your good-boy characters. But neither is he, as Richard is, a hero, a man of mighty strength of mind. He is, according to his own admission, as 'unlike Hercules' as possible. He does not, as a great and energetic mind does, exult under the greatness of a grand object. He is weak, so miserably weak as even to complain of his own weakness.

Elaine Showalter, turn-of-the-millennium feminist, as if responding to Byron's remarks about Ophelia:

When Ophelia is mad, Gertrude says that 'Her speech is nothing,' mere 'unshaped use'. Ophelia's speech thus represents the horror of having nothing to say in the public terms defined by the court. Deprived of thought, sexuality, language, Ophelia's story becomes the Story of O – the zero, the empty circle or mystery of feminine difference, the cipher of female sexuality ... we could provide a manual of female insanity by chronicling the illustrations of Ophelia; this is so because the illustrations of Ophelia have played a major role in the theoretical construction of female insanity.

Søren Kierkegaard, melancholy Danish philosopher, himself a Hamlet wracked by sexual guilt, coming perhaps to the heart of the mystery: 'Hamlet is deeply tragic because he *suspects* his mother's guilt.'

Sigmund Freud, inaugurating the language of psychoanalytic criticism which Showalter has been employing and Kierkegaard subtly anticipating: 'In Sophocles' *Oedipus* the child's wishful fantasy that underlies it is brought out into the open and realized as it would be in a dream. In *Hamlet* it remains repressed; and just as in the case of a neurosis, we only learn of its existence from its inhibiting consequences...Hamlet is able to do anything – except take vengeance on the man who did away with his father and took that father's place with his mother, the man who shows him the repressed wishes of his childhood realized.'

James Joyce, Shakespeare-soaked Irish novelist, in the voice of Stephen Dedalus in *Ulysses*, weaving a somewhat Freudian reading into a biographical fantasy:

> The play begins. A player comes on under the shadow, made up in the cast-off mail of a court buck, a well-set man with a bass voice. It is the ghost, the king, a king and no king, and the player is Shakespeare who has studied Hamlet all the years of his life which were not vanity in order to play the part of the spectre. He speaks the words to Burbage, the young player who stands before him beyond the rack of cerecloth, calling him by a name: 'Hamlet, I am thy father's spirit', bidding him list. To a son he speaks, the son of his soul, the prince, young Hamlet and to the son of his body, Hamnet Shakespeare, who has died in Stratford that his namesake may live for ever. Is it possible that that player Shakespeare, a ghost by absence, and in the vesture of buried Denmark, a ghost by death, speaking his own words to his own son's name (had Hamnet Shakespeare lived he would have been prince Hamlet's twin), is it possible, I want to know, or probable that he did not draw or foresee the logical conclusion of those premises: you are the dispossessed son: I am the murdered father: your mother is the guilty queen. Ann Shakespeare, born Hathaway?

T. S. Eliot, poet and stern critic, dissatisfied with the Freudian solution, but agreeing that there is a problem: 'Shakespeare's *Hamlet*, so far as it is Shakespeare's, is a play dealing with the effect of a mother's guilt upon her son, and...Shakespeare was unable to impose this motive successfully upon the "intractable" material of the old play.... So far from being Shakespeare's masterpiece, the play is most certainly an artistic failure.'

Jan Kott, Polish critic, writing under tyranny, swinging away from psychology to politics: his Hamlet is not 'the moralist, unable to draw a clear-cut line between good and evil' or 'the intellectual, unable to find a sufficient reason for action' or 'the philosopher, to whom the world's existence is a matter of doubt', but rather 'the youth, deeply involved in politics, rid of illusions, sarcastic, passionate and brutal . . . a born conspirator . . . a young rebel who has about him something of the charm of James Dean'.

From Wilhelm Meister to Stephen Dedalus to James Dean and beyond, Hamlet is always our contemporary. To be or not to be Hamlet? That is the question for every young aspiring intellectual or actor. Or indeed actress: of all Shakespeare's major male roles, it is the one that has most often and most effectively been played by women. In Renaissance terms, action was the prerogative of the male and feeling of the female, so perhaps Hamlet's intense gift of feeling, and talking about his feelings, makes him a 'feminine' character.

For those who do not get to play the part itself, there is the compensation of imagining themselves in a supporting role. Tom Stoppard's razor-sharp existential tragicomedy *Rosencrantz and Guildenstern are Dead* (1966) rewrites the drama from the point of view of the two men on the margins who are cogs in the wheel, and in the cult film *Withnail and I* (1986), an old actor (Uncle Monty, played by Richard Griffiths) is broken by the realization that he will never 'play the Dane' (he has only managed to secure the tiny part of Marcellus the nightwatchman) and a young unemployed actor (Withnail, played by Richard E. Grant) ends up in London Zoo reciting Hamlet's great prose discourse 'I have of late – but wherefore I know not – lost all my mirth' (2.2.308–322) to an enclosure of bedraggled wolves. Hardly the 'paragon of animals' and yet, because of Hamlet, still he can dream.

Further selections from critical commentaries on the play, with linking narrative, are available on the edition website, www.rscshakespeare.co.uk.

ABOUT THE TEXT

Shakespeare endures through history. He illuminates later times as well as his own. He helps us to understand the human condition. But he cannot do this without a good text of the plays. Without editions there would be no Shakespeare. That is why every twenty years or so throughout the last three centuries there has been a major new edition of his complete works. One aspect of editing is the process of keeping the texts up to date – modernizing the spelling, punctuation and typography (though not, of course, the actual words), providing explanatory notes in the light of changing educational practices (a generation ago, most of Shakespeare's classical and biblical allusions could be assumed to be generally understood, but now they can't).

But because Shakespeare did not personally oversee the publication of his plays, editors also have to make decisions about the relative authority of the early printed editions. Half of the sum of his plays only appeared posthumously, in the elaborately produced First Folio text of 1623, the original 'Complete Works' prepared for the press by Shakespeare's fellow-actors, the people who knew the plays better than anyone else. The other half had appeared in print in his lifetime, in the more compact and cheaper form of 'Quarto' editions, some of which reproduced good quality texts, others of which were to a greater or lesser degree garbled and error-strewn. In the case of *Hamlet*, there are hundreds of differences between each of the three early editions: two Quartos (one short and frequently corrupt, the other very long and generally well printed) and the Folio. As explained earlier in the discussion of 'How Many *Hamlets?*' (pp. 10–12), some of the differences are far from trivial.

Generations of editors have adopted a 'pick and mix' approach, moving between Quarto and Folio readings, making choices on either aesthetic or bibliographic grounds, and creating a composite text that Shakespeare never actually wrote. Not until the 1980s did editors follow the logic of what ought to have been obvious to anyone who works in the theatre: that the two Quarto and the Folio texts represent three discrete moments in the life of *Hamlet*, that plays change in the course of rehearsal, production and revival, and that the major variants between the early printed versions almost certainly reflect this process.

If you look at printers' handbooks from the age of Shakespeare, you quickly discover that one of the first rules was that, whenever possible, compositors were recommended to set their type from existing printed books rather than manuscripts. This was the age before mechanical typesetting, where each individual letter had to be picked out by hand from the compositor's case and placed on a stick (upside down and back to front) before being laid on the press. It was an age of murky rush-light and of manuscripts written in a secretary hand which had dozens of different, hard-to-decipher forms. Printers' lives were a lot easier when they were reprinting existing books rather than struggling with handwritten copy. Easily the quickest way to have created the First Folio would have been simply to reprint those eighteen plays that had already appeared in Quarto and only work from manuscript on the other eighteen.

But that is not what happened. Whenever Quartos were used, playhouse 'promptbooks' were also consulted and stage directions copied in from them. And in the case of several major plays where a well-printed Quarto was available, *Hamlet* notable among them, the Folio printers were instructed to work from an alternative, playhouse-derived manuscript. This meant that the whole process of producing the first complete Shakespeare took months, even years, longer than it might have done. But for the men overseeing the project, John Hemings and Henry Condell, friends and fellow-actors who had been remembered in Shakespeare's will, the additional labour and cost were worth the effort for the sake of producing an edition that was close to the practice of the theatre. They wanted all the plays in print so that people could, as they wrote in their prefatory address to the reader, 'read him and again and again', but they also wanted 'the great variety of readers' to work from texts that were close to the theatre-life for which Shakespeare originally intended them. For this reason, the *RSC Shakespeare*, in both *Complete Works* and individual volumes, uses the Folio as base text wherever possible. Significant Quarto variants are, however, noted in the Textual Notes, and Quarto-only passages are appended after the text of *Hamlet*.

The following notes highlight various aspects of the editorial process and indicate conventions used in the text of this edition:

Lists of Parts are supplied in the First Folio for only six plays, not including *Hamlet*, so the list at the beginning of the play is provided by the editors, arranged by groups of character. Capitals indicate that part of the name which is used for speech headings in the script (thus 'HAMLET, Prince of Denmark').

Locations are provided by the Folio for only two plays. Eighteenth-century editors, working in an age of elaborately realistic stage sets, were the first to provide detailed locations. Given that Shakespeare wrote for a bare stage and often an imprecise sense of place, we have relegated locations to the explanatory notes at the foot of the page, where they are given at the beginning of each scene where the imaginary location is different from the one before. We have emphasized broad geographical settings rather than specifics of the kind that suggest anachronistically realistic staging. We have therefore avoided such niceties as 'another room in the palace'.

Act and Scene Divisions were provided in the Folio in a much more thoroughgoing way than in the Quartos. Sometimes, however, they were erroneous or omitted; corrections and additions supplied by editorial tradition are indicated by square brackets. Five-act division is based on a classical model, and act breaks provided the opportunity to replace the candles in the indoor Blackfriars playhouse which the King's Men used after 1608, but Shakespeare did not necessarily think in terms of a five-part structure of dramatic composition. The Folio convention is that a scene ends when the stage is empty. Nowadays, partly under the influence of film, we tend to consider a scene to be a dramatic unit that ends with either a change of imaginary location or a significant passage of time within the narrative. Shakespeare's fluidity of composition accords well with this convention, so in addition to act and scene numbers we provide a *running scene* count in the right margin at the beginning of each new scene, in the typeface used for editorial directions. Where there is a scene break caused by a momentary bare stage, but the location does not change and extra time does not pass, we use the convention *running scene continues*. There is inevitably a degree of editorial judgement in making such calls, but the system is very valuable in suggesting the pace of the plays.

Speakers' Names are often inconsistent in Folio. We have regularized speech headings, but retained an element of deliberate inconsistency in entry directions, in order to give the flavour of Folio.

Verse is indicated by lines that do not run to the right margin and by capitalization of each line. The Folio printers sometimes set verse as prose, and vice versa (either out of misunderstanding or for reasons of space). We have silently corrected in such cases, although in some instances there is ambiguity, in which case we have leaned towards the preservation of Folio layout. Folio sometimes uses contraction ('turnd' rather than 'turned') to indicate whether or not the final '-ed' of a past participle is sounded, an area where there is variation for the sake of the five-beat iambic pentameter rhythm. We use the convention of a grave accent to indicate sounding (thus 'turnèd' would be two syllables), but would urge actors not to overstress. In cases where one speaker ends with a verse half-line and the next begins with the other half of the pentameter, editors since the late eighteenth century have indented the second line. We have abandoned this convention, since the Folio does not use it, and nor did actors' cues in the Shakespearean theatre. An exception is made when the second speaker actively interrupts or completes the first speaker's sentence.

Spelling is modernized, but older forms are occasionally maintained where necessary for rhythm or aural effect.

Punctuation in Shakespeare's time was as much rhetorical as grammatical. 'Colon' was originally a term for a unit of thought in an argument. The semi-colon was a new unit of punctuation (some of the Quartos lack them altogether). We have modernized punctuation throughout, but have given more weight to Folio punctuation than many editors, since, though not Shakespearean, it reflects the usage of his period. In particular, we have used the colon far more than many editors: it is exceptionally useful as a way of indicating how many Shakespearean speeches unfold clause by clause in a developing argument that gives the illusion of enacting the process of thinking in the moment. We have also kept in mind the origin of punctuation in classical times as a way of assisting the actor and orator: the comma suggests the briefest of pauses for breath, the colon a middling one and a full stop or period a longer pause. Semi-colons, by contrast, belong to an era of punctuation that was only just coming in during Shakespeare's time and that is coming to an end now: we have accordingly only used them where they occur in our copy-texts (and not always then). Dashes are sometimes used for parenthetical interjections where the Folio has brackets. They are also used for interruptions and changes in train of thought. Where a change of addressee occurs within a speech, we have used a dash preceded by a full stop (or occasionally another form of punctuation). Often the identity of the respective addressees is obvious from the context. When it is not, this has been indicated in a marginal stage direction.

Entrances and Exits are fairly thorough in Folio, which has accordingly been followed as faithfully as possible. Where characters are omitted or corrections are necessary, this is indicated by square brackets (e.g. '[*and Attendants*]'). *Exit* is sometimes silently normalized to *Exeunt* and *Manet* anglicized to 'remains'. We trust Folio positioning of entrances and exits to a greater degree than most editors.

Editorial Stage Directions such as stage business, asides, indications of addressee and of characters' position on the gallery stage are only used sparingly in Folio. Other editions mingle directions of this kind with original Folio and Quarto directions, sometimes marking them by means of square brackets. We have sought to distinguish what could be described as *directorial* interventions of this kind from Folio-style directions (either original or supplied) by placing them in the right margin in a different typeface. There is a degree of subjectivity about which directions are of which kind, but the procedure is intended as a reminder to the reader and the actor that Shakespearean stage directions are often dependent upon editorial inference alone and are not set in stone. We also depart from editorial tradition in sometimes admitting uncertainty and thus printing permissive stage-directions, such as an *Aside?* (often a line may be equally effective as an aside or a direct address – it is for each production or reading to make its own decision) or a *may exit* or a piece of business placed between arrows to indicate that it may occur at various different moments within a scene.

Line Numbers in the left margin are editorial, for reference and to key the explanatory and textual notes.

Explanatory Notes at the foot of each page explain allusions and gloss obsolete and difficult words, confusing phraseology, occasional major textual cruces, and so on. Particular attention is given to non-standard usage, bawdy innuendo and technical terms (e.g. legal and military language). Where more than one sense is given, commas indicate shades of related meaning, slashes alternative or double meanings.

Textual Notes at the end of the play indicate major departures from the Folio. They take the following form: the reading of our text is given in bold and its source given after an equals sign, with 'Q' indicating that it derives from the principal Quarto (Q2 in the case of *Hamlet*, though we also record some significant Q1 readings) and 'Ed' that it derives from the editorial tradition. The rejected Folio ('F') reading is then given. A selection of Quarto variants and plausible unadopted editorial readings are also included. Thus, for example, '**3.4.180 bloat** = Ed. F = blunt. Q = blowt', indicates that we have adopted the editorial reading 'bloat' where Folio has 'blunt' and Quarto 'blowt'.

KEY FACTS

MAJOR PARTS: (*with percentage of lines/number of speeches/scenes on stage*) Hamlet (37%/341/12), King (14%/100/11), Polonius (9%/86/8), Horatio (7%/105/9), Laertes (5%/60/6), Ophelia (4%/58/5), Gertrude (4%/70/10), Rosencrantz (2%/44/6), First Player (2%/8/2), Ghost (2%/15/2), First Clown (2%/34/1), Marcellus (2%/34/4), Guildenstern (1%/29/5), Osric (1%/19/1).

LINGUISTIC MEDIUM: 75% verse, 25% prose.

DATE: 1600? Not mentioned by Meres in 1598; registered for publication in summer 1602. Allusions to *Julius Caesar* (1599) in the dialogue suggest that it was performed after that play; a reference to Shakespeare's *Hamlet* by the Cambridge academic Gabriel Harvey seems to date from before February 1601. The exchange concerning boy-actors alludes to rivalries in the London theatres during 1600 and 1601, but it may have been inserted in the play some time after its original composition (the passage is absent from the Second Quarto text). An old *Hamlet* play, of unknown authorship and now lost, was extant in the late 1580s to mid-1590s; it is not known whether Shakespeare had any direct involvement with it.

SOURCES: Given the frequency with which Shakespeare reworked old plays, it may be assumed that the old *Hamlet* play was his chief source. The Danish prince Amleth is a revenger in the twelfth-century *Historiae Danicae* of Saxo Grammaticus, familiar to Elizabethan readers via a retelling in François de Belleforest's *Histoires tragiques* (1570). In Belleforest, the Gertrude figure definitely begins her affair with her husband's brother before the murder, in which she is suspected of complicity. The Player's speech on the fall of Troy is influenced by the language of Christopher Marlowe's *Dido Queen of Carthage*; Hamlet's philosophizing sometimes resembles the tone of Michel de Montaigne's *Essais*, but a direct link has not been proved.

TEXT: The First Quarto was published in 1603 under the title *The Tragicall Historie of HAMLET Prince of Denmarke by William Shakespeare. As it hath beene diuerse times acted by his Highnesse seruants in the Cittie of London: as also in the two Vniuersities of Cambridge and Oxford, and else-where.* Much shorter than the later texts, and with many garbled lines, it seems to be a reconstruction of an acting version. There are some notable differences from the later texts (e.g. Polonius called Corambis, 'To be or not to be' and the 'nunnery' dialogue positioned with the 'fishmonger' exchange, not after the arrival of the players), but some of the stage directions are valuable (e.g. *'Enter Ofelia playing on a Lute, and her haire downe singing'* for the mad scene). The Second Quarto, published in 1604/ 05, was clearly an 'authorized' text, intended to displace the First Quarto, as may be seen from its title-page claim, 'Newly imprinted and enlarged to almost as much againe as it was, according to the true and perfect Coppie.' Most scholars believe that the text derives from Shakespeare's manuscript; over 4000 lines long, it is unlikely to have been staged in full. The text in the 1623 Folio seems to have been set from the theatre promptbook or a transcript of it. It has much fuller stage directions than the Second Quarto, and considerable textual variations: about 70 new lines are present, while about 230 Quarto lines are absent, including the whole of Hamlet's last major soliloquy, 'How all occasions do inform against me' – in Folio, he is not there to witness Fortinbras' army. Hundreds of individual readings differ, strongly suggesting that the Second Quarto and Folio represent different stages in the play's life. Some scholars regard the revision as systematic (e.g. making subtle changes to Hamlet's relationship with Rosencrantz and Guilden-stern), but it may have been more incremental and haphazard. Given the major differences, the editorial practice of conflation, which began with Nicholas Rowe's insertion of the Second Quarto's final soliloquy in his Folio-based text of 1709, has recently fallen into disrepute. We edit the Folio text, but include the Quarto-only passages (edited and annotated) independently at the end. Though Folio seems to have been set from a theatrical manuscript, it was also influenced by the Quarto tradition; so too, a modern edition of Folio can benefit from Quarto readings when the Folio text is manifestly erroneous, as it is on numerous occasions.

THE TRAGEDY OF HAMLET, PRINCE OF DENMARK

HAMLET, Prince of Denmark

KING of Denmark, Hamlet's uncle

GHOST of old Hamlet, former King of Denmark, Hamlet's father

GERTRUDE, queen of Denmark, Hamlet's mother

POLONIUS, councillor to the state of Denmark

LAERTES, Polonius' son

OPHELIA, Polonius' daughter

REYNALDO, Polonius' servant

HORATIO, Hamlet's friend and fellow-student

ROSENCRANTZ *and* **GUILDENSTERN** } two courtiers, former schoolfellows of Hamlet

VOLTEMAND *and* **CORNELIUS** } ambassadors to Norway

MARCELLUS **BARNARDO** } sentinels of the king's guard, seemingly also friends and fellow-students of Hamlet and Horatio

FRANCISCO, another sentinel of the king's guard

OSRIC, a courtier

PLAYERS, who take the roles of **PROLOGUE**, **PLAYER KING**, **BAPTISTA** and **LUCIANUS**

FORTINBRAS, Prince of Norway

A **CAPTAIN** in his army

Two **CLOWNS**, a gravedigger and his companion

Two **MESSENGERS**

A **SAILOR**

A **PRIEST**

AMBASSADOR from England

Lords, Soldiers, Attendants, Servants, Followers of Laertes

List of parts   KING called Claudius in his first entry direction, but never named in the dialogue, so a theatre audience would not know what he is called

Act 1 Scene 1

Enter Barnardo and Francisco, two sentinels   *Meeting*

BARNARDO Who's there?

FRANCISCO Nay, answer me: stand and unfold yourself.

BARNARDO Long live the king!

FRANCISCO Barnardo?

5 **BARNARDO** He.

FRANCISCO You come most carefully upon your hour.

BARNARDO 'Tis now struck twelve: get thee to bed,
Francisco.

FRANCISCO For this relief much thanks: 'tis bitter cold,
And I am sick at heart.

10 **BARNARDO** Have you had quiet guard?

FRANCISCO Not a mouse stirring.

BARNARDO Well, goodnight.
If you do meet Horatio and Marcellus,
The rivals of my watch, bid them make haste.

Enter Horatio and Marcellus

15 **FRANCISCO** I think I hear them.— Stand! Who's there?

HORATIO Friends to this ground.

MARCELLUS And liegemen to the Dane.

FRANCISCO Give you goodnight.

MARCELLUS O, farewell, honest soldier. Who hath
relieved you?

20 **FRANCISCO** Barnardo has my place. Give you goodnight.

Exit Francisco

MARCELLUS Holla! Barnardo!

BARNARDO Say, what, is Horatio there?

HORATIO A piece of him.

BARNARDO Welcome, Horatio: welcome, good Marcellus.

25 **MARCELLUS** What, has this thing appeared again
tonight?

BARNARDO I have seen nothing.

MARCELLUS Horatio says 'tis but our fantasy,
And will not let belief take hold of him
Touching this dreaded sight twice seen of us:

30 Therefore I have entreated him along

1.1 *Location: the gun terrace of the royal castle at Elsinore, Denmark*   **2 me** Francisco asserts that, as
the sentry on guard, he is the one who should be making the challenge   **unfold** reveal/identify
6 carefully . . . hour responsibly at your appointed time   **14 rivals** partners   **16 ground** country
17 liegemen . . . Dane sworn servants of the Danish king   **18 Give** God give   **27 fantasy** imagination
29 Touching concerning   **of** by   **30 along** to come along

With us to watch the minutes of this night,
That if again this apparition come,
He may approve our eyes and speak to it.

HORATIO Tush, tush, 'twill not appear.

35 **BARNARDO** Sit down awhile,
And let us once again assail your ears,
That are so fortified against our story,
What we two nights have seen.

HORATIO Well, sit we down,
40 And let us hear Barnardo speak of this.

BARNARDO Last night of all,
When yond same star that's westward from the pole
Had made his course t'illume that part of heaven
Where now it burns, Marcellus and myself,
45 The bell then beating one—

MARCELLUS Peace, break thee off.

Enter the Ghost

Look where it comes again.

BARNARDO In the same figure like the king that's dead.

MARCELLUS Thou art a scholar; speak to it, Horatio.

BARNARDO Looks it not like the king? Mark it, Horatio.

50 **HORATIO** Most like: it harrows me with fear and wonder.

BARNARDO It would be spoke to.

MARCELLUS Question it, Horatio.

HORATIO What art thou that usurp'st this time of night,
Together with that fair and warlike form
55 In which the majesty of buried Denmark
Did sometimes march? By heaven I charge thee
speak!

MARCELLUS It is offended.

BARNARDO See, it stalks away.

HORATIO Stay! Speak, speak! I charge thee, speak!

Exit the Ghost

60 **MARCELLUS** 'Tis gone and will not answer.

BARNARDO How now, Horatio? You tremble and look
pale.
Is not this something more than fantasy?
What think you on't?

---

31 **watch** remain awake during/keep guard through   33 **approve** corroborate the reliability of   36 **assail** attack   41 **Last . . . all** this very night past   42 **yond** yonder, that   **pole** Pole Star (i.e. North Star) 43 **t'illume** to illuminate   47 **figure** appearance/likeness   48 **scholar** i.e. one knowledgeable enough to know how to address a ghost; a ghost was thought to be unable to speak until spoken to   49 **Mark it** observe it closely   50 **harrows** wounds/distresses   51 **would** wants to   53 **usurp'st** wrongfully occupies (both the night and the form of the dead king)   55 **Denmark** the King of Denmark   56 **sometimes** formerly **charge** order   63 **on't** of it

HORATIO Before my God, I might not this believe
65   Without the sensible and true avouch
        Of mine own eyes.
MARCELLUS Is it not like the king?
HORATIO As thou art to thyself.
        Such was the very armour he had on
70   When he th'ambitious Norway combated:
        So frowned he once when, in an angry parle,
        He smote the steelèd pole-axe on the ice.
        'Tis strange.
MARCELLUS Thus twice before, and just at this dead
            hour,
75   With martial stalk hath he gone by our watch.
HORATIO In what particular thought to work I know not,
        But in the gross and scope of my opinion,
        This bodes some strange eruption to our state.
MARCELLUS Good now, sit down and tell me, he that
            knows,
80   Why this same strict and most observant watch
        So nightly toils the subject of the land,
        And why such daily cast of brazen cannon
        And foreign mart for implements of war:
        Why such impress of shipwrights, whose sore task
85   Does not divide the Sunday from the week:
        What might be toward, that this sweaty haste
        Doth make the night joint-labourer with the day:
        Who is't that can inform me?
HORATIO That can I,
90   At least, the whisper goes so: our last king,
        Whose image even but now appeared to us,
        Was, as you know, by Fortinbras of Norway,
        Thereto pricked on by a most emulate pride,
        Dared to the combat, in which our valiant Hamlet —
95   For so this side of our known world esteemed him —
        Did slay this Fortinbras, who by a sealed compact,
        Well ratified by law and heraldry,

---

65 sensible perceptible to the senses   avouch assurance   70 Norway King of Norway   71 parle
negotiation   72 steelèd pole-axe halberd or similar long-handled weapon (tempered with steel) carried by
the bodyguard of a king   76 In…not i.e. I don't know exactly what to think   work occupy myself,
engage   77 gross and scope general drift   78 eruption disturbance, turmoil   79 Good now a polite
entreaty for attention   81 toils causes to toil   subject subjects   82 cast casting, manufacturing   brazen
brass   83 mart trading   84 impress conscription   85 Does…week i.e. they work seven days a week
including Sundays   86 toward impending/afoot   90 whisper rumour   93 Thereto…pride refers to
Fortinbras, not Hamlet, the Danish king   pricked spurred   emulate ambitious, rivalrous   96 sealed
compact formally certified agreement

Did forfeit, with his life, all those his lands
Which he stood seized on to the conqueror:
100 Against the which, a moiety competent
Was gagèd by our king, which had returned
To the inheritance of Fortinbras,
Had he been vanquisher, as, by the same cov'nant,
And carriage of the article designed,
105 His fell to Hamlet. Now, sir, young Fortinbras,
Of unimprovèd mettle hot and full,
Hath in the skirts of Norway here and there
Sharked up a list of landless resolutes
For food and diet to some enterprise
110 That hath a stomach in't, which is no other —
And it doth well appear unto our state —
But to recover of us, by strong hand
And terms compulsative, those foresaid lands
So by his father lost: and this, I take it,
115 Is the main motive of our preparations,
The source of this our watch and the chief head
Of this post-haste and rummage in the land.

Enter Ghost again

But soft, behold! Lo, where it comes again!
I'll cross it, though it blast me. Stay, illusion!
120 If thou hast any sound or use of voice,
Speak to me:
If there be any good thing to be done
That may to thee do ease and grace to me,
Speak to me:
125 If thou art privy to thy country's fate —
Which, haply, foreknowing may avoid — O, speak!
Or if thou hast uphoarded in thy life
Extorted treasure in the womb of earth —   ↓*A cock crows*↓
For which, they say, you spirits oft walk in death —
130 Speak of it: stay and speak!— Stop it, Marcellus.

99 seized on legally possessed of   **100 moiety competent** sufficient portion   **101 gagèd** pledged   **had returned** would have gone   **103 cov'nant** i.e. the sealed compact   **104 carriage . . . designed** carrying out of the clause that had been drawn up in it   **106 unimprovèd** untested/undisciplined/uncensured   **mettle** temperament, spirit   **107 skirts** outlying parts   **108 Sharked up** gathered up indiscriminately, as a shark does fish/seized upon like a predator   **list** troop   **resolutes** resolved people/desperadoes   **109 For . . . enterprise** i.e. men who will serve in return for food/men who will serve to feed the enterprise   **110 a stomach** courage/an appetite   **111 state** governing powers   **113 compulsative** compulsory   **116 head** origin   **117 post-haste** great speed   **rummage** turmoil, bustle   **118 soft** wait a moment   **Lo** look   **119 cross it** challenge it/make the sign of the cross at it/cross its path (believed to expose one to evil influence)   **blast** wither/destroy   **126 haply** perhaps   **127 uphoarded** hoarded up   **128 Extorted** wrongfully obtained

MARCELLUS Shall I strike at it with my partisan?
HORATIO Do, if it will not stand.   *They attempt to strike it*
BARNARDO 'Tis here!
HORATIO 'Tis here!
135 MARCELLUS 'Tis gone!   *Exit Ghost*
    We do it wrong, being so majestical,
    To offer it the show of violence,
    For it is as the air invulnerable,
    And our vain blows malicious mockery.
140 BARNARDO It was about to speak when the cock crew.
    HORATIO And then it started like a guilty thing
    Upon a fearful summons. I have heard
    The cock, that is the trumpet to the day,
    Doth with his lofty and shrill-sounding throat
145 Awake the god of day, and at his warning,
    Whether in sea or fire, in earth or air,
    Th'extravagant and erring spirit hies
    To his confine: and of the truth herein
    This present object made probation.
150 MARCELLUS It faded on the crowing of the cock.
    Some say that ever gainst that season comes
    Wherein our Saviour's birth is celebrated,
    The bird of dawning singeth all night long,
    And then, they say, no spirit can walk abroad:
155 The nights are wholesome, then no planets strike,
    No fairy talks, nor witch hath power to charm,
    So hallowed and so gracious is the time.
    HORATIO So have I heard and do in part believe it.
    But, look, the morn in russet mantle clad,
160 Walks o'er the dew of yon high eastern hill.
    Break we our watch up, and by my advice,
    Let us impart what we have seen tonight
    Unto young Hamlet, for upon my life,
    This spirit, dumb to us, will speak to him.
165 Do you consent we shall acquaint him with it,
    As needful in our loves, fitting our duty?
    MARCELLUS Let's do't, I pray, and I this morning know
    Where we shall find him most conveniently. *Exeunt*

---

131 **partisan** long-handled spear   132 **stand** stop, remain   147 **Th'extravagant and erring** the wandering and straying (out of bounds)   **hies** hastens   148 **confine** specific region/place of confinement   149 **probation** proof   151 **gainst** in anticipation of/just before   152 **our Saviour** i.e. Jesus Christ   153 **bird of dawning** i.e. the cock   155 **wholesome** healthy (damp night air was usually viewed as noxious)   **strike** destroy with evil influence   156 **talks** whispers spells (some editors prefer Quarto's 'takes', enchants/steals)   **charm** cast spells   157 **hallowed** holy   **gracious** full of divine grace   159 **russet** reddish-brown (from the coarse cloth of that colour)

Act 1 Scene 2

Enter Claudius King of Denmark, Gertrude the Queen,
Hamlet, Polonius, Laertes and his sister Ophelia, Lords
Attendant

KING Though yet of Hamlet our dear brother's death
    The memory be green, and that it us befitted
    To bear our hearts in grief and our whole kingdom
    To be contracted in one brow of woe,
5   Yet so far hath discretion fought with nature
    That we with wisest sorrow think on him
    Together with remembrance of ourselves.
    Therefore our sometime sister, now our queen,
    Th'imperial jointress of this warlike state,
10   Have we, as 'twere with a defeated joy,
    With one auspicious and one dropping eye,
    With mirth in funeral and with dirge in marriage,
    In equal scale weighing delight and dole,
    Taken to wife; nor have we herein barred
15   Your better wisdoms, which have freely gone
    With this affair along. For all, our thanks.
    Now follows that you know young Fortinbras,
    Holding a weak supposal of our worth,
    Or thinking by our late dear brother's death
20   Our state to be disjoint and out of frame,
    Colleaguèd with the dream of his advantage,
    He hath not failed to pester us with message
    Importing the surrender of those lands
    Lost by his father, with all bonds of law,
25   To our most valiant brother. So much for him.
    Enter Voltemand and Cornelius
    Now for ourself and for this time of meeting,
    Thus much the business is: we have here writ
    To Norway, uncle of young Fortinbras —
    Who, impotent and bedrid, scarcely hears
30   Of this his nephew's purpose — to suppress

1.2 *Location: the royal castle at Elsinore* **2 green** fresh **4 contracted** knit together **5 discretion**
good judgement, reason **8 sometime** former **9 jointress** widow with rights to property that she formerly
owned with her husband **11 one ... eye** one eye looking cheerfully to the future and the other downcast
and tearful **13 dole** sorrow **14 barred** ignored/excluded **17 that you know** what you should know,
that/what you already know **18 supposal** estimate **21 Colleaguèd** joined, allied **dream ...**
advantage illusion of his superior position/dream of what he might gain **23 Importing** concerning
29 impotent powerless, frail **bedrid** bedridden

His further gait herein, in that the levies,
The lists and full proportions, are all made
Out of his subject. And we here dispatch
You, good Cornelius, and you, Voltemand,
35   For bearing of this greeting to old Norway,
Giving to you no further personal power
To business with the king, more than the scope
Of these dilated articles allow.   *Gives a paper*
Farewell, and let your haste commend your duty.
40   VOLTEMAND In that, and all things, will we show our
        duty.
KING We doubt it nothing: heartily farewell.—
                        Exeunt Voltemand and Cornelius
And now, Laertes, what's the news with you?
You told us of some suit: what is't, Laertes?
You cannot speak of reason to the Dane
45   And lose your voice: what wouldst thou beg, Laertes,
That shall not be my offer, not thy asking?
The head is not more native to the heart,
The hand more instrumental to the mouth,
Than is the throne of Denmark to thy father.
50   What wouldst thou have, Laertes?
LAERTES Dread my lord,
Your leave and favour to return to France,
From whence though willingly I came to Denmark
To show my duty in your coronation,
55   Yet now I must confess, that duty done,
My thoughts and wishes bend again towards France
And bow them to your gracious leave and pardon.
KING Have you your father's leave? What says Polonius?
POLONIUS He hath, my lord:
60   I do beseech you, give him leave to go.
KING Take thy fair hour, Laertes: time be thine,
And thy best graces spend it at thy will.—
But now, my cousin Hamlet, and my son—

31 His i.e. Fortinbras' gait proceeding in...subject since the full number of troops mustered is
drawn from his (the king's) subjects 37 To for 38 dilated articles detailed, fully expressed terms
39 haste...duty speedy departure, rather than words, convey your dutifulness 41 nothing not at all
43 suit formal request 44 Dane Danish king 45 lose your voice waste your words 46 That...asking
that I shall not give you rather than have you ask for it 47 native closely related 48 instrumental
serviceable 51 Dread my lord my revered lord 52 leave and favour kind permission 57 bow them
submit themselves leave and pardon indulgent permission 62 graces qualities/virtues 63 cousin a
general term for a relative

HAMLET A little more than kin and less than kind.

65 KING How is it that the clouds still hang on you?

HAMLET Not so, my lord:— I am too much i'th'sun.   *Aside?*

GERTRUDE Good Hamlet, cast thy nightly colour off,
　　　And let thine eye look like a friend on Denmark.
　　　Do not forever with thy veilèd lids
70 　　Seek for thy noble father in the dust:
　　　Thou know'st 'tis common, all that lives must die,
　　　Passing through nature to eternity.

HAMLET Ay, madam, it is common.

GERTRUDE If it be,
75 　　Why seems it so particular with thee?

HAMLET 'Seems', madam? Nay it is: I know not 'seems'.
　　　'Tis not alone my inky cloak, good mother,
　　　Nor customary suits of solemn black,
　　　Nor windy suspiration of forced breath,
80 　　No, nor the fruitful river in the eye,
　　　Nor the dejected 'haviour of the visage,
　　　Together with all forms, moods, shows of grief,
　　　That can denote me truly: these indeed seem,
　　　For they are actions that a man might play,
85 　　But I have that within which passeth show;
　　　These but the trappings and the suits of woe.

KING 'Tis sweet and commendable in your nature, Hamlet,
　　　To give these mourning duties to your father:
　　　But you must know your father lost a father,
90 　　That father lost, lost his, and the survivor bound
　　　In filial obligation for some term
　　　To do obsequious sorrow. But to persever
　　　In obstinate condolement is a course
　　　Of impious stubbornness: 'tis unmanly grief:
95 　　It shows a will most incorrect to heaven,
　　　A heart unfortified, a mind impatient,
　　　An understanding simple and unschooled.
　　　For what we know must be and is as common
　　　As any the most vulgar thing to sense,

---

64 A...kind i.e. after his marriage to Gertrude, Claudius has become more closely (too closely) related to Hamlet, but the relationship is lacking in natural feeling   kind natural/familial/affectionate   67 nightly colour dark mourning clothes/gloomy demeanour   69 veilèd lids lowered eyes   71 common universal; in his reply, Hamlet engineers a dig at Gertrude by playing on the senses of 'vulgar/whorish'   75 particular specific, personal   78 customary habitual to me/socially conventional   79 suspiration sighing 81 'haviour...visage facial expression   82 moods outward expressions of mood   83 denote depict 85 passeth surpasses, exceeds   92 obsequious relating to obsequies (commemorative rites for the dead) persever persevere   93 condolement grieving   95 incorrect disobedient   96 impatient unwilling to endure (suffering)   99 any...sense the most ordinary thing we may experience

100   Why should we in our peevish opposition
       Take it to heart? Fie, 'tis a fault to heaven,
       A fault against the dead, a fault to nature,
       To reason most absurd, whose common theme
       Is death of fathers, and who still hath cried,
105   From the first corpse till he that died today,
       'This must be so.' We pray you throw to earth
       This unprevailing woe, and think of us
       As of a father; for let the world take note,
       You are the most immediate to our throne,
110   And with no less nobility of love
       Than that which dearest father bears his son,
       Do I impart towards you. For your intent
       In going back to school in Wittenberg,
       It is most retrograde to our desire,
115   And we beseech you bend you to remain
       Here in the cheer and comfort of our eye,
       Our chiefest courtier, cousin, and our son.
       GERTRUDE Let not thy mother lose her prayers, Hamlet:
       I prithee stay with us, go not to Wittenberg.
120   HAMLET I shall in all my best obey you, madam.
       KING Why, 'tis a loving and a fair reply.
       Be as ourself in Denmark.— Madam, come:
       This gentle and unforced accord of Hamlet
       Sits smiling to my heart, in grace whereof,
125   No jocund health that Denmark drinks today
       But the great cannon to the clouds shall tell,
       And the king's rouse the heavens shall bruit again,
       Re-speaking earthly thunder. Come away.
                                    Exeunt. Hamlet remains
       HAMLET O, that this too too solid flesh would melt,
130   Thaw and resolve itself into a dew!
       Or that the Everlasting had not fixed
       His canon gainst self-slaughter! O God, O God!
       How weary, stale, flat and unprofitable
       Seem to me all the uses of this world!
135   Fie on't! O, fie, fie! 'Tis an unweeded garden

100 **peevish** stubborn, wilful   101 **Fie** expression of disgust or indignation   104 **still** always
107 **unprevailing** unavailing, pointless   109 **most immediate** i.e. heir   112 **For** as for   113 **Wittenberg** city in Germany, home to a well-known Protestant university   114 **retrograde** contrary   115 **bend you** incline yourself   123 **gentle** kind/noble   **accord** consent   124 **grace whereof** thanksgiving for which   125 **jocund health** merry toast   **Denmark** i.e. himself, King of Denmark   126 **tell** report/count out (i.e. a celebratory cannon shot will be fired for each toast)   127 **rouse** (drinking of a) full draught of liquor   **bruit** proclaim/celebrate   128 **Re-speaking** echoing, repeating   130 **resolve** dissolve   131 **Everlasting** i.e. God   132 **canon** law, decree   134 **uses** habits, customary practices

That grows to seed: things rank and gross in nature
Possess it merely. That it should come to this!
But two months dead: nay, not so much, not two.
So excellent a king, that was to this
140   Hyperion to a satyr, so loving to my mother
That he might not beteem the winds of heaven
Visit her face too roughly. Heaven and earth,
Must I remember? Why, she would hang on him
As if increase of appetite had grown
145   By what it fed on, and yet within a month —
Let me not think on't: frailty, thy name is woman! —
A little month, or ere those shoes were old
With which she followed my poor father's body,
Like Niobe, all tears: why she, even she —
150   O, heaven! A beast that wants discourse of reason
Would have mourned longer — married with mine
        uncle,
My father's brother but no more like my father
Than I to Hercules. Within a month?
Ere yet the salt of most unrighteous tears
155   Had left the flushing of her gallèd eyes,
She married. O, most wicked speed, to post
With such dexterity to incestuous sheets!
It is not nor it cannot come to good:
But break my heart, for I must hold my tongue.
Enter Horatio, Barnardo and Marcellus
160   **HORATIO** Hail to your lordship!
HAMLET I am glad to see you well:
        Horatio — or I do forget myself.   *Recognizes him*
HORATIO The same, my lord, and your poor servant ever.
HAMLET Sir, my good friend, I'll change that name with
        you.
165   And what make you from Wittenberg, Horatio?—
        Marcellus.
MARCELLUS My good lord.

---

136 **rank and gross** coarsely profuse in growth   137 **merely** completely   139 **to** compared to
140 **Hyperion** Greek god of the sun, and one of the Titans   **satyr** mythological creature, part-man and part-
goat (often associated with lechery)   141 **beteem** permit   147 **or ere** before   149 **Niobe** for boasting that
she had more children than the goddess Leto, Niobe's offspring were killed; she grieved until she was turned
into a stone, from which tears continued to stream   150 **wants . . . reason** lacks the faculty of reason
153 **Hercules** famously strong Greek hero who completed twelve arduous labours   154 **unrighteous**
wicked/insincere   155 **flushing** redness   **gallèd** sore, irritated   156 **post** rush (literally, ride swiftly)
164 **change . . . you** exchange the name of **servant** for that of **friend**/exchange the name of servant with you
(and become yours)/mutually exchange the name of friend with you   165 **make you from** are you doing
away from

HAMLET I am very glad to see you.— Good even, sir.—   *To Barnardo*
    But what in faith make you from Wittenberg?   *To Horatio*

170 HORATIO A truant disposition, good my lord.

HAMLET I would not have your enemy say so,
    Nor shall you do mine ear that violence,
    To make it truster of your own report
    Against yourself: I know you are no truant.
175   But what is your affair in Elsinore?
    We'll teach you to drink deep ere you depart.

HORATIO My lord, I came to see your father's funeral.

HAMLET I pray thee do not mock me, fellow student:
    I think it was to see my mother's wedding.

180 HORATIO Indeed, my lord, it followed hard upon.

HAMLET Thrift, thrift, Horatio! The funeral baked meats
    Did coldly furnish forth the marriage tables.
    Would I had met my dearest foe in heaven
    Ere I had ever seen that day, Horatio.
185   My father, methinks I see my father.

HORATIO O, where, my lord?

HAMLET In my mind's eye, Horatio.

HORATIO I saw him once; he was a goodly king.

HAMLET He was a man, take him for all in all:
190   I shall not look upon his like again.

HORATIO My lord, I think I saw him yesternight.

HAMLET Saw who?

HORATIO My lord, the king your father.

HAMLET The king my father?

195 HORATIO Season your admiration for a while
    With an attent ear till I may deliver,
    Upon the witness of these gentlemen,
    This marvel to you.

HAMLET For heaven's love, let me hear.

200 HORATIO Two nights together had these gentlemen,
    Marcellus and Barnardo, on their watch,
    In the dead waste and middle of the night,
    Been thus encountered. A figure like your father,
    Armed at all points exactly, cap-à-pie,
205   Appears before them, and with solemn march
    Goes slow and stately: by them thrice he walked,

168 even evening (also used in the afternoon) **170 truant** lazy, negligent **176 ere** before **180 hard close** **181 Thrift** economy **baked meats** meat pies, pastries **183 dearest** closest, greatest **191 yesternight** last night **195 Season your admiration** control your astonishment **196 attent** attentive **deliver** report **202 waste** desolate expanse (puns on 'waist') **204 at all points** in every respect **cap-à-pie** from head to foot **206 Goes** walks/passes along

By their oppressed and fear-surprisèd eyes
Within his truncheon's length, whilst they, distilled
Almost to jelly with the act of fear
210 Stand dumb and speak not to him. This to me
In dreadful secrecy impart they did,
And I with them the third night kept the watch,
Where, as they had delivered, both in time,
Form of the thing, each word made true and good,
215 The apparition comes. I knew your father:
These hands are not more like.

HAMLET But where was this?

MARCELLUS My lord, upon the platform where we
watched.

HAMLET Did you not speak to it?

220 **HORATIO** My lord, I did;
But answer made it none. Yet once methought
It lifted up its head and did address
Itself to motion, like as it would speak:
But even then the morning cock crew loud,
225 And at the sound it shrunk in haste away
And vanished from our sight.

HAMLET 'Tis very strange.

HORATIO As I do live, my honoured lord, 'tis true;
And we did think it writ down in our duty
230 To let you know of it.

HAMLET Indeed, indeed, sirs; but this troubles me.
Hold you the watch tonight?

MARCELLUS *and* **BARNARDO** We do, my lord.

HAMLET Armed, say you?

235 **MARCELLUS** *and* **BARNARDO** Armed, my lord.

HAMLET From top to toe?

MARCELLUS *and* **BARNARDO** My lord, from head to foot.

HAMLET Then saw you not his face?

HORATIO O, yes, my lord, he wore his beaver up.

240 **HAMLET** What, looked he frowningly?

HORATIO A countenance more in sorrow than in anger.

HAMLET Pale or red?

HORATIO Nay, very pale.

HAMLET And fixed his eyes upon you?

207 **oppressed and fear-surprisèd** overcome and taken prisoner by fear   208 **truncheon** staff carried as
a symbol of military authority   **distilled** dissolved   209 **act** action/influence   211 **dreadful** full of dread
and fear   216 **These ... like** my two hands are not more alike than the ghost was like your father
218 **platform** terrace on which guns were mounted   222 **address ... speak** prepare itself for action as if it
were about to speak   239 **beaver** visor of a helmet   241 **countenance** facial expression

245   **HORATIO** Most constantly.
      HAMLET I would I had been there.
      HORATIO It would have much amazed you.
      HAMLET Very like, very like. Stayed it long?
      HORATIO While one with moderate haste might tell a
          hundred.
250 **MARCELLUS** *and* **BARNARDO** Longer, longer.
      HORATIO Not when I saw't.
      HAMLET His beard was grizzly, no?
      HORATIO It was, as I have seen it in his life,
          A sable silvered.
255 **HAMLET** I'll watch tonight; perchance 'twill walk again.
      HORATIO I warrant you it will.
      HAMLET If it assume my noble father's person,
          I'll speak to it though hell itself should gape
          And bid me hold my peace. I pray you all,
260   If you have hitherto concealed this sight,
          Let it be tenable in your silence still,
          And whatsoever else shall hap tonight,
          Give it an understanding but no tongue.
          I will requite your loves. So, fare ye well:
265   Upon the platform 'twixt eleven and twelve
          I'll visit you.
      ALL Our duty to your honour.   *Exeunt [all but Hamlet]*
      HAMLET Your love, as mine to you: farewell.—
          My father's spirit in arms? All is not well:
270   I doubt some foul play. Would the night were come.
          Till then, sit still my soul: foul deeds will rise,
          Though all the earth o'erwhelm them, to men's eyes.
                       Exit

Act 1 Scene 3   *running scene 3*

Enter Laertes and Ophelia

      LAERTES My necessaries are embarked, farewell:
          And, sister, as the winds give benefit
          And convoy is assistant, do not sleep
          But let me hear from you.
5   **OPHELIA** Do you doubt that?

---

249 **tell** count   252 **grizzly** grey   254 **sable silvered** black mixed with silver hairs   256 **warrant** assure
261 **tenable** capable of being held   **still** plays on the sense of 'silent'   264 **requite** reward   270 **doubt**
suspect/fear   **1.3** *Location: within the castle*   2 **as** whenever   3 **convoy is assistant** transport (for
letters) is available

LAERTES For Hamlet and the trifling of his favours,
Hold it a fashion and a toy in blood,
A violet in the youth of primy nature,
Froward, not permanent, sweet, not lasting,
10   The suppliance of a minute, no more.
OPHELIA No more but so?
LAERTES Think it no more,
For nature crescent does not grow alone
In thews and bulk, but as his temple waxes,
15   The inward service of the mind and soul
Grows wide withal. Perhaps he loves you now,
And now no soil nor cautel doth besmirch
The virtue of his will: but you must fear,
His greatness weighed, his will is not his own;
20   For he himself is subject to his birth:
He may not, as unvalued persons do,
Carve for himself, for on his choice depends
The sanctity and health of the whole state,
And therefore must his choice be circumscribed
25   Unto the voice and yielding of that body
Whereof he is the head. Then if he says he loves you,
It fits your wisdom so far to believe it
As he in his peculiar sect and force
May give his saying deed, which is no further
30   Than the main voice of Denmark goes withal.
Then weigh what loss your honour may sustain
If with too credent ear you list his songs,
Or lose your heart, or your chaste treasure open
To his unmastered importunity.
35   Fear it, Ophelia, fear it, my dear sister,
And keep within the rear of your affection,
Out of the shot and danger of desire.
The chariest maid is prodigal enough

7 toy in blood amorous whim   **8 primy** in its prime/early/wonderful/sexually excited   **9 Froward** perverse/obstinate/wilful/ungovernable   **10 suppliance** fulfilment/pastime   **11 but so** than that   **13 crescent** growing   **14 thews** bodily proportions, muscles   **temple** i.e. body (the temple of the soul)   **16 withal** with it   **17 soil nor cautel** stain nor deceit   **18 will** intent/(sexual) desire   **19 weighed** being considered   **21 unvalued** i.e. without rank   **22 Carve** choose (from the image of serving oneself meat; with sexual connotations)   **23 sanctity** inviolability/worthiness of religious respect   **25 yielding** consent   **28 peculiar . . . force** particular circumstances of rank and power   **30 main voice** general agreement   **withal** along with   **32 credent** credulous, trusting   **list** listen to   **33 chaste treasure** i.e. virginity (**treasure** was slang for 'vagina')   **34 unmastered importunity** unrestrained persistence   **36 keep . . . affection** i.e. do not advance headlong into the dangerous territory your affection might lead you into   **rear** back portion of an army, which moves last   **37 shot** maintains the military image, with suggestions of phallic attack   **38 chariest** most modest/cautious/frugal

If she unmask her beauty to the moon:
40   Virtue itself scapes not calumnious strokes:
The canker galls the infants of the spring
Too oft before the buttons be disclosed,
And in the morn and liquid dew of youth
Contagious blastments are most imminent.
45   Be wary then: best safety lies in fear.
Youth to itself rebels, though none else near.

OPHELIA   I shall th'effect of this good lesson keep
As watchman to my heart. But, good my brother,
Do not, as some ungracious pastors do,
50   Show me the steep and thorny way to heaven,
Whilst, like a puffed and reckless libertine
Himself the primrose path of dalliance treads,
And recks not his own rede.

LAERTES   O, fear me not.

Enter Polonius

55   I stay too long. But here my father comes.
A double blessing is a double grace;
Occasion smiles upon a second leave.

POLONIUS   Yet here, Laertes? Aboard, aboard, for shame!
The wind sits in the shoulder of your sail,
60   And you are stayed for there. My blessing with you!
And these few precepts in thy memory
See thou character. Give thy thoughts no tongue,
Nor any unproportioned thought his act.
Be thou familiar, but by no means vulgar.
65   The friends thou hast, and their adoption tried,
Grapple them to thy soul with hoops of steel,
But do not dull thy palm with entertainment
Of each new-hatched, unfledged comrade: beware
Of entrance to a quarrel, but being in,
70   Bear't that th'opposèd may beware of thee.
Give every man thine ear, but few thy voice:
Take each man's censure, but reserve thy judgement:

39 If she i.e. if she does no more than   moon symbol of chastity   40 scapes escapes   calumnious strokes slanderous blows   41 canker canker-worm, a grub that destroys plants   galls wounds, destroys infants...spring i.e. young plants   42 buttons be disclosed buds be open   44 blastments blights/ withering   46 to against   49 ungracious ungodly   51 puffed swollen with pride and vanity   53 recks heeds   rede advice   54 fear me not do not worry about me   55 stay delay   56 double blessing i.e. a second chance to say goodbye to and receive the blessing of Polonius   57 Occasion opportunity   leave leave-taking, farewell   60 stayed waited   62 See thou character make sure that you inscribe 63 unproportioned immoderate/unruly   his its   64 familiar friendly, sociable   65 adoption tried worthiness to be adopted as friends having been tested   66 Grapple fasten firmly   67 dull thy palm i.e. by shaking hands too often   68 unfledged still unfeathered (i.e. new, untried)   70 Bear't that th'opposèd manage it so that your opponent   72 censure judgement/opinion

Costly thy habit as thy purse can buy,
But not expressed in fancy; rich, not gaudy:
75   For the apparel oft proclaims the man,
And they in France of the best rank and station
Are of a most select and generous chief in that.
Neither a borrower nor a lender be,
For loan oft loses both itself and friend,
80   And borrowing dulls the edge of husbandry.
This above all: to thine own self be true,
And it must follow, as the night the day,
Thou canst not then be false to any man.
Farewell: my blessing season this in thee!
85   **LAERTES** Most humbly do I take my leave, my lord.
POLONIUS The time invites you. Go, your servants tend.
LAERTES Farewell, Ophelia, and remember well
What I have said to you.
OPHELIA 'Tis in my memory locked,
90   And you yourself shall keep the key of it.
LAERTES Farewell.   *Exit Laertes*
POLONIUS What is't, Ophelia, he hath said to you?
OPHELIA So please you, something touching the lord
Hamlet.
POLONIUS Marry, well bethought.
95   'Tis told me, he hath very oft of late
Given private time to you; and you yourself
Have of your audience been most free and bounteous:
If it be so, as so 'tis put on me,
And that in way of caution, I must tell you
100   You do not understand yourself so clearly
As it behoves my daughter and your honour.
What is between you? Give me up the truth.
OPHELIA He hath, my lord, of late made many tenders
Of his affection to me.
105   **POLONIUS** Affection? Puh! You speak like a green girl,
Unsifted in such perilous circumstance.
Do you believe his tenders, as you call them?
OPHELIA I do not know, my lord, what I should think.

---

73 habit clothing   **74 fancy** elaborate, fanciful style   **77 Are . . . that** are of a most distinguished and noble
pre-eminence in their choice garments   **80 husbandry** economy   **83 false** dishonest, disloyal   **84 season**
ripen   **this** i.e. his advice   **86 tend** await   **93 touching** concerning   **94 Marry** by the Virgin Mary
bethought thought of   **97 audience** hearing, reception   **98 put on** conveyed to/impressed upon
101 behoves befits, is appropriate for   **103 tenders** offers (Polonius subsequently shifts the sense to 'offers
of money')   **105 green** inexperienced/gullible   **106 Unsifted** untested

POLONIUS Marry, I'll teach you: think yourself a baby
110   That you have ta'en his tenders for true pay
        Which are not sterling. Tender yourself more dearly;
        Or — not to crack the wind of the poor phrase,
        Running it thus — you'll tender me a fool.

OPHELIA My lord, he hath importuned me with love
115   In honourable fashion.

POLONIUS Ay, fashion you may call it. Go to, go to.

OPHELIA And hath given countenance to his speech,
        My lord, with all the vows of heaven.

POLONIUS Ay, springes to catch woodcocks. I do know,
120   When the blood burns, how prodigal the soul
        Lends the tongue vows: these blazes, daughter,
        Giving more light than heat, extinct in both
        Even in their promise, as it is a-making,
        You must not take for fire. For this time, daughter,
125   Be somewhat scanter of your maiden presence;
        Set your entreatments at a higher rate
        Than a command to parley. For Lord Hamlet,
        Believe so much in him that he is young
        And with a larger tether may he walk
130   Than may be given you: in few, Ophelia,
        Do not believe his vows, for they are brokers,
        Not of the dye which their investments show,
        But mere implorators of unholy suits,
        Breathing like sanctified and pious bawds,
135   The better to beguile. This is for all:
        I would not, in plain terms, from this time forth,
        Have you so slander any moment leisure,
        As to give words or talk with the Lord Hamlet.
        Look to't, I charge you. Come your ways.

140 OPHELIA I shall obey, my lord.   *Exeunt*

111 sterling true currency   Tender . . . dearly take greater care of yourself/value yourself more highly/offer yourself at a higher rate   112 crack . . . of make broken-winded, i.e. wear out   113 Running the image is of urging a horse   tender . . . fool show yourself up to be a fool/show me to be a fool/present me with an illegitimate baby   114 importuned entreated persistently   116 fashion shifts the sense from Ophelia's 'manner' to 'mere form/passing fancy'   Go to expression of dismissive impatience   117 countenance authority/confirmation   119 springes snares   woodcocks birds which were easily caught, hence regarded as stupid, gullible   120 prodigal prodigally, liberally   122 extinct . . . a-making i.e. both light and heat are extinguished in such passionate declarations even as they are being uttered   124 For this time for the time being   125 scanter more sparing   126 entreatments discussions/military negotiations   127 command to parley call from the enemy for the negotiation of terms (i.e. Ophelia is not obliged to meet with and possibly discuss surrender to Hamlet simply because he requests it)   130 in few in short   131 brokers negotiators/go-betweens/pimps   132 investments clothes   133 mere implorators out-and-out pleaders   suits requests/courtship (plays on the sense of 'clothing')   134 bawds procurers, pimps   135 beguile deceive   for all once for all/in sum   137 moment moment of   139 Come your ways come along

[Act 1 Scene 4]

Enter Hamlet, Horatio, Marcellus

HAMLET The air bites shrewdly: is it very cold?
HORATIO It is a nipping and an eager air.
HAMLET What hour now?
HORATIO I think it lacks of twelve.
5 **HAMLET** No, it is struck.
HORATIO Indeed? I heard it not: then it draws near the
    season
    Wherein the spirit held his wont to walk.   *A flourish of trumpets and*
    What does this mean, my lord?   *drums, perhaps also cannon*
HAMLET The king doth wake tonight and takes his rouse,
10   Keeps wassail, and the swaggering upspring reels:
    And as he drains his draughts of Rhenish down,
    The kettledrum and trumpet thus bray out
    The triumph of his pledge.
HORATIO Is it a custom?
15 **HAMLET** Ay, marry, is't:
    And to my mind, though I am native here
    And to the manner born, it is a custom
    More honoured in the breach than the observance.
Enter Ghost
HORATIO Look, my lord, it comes!
20 **HAMLET** Angels and ministers of grace defend us!
    Be thou a spirit of health or goblin damned,
    Bring with thee airs from heaven or blasts from hell,
    Be thy intents wicked or charitable,
    Thou com'st in such a questionable shape
25   That I will speak to thee: I'll call thee Hamlet,
    King, father, royal Dane. O, O, answer me!
    Let me not burst in ignorance, but tell
    Why thy canonized bones, hearsèd in death,
    Have burst their cerements, why the sepulchre

1.4 *Location: the gun terrace of the royal castle at Elsinore* **1 shrewdly** sharply, keenly **2 eager** biting **4 lacks of** is just before **7 held his wont** has been accustomed *flourish* trumpet fanfare accompanying a person in authority **9 wake** stay up/revel **takes his rouse** carouses **10 Keeps wassail** revels/drinks heartily **the . . . reels** drunkenly dances the upspring, a German dance **11 Rhenish** German wine from the area around the River Rhine **12 kettledrum** type of drum often associated with the Danes **bray . . . pledge** i.e. raucously celebrate the king's fulfilment of his earlier promise to drain a full draught of liquor **17 manner** custom **18 More . . . observance** better being broken than observed **20 ministers of grace** God's messengers, angels **21 Be thou** whether you are **health** benevolence/salvation **goblin** demon **24 questionable shape** form that invites question **28 canonized** consecrated, buried according to Christian rite (three syllables, stress on second) **hearsèd** entombed **29 cerements** grave clothes **sepulchre** tomb

30   Wherein we saw thee quietly inurned,
        Hath oped his ponderous and marble jaws
        To cast thee up again. What may this mean,
        That thou, dead corpse, again in complete steel
        Revisits thus the glimpses of the moon,
35   Making night hideous, and we fools of nature
        So horridly to shake our disposition
        With thoughts beyond the reaches of our souls?
        Say, why is this? Wherefore? What should we do?
Ghost beckons Hamlet
HORATIO It beckons you to go away with it,
40   As if it some impartment did desire
        To you alone.
MARCELLUS Look, with what courteous action
        It wafts you to a more removèd ground:
        But do not go with it.
45   **HORATIO** No, by no means.
HAMLET It will not speak; then will I follow it.
HORATIO Do not, my lord.
HAMLET Why, what should be the fear?
        I do not set my life at a pin's fee;
50   And for my soul, what can it do to that,
        Being a thing immortal as itself?
        It waves me forth again: I'll follow it.
HORATIO What if it tempt you toward the flood, my lord,
        Or to the dreadful summit of the cliff
55   That beetles o'er his base into the sea,
        And there assumes some other horrible form
        Which might deprive your sovereignty of reason
        And draw you into madness? Think of it.
HAMLET It wafts me still.— Go on, I'll follow thee.
60   **MARCELLUS** You shall not go, my lord.   *Holds him back*
HAMLET Hold off your hand.
HORATIO Be ruled: you shall not go.
HAMLET My fate cries out,
        And makes each petty artery in this body

---

30 **inurned** enclosed/buried   31 **ponderous** weighty   32 **cast** vomit   33 **complete steel** full armour
34 **glimpses...moon** earth by moonlight, literally 'flashes of moonlight'   35 **hideous** frightening, full of
horror   **fools of nature** ignorant mortals/playthings of nature   36 **horridly** dreadfully/with horror
disposition ordinary temperaments/mental composure   38 **Wherefore?** Why?   40 **impartment**
communication   43 **wafts** waves, beckons   49 **a pin's fee** the (tiny) worth of a pin   53 **flood** sea
55 **beetles o'er** overhangs (like frowning eyebrows)   57 **deprive...reason** remove your reason from its
position of control   64 **artery** thought not to convey blood, but the ethereal fluid known as 'vital spirits'

65   As hardy as the Nemean lion's nerve.—
        Still am I called?— Unhand me, gentlemen.
        By heav'n, I'll make a ghost of him that lets me!
        I say, away!— Go on, I'll follow thee.

                               Exeunt Ghost and Hamlet

HORATIO He waxes desperate with imagination.

70 **MARCELLUS** Let's follow; 'tis not fit thus to obey him.
HORATIO Have after. To what issue will this come?
MARCELLUS Something is rotten in the state of Denmark.
HORATIO Heaven will direct it.
MARCELLUS Nay, let's follow him.   *Exeunt*

[Act 1 Scene 5]   *running scene 4 continues*

Enter Ghost and Hamlet

HAMLET Where wilt thou lead me? Speak; I'll go no further.
GHOST Mark me.
HAMLET I will.
GHOST My hour is almost come,

5   When I to sulphurous and tormenting flames
        Must render up myself.

HAMLET Alas, poor ghost!
GHOST Pity me not, but lend thy serious hearing
        To what I shall unfold.

10 **HAMLET** Speak: I am bound to hear.
GHOST So art thou to revenge, when thou shalt hear.
HAMLET What?
GHOST I am thy father's spirit,
        Doomed for a certain term to walk the night,

15   And for the day confined to fast in fires,
        Till the foul crimes done in my days of nature
        Are burnt and purged away. But that I am forbid
        To tell the secrets of my prison-house,
        I could a tale unfold whose lightest word

20   Would harrow up thy soul, freeze thy young blood,
        Make thy two eyes like stars start from their spheres,
        Thy knotty and combinèd locks to part
        And each particular hair to stand on end

---

65 Nemean lion supposedly invincible beast strangled by Hercules as one of his twelve labours   **nerve** sinew, tendon   **67 lets** hinders   **69 waxes** grows   **71 Have after** let's follow   **issue** outcome   **73 it** i.e. the **issue**   **1.5**   **2 Mark** listen, pay attention to   **9 unfold** reveal   **10 bound** ready/under obligation **17 But** were it not   **20 harrow up** distress/tear up   **21 like ... spheres** individual stars and planets were thought to be contained within concentric hollow spheres that revolved around the earth   **22 knotty ... locks** neat and carefully styled hair

                Like quills upon the fretful porpentine.
25   But this eternal blazon must not be
                To ears of flesh and blood. List, Hamlet, O, list!
                If thou didst ever thy dear father love—
        HAMLET O heaven!
        GHOST Revenge his foul and most unnatural murder.
30   **HAMLET** Murder?
        GHOST Murder most foul, as in the best it is,
                But this most foul, strange and unnatural.
        HAMLET Haste, haste me to know it, that I with wings as
                    swift
                As meditation or the thoughts of love
35   May sweep to my revenge.
        GHOST I find thee apt,
                And duller shouldst thou be than the fat weed
                That roots itself in ease on Lethe wharf,
                Wouldst thou not stir in this. Now, Hamlet, hear:
40   It's given out that, sleeping in mine orchard,
                A serpent stung me, so the whole ear of Denmark
                Is by a forgèd process of my death
                Rankly abused. But know thou, noble youth,
                The serpent that did sting thy father's life
45   Now wears his crown.
        HAMLET O, my prophetic soul! Mine uncle!
        GHOST Ay, that incestuous, that adulterate beast,
                With witchcraft of his wit, with traitorous gifts —
                O, wicked wit and gifts, that have the power
50   So to seduce! — won to his shameful lust
                The will of my most seeming-virtuous queen.
                O Hamlet, what a falling-off was there!
                From me, whose love was of that dignity
                That it went hand in hand even with the vow
55   I made to her in marriage, and to decline
                Upon a wretch whose natural gifts were poor
                To those of mine!
                But virtue, as it never will be moved,
                Though lewdness court it in a shape of heaven,
60   So lust, though to a radiant angel linked,

24 **porpentine** porcupine   25 **eternal blazon** revelation of the secrets of the eternal world   26 **List** listen
31 **in the best** even at best   34 **meditation** thought   35 **sweep** swoop in sudden attack   36 **apt** fit/
ready/responsive   37 **duller . . . be** you would be more sluggish   38 **Lethe wharf** the banks of the Lethe,
the river of forgetfulness in the classical underworld   40 **orchard** garden   42 **forgèd process** fabricated
account   43 **Rankly** excessively/foully   47 **adulterate** adulterous   48 **gifts** natural talents/presents
51 **will** sexual desire   53 **dignity** worth, excellence   55 **decline Upon** sink to   58 **virtue, as it** as virtue

Will sate itself in a celestial bed,
And prey on garbage.
But, soft, methinks I scent the morning's air;
Brief let me be. Sleeping within mine orchard,
65 My custom always in the afternoon,
Upon my secure hour thy uncle stole,
With juice of cursèd hebenon in a vial,
And in the porches of mine ears did pour
The leperous distilment, whose effect
70 Holds such an enmity with blood of man
That swift as quicksilver it courses through
The natural gates and alleys of the body,
And with a sudden vigour it doth posset
And curd, like eager droppings into milk,
75 The thin and wholesome blood: so did it mine,
And a most instant tetter barked about,
Most lazar-like, with vile and loathsome crust,
All my smooth body.
Thus was I, sleeping, by a brother's hand
80 Of life, of crown and queen, at once dispatched:
Cut off even in the blossoms of my sin,
Unhouseled, disappointed, unaneled,
No reckoning made, but sent to my account
With all my imperfections on my head.
85 O horrible, O horrible, most horrible!
If thou hast nature in thee, bear it not;
Let not the royal bed of Denmark be
A couch for luxury and damnèd incest.
But, howsoever thou pursuest this act,
90 Taint not thy mind nor let thy soul contrive
Against thy mother aught; leave her to heaven
And to those thorns that in her bosom lodge,
To prick and sting her. Fare thee well at once;
The glow-worm shows the matin to be near,

61 **sate itself** become satiated/grow weary   62 **garbage** filth/animal entrails   66 **secure** carefree,
unsuspecting   67 **hebenon** a poisonous substance – possibly 'henbane' or 'yew' (*hebenus*)   69 **leperous
distilment** distillation causing leprosy-like symptoms (i.e. corrosion of the skin)   71 **quicksilver** liquid
mercury   73 **posset And curd** clot, curdle   74 **eager** sour/acid   76 **tetter** eruption of the skin   **barked
about** covered with a bark-like crust   77 **lazar-like** leper-like   80 **dispatched** deprived through death
82 **Unhouseled, disappointed, unaneled** without having received Holy Communion (the 'housel'),
unprepared, and without having received extreme unction (being anointed with holy oil before death)
83 **reckoning** settling of debts   **account** i.e. judgement   86 **nature** natural feeling   88 **luxury** lust
90 **Taint** pollute   91 **aught** anything   94 **matin** morning

95   And 'gins to pale his uneffectual fire.
     Adieu, adieu, Hamlet: remember me.   *Exit*
     HAMLET O all you host of heaven! O earth! What else?
     And shall I couple hell? O, fie! Hold, my heart;
     And you, my sinews, grow not instant old,
100 But bear me stiffly up. Remember thee?
     Ay, thou poor ghost, while memory holds a seat
     In this distracted globe. Remember thee?
     Yea, from the table of my memory
     I'll wipe away all trivial fond records,
105 All saws of books, all forms, all pressures past
     That youth and observation copied there;
     And thy commandment all alone shall live
     Within the book and volume of my brain,
     Unmixed with baser matter: yes, yes, by heaven!
110 O most pernicious woman!
     O villain, villain, smiling, damnèd villain!
     My tables,
     My tables: meet it is I set it down
     That one may smile and smile and be a villain;
115 At least I'm sure it may be so in Denmark.   *Writes*
     So, uncle, there you are. Now to my word:
     It is 'Adieu, adieu, remember me.'
     I have sworn't.
     HORATIO *and* **MARCELLUS** My lord, my lord!   *Within*
     Enter Horatio and Marcellus
120 **MARCELLUS** Lord Hamlet!
     HORATIO Heaven secure him.
     HAMLET So be it.
     HORATIO Hillo, ho, ho, my lord!
     HAMLET Hillo, ho, ho, boy! Come, bird, come.
125 **MARCELLUS** How is't, my noble lord?
     HORATIO What news, my lord?
     HAMLET O, wonderful!
     HORATIO Good my lord, tell it.
     HAMLET No, you'll reveal it.
130 **HORATIO** Not I, my lord, by heaven.
     MARCELLUS Nor I, my lord.

95 **'gins** begins   **uneffectual** i.e. no longer providing light   97 **host** angels   98 **couple** add (to **heaven** and **earth**)   102 **distracted** distressed, agitated   **globe** world/head (plays on the name of the Globe theatre)   103 **table** writing tablet, slate   104 **fond** foolish   **records** memories/written accounts   105 **saws** sayings, maxims   **pressures** impressions, stamps   110 **pernicious** destructive/wicked   113 **meet** fitting   116 **word** watchword/motto   124 **Hillo...come** Hamlet mockingly responds as if Horatio's call were that of a falconer summoning his bird to return   125 **How is't** how is it with you, how are you   127 **wonderful** astonishing, extraordinary

HAMLET How say you, then, would heart of man once
    think it?
  But you'll be secret?

BOTH Ay, by heaven, my lord.

135 **HAMLET** There's ne'er a villain dwelling in all Denmark
    But he's an arrant knave.

HORATIO There needs no ghost, my lord, come from the
    grave
  To tell us this.

HAMLET Why, right, you are i'th'right;
140   And so, without more circumstance at all,
    I hold it fit that we shake hands and part:
    You, as your business and desires shall point you,
    For every man has business and desire,
    Such as it is: and for mine own poor part,
145   Look you, I'll go pray.

HORATIO These are but wild and whirling words, my lord.

HAMLET I'm sorry they offend you, heartily:
  Yes, faith, heartily.

HORATIO There's no offence, my lord.

150 **HAMLET** Yes, by Saint Patrick, but there is, Horatio,
    And much offence too. Touching this vision here,
    It is an honest ghost, that let me tell you:
    For your desire to know what is between us,
    O'ermaster't as you may. And now, good friends,
155   As you are friends, scholars and soldiers,
    Give me one poor request.

HORATIO What is't, my lord? We will.

HAMLET Never make known what you have seen tonight.

BOTH My lord, we will not.

160 **HAMLET** Nay, but swear't.

HORATIO In faith, my lord, not I.

MARCELLUS Nor I, my lord, in faith.

HAMLET Upon my sword.   *Holds out his sword*

MARCELLUS We have sworn, my lord, already.

165 **HAMLET** Indeed, upon my sword, indeed.

GHOST Swear.   *Ghost cries under the stage*

---

132 **once** ever   136 **arrant** downright/notorious   140 **circumstance** roundabout talk/details   142 **as**
i.e. in the direction that   150 **Saint Patrick** the keeper of Purgatory   152 **honest** genuine (i.e. not an evil
spirit)   154 **O'ermaster't** repress it   161 **not I** i.e. I will not tell (not 'I will not swear')   163 **sword** i.e. the
hilt of the sword (the shape of a cross)   *under the stage* accessed through the trapdoor, this region was
often associated with hell

HAMLET Ah ha, boy, say'st thou so? Art thou there,
    truepenny?—
    Come on, you hear this fellow in the cellarage:
    Consent to swear.
170 HORATIO Propose the oath, my lord.
HAMLET Never to speak of this that you have seen,
    Swear by my sword.
GHOST Swear.   *They swear*
HAMLET *Hic et ubique?* Then we'll shift our ground.   *Moves*
175   Come hither, gentlemen,
    And lay your hands again upon my sword:
    Never to speak of this that you have heard,
    Swear by my sword.
GHOST Swear.   *They swear*
180 HAMLET Well said, old mole. Canst work i'th'ground so
    fast?
    A worthy pioneer! Once more remove, good friends.
HORATIO O, day and night, but this is wondrous strange!
HAMLET And therefore as a stranger give it welcome.
    There are more things in heaven and earth, Horatio, *Aside to Horatio?*
185   Than are dreamt of in our philosophy.— But come,
    Here, as before, never, so help you mercy,
    How strange or odd soe'er I bear myself —
    As I perchance hereafter shall think meet
    To put an antic disposition on —
190   That you, at such time seeing me, never shall,
    With arms encumbered thus, or thus headshake,
    Or by pronouncing of some doubtful phrase,
    As 'Well, we know' or 'We could, an if we would'
    Or 'If we list to speak' or 'There be, an if they might'
195   Or such ambiguous giving out, to note
    That you know aught of me: this not to do,
    So grace and mercy at your most need help you. Swear.
GHOST Swear.   *They swear*
HAMLET Rest, rest, perturbèd spirit!— So, gentlemen,
200   With all my love I do commend me to you:
    And what so poor a man as Hamlet is

---

167 **truepenny** honest fellow   168 **cellarage** cellars   174 *Hic et ubique*? 'Here and everywhere?' (Latin)
181 **pioneer** soldier whose responsibility it was to dig trenches   **remove** move   183 **stranger** i.e. one in
need of hospitality   186 **never...mercy** never, as you hope for God's mercy (Hamlet begins the oath)
187 **How...soe'er** however strangely or oddly   189 **antic** grotesque/fantastic/bizarre   191 **encumbered**
entangled (i.e. folded)   **headshake** shaking the head   192 **doubtful** ambiguous   193 **an if** if   194 **list**
wished   **'There...might'** there are those who might tell, if they could   195 **giving out** utterance/
suggestion   **note** indicate   200 **commend me** entrust myself   201 **what** whatever

May do t'express his love and friending to you,
God willing, shall not lack. Let us go in together:
And still your fingers on your lips, I pray.
205 The time is out of joint: O, cursèd spite
That ever I was born to set it right!
Nay, come, let's go together.   *Exeunt*

Act 2 Scene 1   *running scene 5*

Enter Polonius and Reynaldo

POLONIUS Give him this money and these notes,
    Reynaldo.   *Gives money and papers*
REYNALDO I will, my lord.
POLONIUS You shall do marvellous wisely, good
    Reynaldo,
    Before you visit him, you make inquiry
5   Of his behaviour.
REYNALDO My lord, I did intend it.
POLONIUS Marry, well said; very well said. Look you, sir,
    Inquire me first what Danskers are in Paris,
    And how, and who, what means and where they keep,
10   What company, at what expense, and finding
    By this encompassment and drift of question
    That they do know my son, come you more nearer
    Than your particular demands will touch it:
    Take you, as 'twere, some distant knowledge of him,
15   As thus, 'I know his father and his friends
    And in part him.' Do you mark this, Reynaldo?
REYNALDO Ay, very well, my lord.
POLONIUS 'And in part him, but', you may say, 'not well,
    But if't be he I mean, he's very wild;
20   Addicted so and so', and there put on him
    What forgeries you please: marry, none so rank
    As may dishonour him — take heed of that —
    But, sir, such wanton, wild and usual slips
    As are companions noted and most known
25   To youth and liberty.

202 **friending** friendship   204 **still** always   205 **The time** things generally, the age   **out of joint** dislocated, disordered   2.1   *Location: within the royal castle at Elsinore; this remains the location for all scenes until Act 4 scene 3*   3 **marvellous** marvellously, extremely   4 **you** i.e. if you   8 **Inquire me** inquire (**me** is emphatic)   **Danskers** Danes   9 **keep** lodge   11 **encompassment** roundabout manner of talking   **drift** general aim   12 **come … it** you will come closer to the truth than you would were you to ask specific, pointed questions   14 **Take you** assume, affect   20 **Addicted** devoted or inclined to   21 **forgeries** fabrications   **rank** excessive/coarse   23 **wanton** boisterous/wild/lustful   **slips** flaws, foibles

REYNALDO As gaming, my lord.

POLONIUS Ay, or drinking, fencing, swearing, quarrelling,
    Drabbing: you may go so far.

REYNALDO My lord, that would dishonour him.

30 POLONIUS Faith, no, as you may season it in the charge.
    You must not put another scandal on him,
    That he is open to incontinency;
    That's not my meaning: but breathe his faults so quaintly
    That they may seem the taints of liberty,
35   The flash and outbreak of a fiery mind,
    A savageness in unreclaimèd blood,
    Of general assault.

REYNALDO But, my good lord—

POLONIUS Wherefore should you do this?

40 REYNALDO Ay, my lord, I would know that.

POLONIUS Marry, sir, here's my drift,
    And I believe, it is a fetch of warrant:
    You laying these slight sullies on my son,
    As 'twere a thing a little soiled i'th'working,
45   Mark you, your party in converse, him you would sound,
    Having ever seen in the prenominate crimes
    The youth you breathe of guilty, be assured
    He closes with you in this consequence:
    'Good sir' or so, or 'friend' or 'gentleman',
50   According to the phrase and the addition
    Of man and country.

REYNALDO Very good, my lord.

POLONIUS And then, sir, does he this — he does — what was I about to say? I was about to say something:
55 where did I leave?

REYNALDO At 'closes in the consequence' at 'friend or so' and 'gentleman'.

26 gaming gambling   28 Drabbing using prostitutes   30 season . . . charge moderate the accusation
32 incontinency excessive sexual licence   33 quaintly artfully, skilfully   34 taints of liberty faults
resulting from too much freedom   36 savageness wildness   unreclaimèd untamed   37 Of general
assault by which all men are affected   41 drift intention/plan   42 fetch of warrant legitimate stratagem
44 As 'twere as if he were   i'th'working in the handling, the manufacture   45 party in converse the
person with whom you are conversing   sound question, probe   46 Having ever if he has ever
prenominate aforementioned   47 breathe of speak about (i.e. Laertes)   48 closes . . . consequence
agrees with you in the following way   50 addition form of address

POLONIUS At 'closes in the consequence', ay, marry.
He closes with you thus: 'I know the gentleman,
60   I saw him yesterday, or t'other day',
Or then, or then, with such and such; and, as you say,
There was he gaming, there o'ertook in's rouse,
There falling out at tennis, or perchance,
'I saw him enter such a house of sale',
65   *Videlicet*, a brothel, or so forth.
See you now;
Your bait of falsehood takes this carp of truth:
And thus do we of wisdom and of reach,
With windlasses and with assays of bias,
70   By indirections find directions out:
So by my former lecture and advice,
Shall you my son. You have me, have you not?

REYNALDO My lord, I have.

POLONIUS God buy you; fare you well.

75 **REYNALDO** Good my lord.

POLONIUS Observe his inclination in yourself.

REYNALDO I shall, my lord.

POLONIUS And let him ply his music.

REYNALDO Well, my lord.   *Exit*

Enter Ophelia

80 **POLONIUS** Farewell.— How now, Ophelia, what's the
    matter?

OPHELIA Alas, my lord, I have been so affrighted!

POLONIUS With what, in the name of heaven?

OPHELIA My lord, as I was sewing in my chamber,
Lord Hamlet, with his doublet all unbraced,
85   No hat upon his head, his stockings fouled,
Ungartered, and down-gyvèd to his ankle,
Pale as his shirt, his knees knocking each other,
And with a look so piteous in purport
As if he had been loosèd out of hell
90   To speak of horrors — he comes before me.

---

58 ay, marry yes, by the Virgin Mary, i.e. yes, of course   **62 o'ertook in's rouse** overcome in his carousals (i.e. drunk)   **65 *Videlicet*** 'that is to say' (Latin)   **67 carp** type of fish   **68 we … reach** we who are wise and widely perceptive   **69 windlasses** roundabout routes   **assays of bias** indirect ventures
70 directions the way things are really going   **71 lecture** lesson   **72 have** understand   **74 buy** i.e. be with   **76 Observe … yourself** observe his behaviour in person/go along with his inclinations   **78 ply his music** (literally) practise his musical skills/(metaphorically) go his own way   **79 Well** very well
84 doublet close-fitting jacket with buttons down the front   **unbraced** undone   **85 No hat** Elizabethans usually wore hats indoors when in company   **86 Ungartered** falling down, untied (garters were bands that held the stockings in place)   **down-gyvèd** fallen down and resembling fetters (gyves)   **88 purport** meaning

POLONIUS Mad for thy love?

OPHELIA My lord, I do not know, but truly I do fear it.

POLONIUS What said he?

OPHELIA He took me by the wrist and held me hard;
95   Then goes he to the length of all his arm,
And with his other hand thus o'er his brow
He falls to such perusal of my face
As he would draw it. Long stayed he so.
At last, a little shaking of mine arm
100   And thrice his head thus waving up and down,
He raised a sigh so piteous and profound
That it did seem to shatter all his bulk
And end his being: that done, he lets me go,
And, with his head over his shoulders turned,
105   He seemed to find his way without his eyes,
For out o'doors he went without their help,
And to the last, bended their light on me.

POLONIUS Go with me: I will go seek the king.
This is the very ecstasy of love,
110   Whose violent property fordoes itself
And leads the will to desperate undertakings
As oft as any passion under heaven
That does afflict our natures. I am sorry.
What, have you given him any hard words of late?
115   OPHELIA No, my good lord, but as you did command,
I did repel his letters and denied
His access to me.

POLONIUS That hath made him mad.
I am sorry that with better speed and judgement
120   I had not quoted him: I feared he did but trifle,
And meant to wreck thee. But beshrew my jealousy!
It seems it is as proper to our age
To cast beyond ourselves in our opinions
As it is common for the younger sort
125   To lack discretion. Come, go we to the king:
This must be known, which, being kept close, might
    move
More grief to hide than hate to utter love.   *Exeunt*

95 goes . . . arm he backs away until he stands at arm's length   98 As as if   107 bended their light i.e.
directed their gaze   109 ecstasy frenzy, madness   110 Whose . . . itself the violent nature of which causes
self-destruction   119 speed profit/promptness   120 quoted observed   121 wreck dishonour, ruin
sexually   beshrew my jealousy curse my suspicion   122 proper . . . age i.e. typical of old men   123 cast
beyond ourselves miscalculate/miss the mark (another angling metaphor)   126 close secret   move . . .
love cause more unhappiness by concealment than unpleasantness by coming forward

Act 2 Scene 2

*Enter King, Queen, Rosencrantz and Guildenstern, with
others*

KING Welcome, dear Rosencrantz and Guildenstern.
Moreover that we much did long to see you,
The need we have to use you did provoke
Our hasty sending. Something have you heard
5 Of Hamlet's transformation, so I call it,
Since not th'exterior nor the inward man
Resembles that it was. What it should be,
More than his father's death, that thus hath put him
So much from th'understanding of himself,
10 I cannot deem of. I entreat you both,
That, being of so young days brought up with him,
And since so neighboured to his youth and humour,
That you vouchsafe your rest here in our court
Some little time, so by your companies
15 To draw him on to pleasures, and to gather
So much as from occasions you may glean,
Whether aught, to us unknown, afflicts him thus,
That, opened, lies within our remedy.
GERTRUDE Good gentlemen, he hath much talked of
you,
20 And sure I am two men there are not living
To whom he more adheres. If it will please you
To show us so much gentry and good will
As to expend your time with us awhile,
For the supply and profit of our hope,
25 Your visitation shall receive such thanks
As fits a king's remembrance.
ROSENCRANTZ Both your majesties
Might, by the sovereign power you have of us,
Put your dread pleasures more into command
30 Than to entreaty.
GUILDENSTERN We both obey,
And here give up ourselves in the full bent
To lay our services freely at your feet,
To be commanded.

2.2 **2 Moreover that** in addition to the fact that **10 deem** think, discern/judge **12 neighboured to**
familiar with **humour** temperament **13 vouchsafe your rest** consent to stay **16 occasions**
opportunities **18 opened** revealed **21 more adheres** is more attached **22 gentry** courtesy
24 supply and profit fulfilment and advancement **28 of** over **29 dread pleasures** revered wishes
32 in . . . bent to the utmost

35   **KING** Thanks, Rosencrantz and gentle Guildenstern.
GERTRUDE Thanks, Guildenstern and gentle
        Rosencrantz.
        And I beseech you instantly to visit
        My too much changèd son.— Go, some of ye,
        And bring the gentlemen where Hamlet is.
40   **GUILDENSTERN** Heavens make our presence and our
        practices
        Pleasant and helpful to him.
                Exeunt [Ros. and Guild. with some Attendants]
GERTRUDE Amen.
Enter Polonius
POLONIUS Th'ambassadors from Norway, my good lord,
        Are joyfully returned.
45   **KING** Thou still hast been the father of good news.
POLONIUS Have I, my lord? I assure you, my good liege,
        I hold my duty, as I hold my soul,
        Both to my God and to my gracious king:
        And I do think, or else this brain of mine
50   Hunts not the trail of policy so sure
        As I have used to do, that I have found
        The very cause of Hamlet's lunacy.
KING O, speak of that: that I do long to hear.
POLONIUS Give first admittance to th'ambassadors:
55   My news shall be the fruit to that great feast.
KING Thyself do grace to them and bring them in.—
                        [Exit Polonius]
        He tells me, my sweet queen, that he hath found
        The head and source of all your son's distemper.
GERTRUDE I doubt it is no other but the main:
60   His father's death and our o'erhasty marriage.
Enter Polonius, Voltemand and Cornelius
KING Well, we shall sift him.— Welcome, good friends.
        Say, Voltemand, what from our brother Norway?
VOLTEMAND Most fair return of greetings and desires.
        Upon our first, he sent out to suppress
65   His nephew's levies, which to him appeared
        To be a preparation gainst the Polack,
        But, better looked into, he truly found

It was against your highness: whereat grieved
That so his sickness, age and impotence
70   Was falsely borne in hand, sends out arrests
On Fortinbras, which he, in brief, obeys,
Receives rebuke from Norway, and in fine
Makes vow before his uncle never more
To give th'assay of arms against your majesty.
75   Whereon old Norway, overcome with joy,
Gives him three thousand crowns in annual fee
And his commission to employ those soldiers,
So levied as before, against the Polack,
With an entreaty, herein further shown,   *Gives a paper*
80   That it might please you to give quiet pass
Through your dominions for his enterprise
On such regards of safety and allowance
As therein are set down.
      KING It likes us well,
85   And at our more considered time we'll read,
Answer and think upon this business.
Meantime we thank you for your well-took labour.
Go to your rest: at night we'll feast together.
Most welcome home!   *Exeunt Ambassadors*
90   POLONIUS This business is very well ended.
My liege, and madam, to expostulate
What majesty should be, what duty is,
Why day is day, night night, and time is time,
Were nothing but to waste night, day and time.
95   Therefore, since brevity is the soul of wit,
And tediousness the limbs and outward flourishes,
I will be brief: your noble son is mad:
Mad call I it, for, to define true madness,
What is't but to be nothing else but mad?
100   But let that go—
      GERTRUDE More matter, with less art.
      POLONIUS Madam, I swear I use no art at all.
That he is mad, 'tis true: 'tis true 'tis pity,
And pity it is true: a foolish figure,

69 **impotence** frailty, helplessness   70 **borne in hand** deluded, taken advantage of   **arrests** orders to
cease military activity   72 **fine** conclusion   74 **give...arms** attempt to use force   76 **crowns** gold coins
(of varying values according to the countries they were used in)   77 **commission** authority   80 **quiet
pass** safe passage   82 **On...allowance** i.e. according to conditions regarding the safety of Denmark and
your permission for such an enterprise   84 **likes** pleases   85 **at...time** when we have the time for proper
consideration   91 **expostulate** discuss/ask   95 **wit** intellect/good sense   98 **for...mad** Polonius means
that it would be mad to attempt to define madness, but ends up implying, rather nonsensically, that the
definition of madness is 'being mad'   104 **figure** figure of speech

105   But farewell it, for I will use no art.
         Mad let us grant him, then, and now remains
         That we find out the cause of this effect,
         Or rather say, the cause of this defect,
         For this effect defective comes by cause.
110   Thus it remains, and the remainder thus. Perpend:
         I have a daughter — have whilst she is mine —
         Who, in her duty and obedience, mark,
         Hath given me this: now gather, and surmise.   *Shows a letter*
       The letter
         'To the celestial and my soul's idol, the most   *Reads*
115   beautified Ophelia'— That's an ill phrase, a vile
         phrase: 'beautified' is a vile phrase. But you shall
         hear these, 'in her excellent white bosom', these—
       GERTRUDE Came this from Hamlet to her?
       POLONIUS Good madam, stay awhile: I will be faithful.
120   'Doubt thou the stars are fire,   *Reads*
            Doubt that the sun doth move,
            Doubt truth to be a liar,
            But never doubt I love.
         O dear Ophelia, I am ill at these numbers: I have not
125   art to reckon my groans; but that I love thee best,
         O, most best, believe it. Adieu. Thine evermore, most
         dear lady, whilst this machine is to him, Hamlet.'
         This in obedience hath my daughter showed me,
         And more above, hath his solicitings,
130   As they fell out by time, by means and place,
         All given to mine ear.
       KING But how hath she received his love?
       POLONIUS What do you think of me?
       KING As of a man faithful and honourable.
135   **POLONIUS** I would fain prove so. But what might you
            think,
         When I had seen this hot love on the wing —
         As I perceived it, I must tell you that,
         Before my daughter told me — what might you,
         Or my dear majesty your queen here, think,

---

109 this . . . cause this defective behaviour (Hamlet's madness) has a cause   110 Thus . . . thus this is the current state of affairs, and now for the rest   Perpend consider   113 gather, and surmise collect your thoughts, draw your conclusions (or gather may be a request to Claudius and Gertrude to draw closer and look at the letter)   117 these i.e. this letter/these phrases   119 faithful i.e. to the letter/in reading the letter fully   122 Doubt in this third line the sense shifts to 'suspect'   124 ill . . . numbers poor at writing verse   125 reckon my groans count my groans/make my groans scan poetically   127 machine is to bodily structure belongs to   129 more above moreover   130 fell out occurred   135 fain willingly

140   If I had played the desk or table-book,
     Or given my heart a winking, mute and dumb,
     Or looked upon this love with idle sight?
     What might you think? No, I went round to work,
     And my young mistress thus I did bespeak:
145   'Lord Hamlet is a prince, out of thy star:
     This must not be.' And then I precepts gave her
     That she should lock herself from his resort,
     Admit no messengers, receive no tokens:
     Which done, she took the fruits of my advice,
150   And he, repulsèd — a short tale to make —
     Fell into a sadness, then into a fast,
     Thence to a watch, thence into a weakness,
     Thence to a lightness, and, by this declension
     Into the madness whereon now he raves,
155   And all we wail for.
     KING Do you think 'tis this?   *To Gertrude*
     GERTRUDE It may be, very likely.
     POLONIUS Hath there been such a time — I'd fain know
         that —
     That I have positively said ''Tis so'
160   When it proved otherwise?
     KING Not that I know.
     POLONIUS Take this from this, if this be otherwise: *Points to his head*
     If circumstances lead me, I will find   *and shoulders?*
     Where truth is hid, though it were hid indeed
165   Within the centre.
     KING How may we try it further?
     POLONIUS You know sometimes he walks four hours
         together
     Here in the lobby.
     GERTRUDE So he does indeed.
170   **POLONIUS** At such a time I'll loose my daughter to him:
     Be you and I behind an arras then: *To the King*
     Mark the encounter: if he love her not
     And be not from his reason fall'n thereon,

---

140 played . . . table-book remained silent and withheld the information/assisted in conveying messages between them   **141 given . . . winking** closed the eyes of my heart   **142 with idle sight** complacently/ without recognising its significance   **143 round** roundly, in a forthright manner   **144 bespeak** address/ speak angrily to   **145 out . . . star** beyond your reach/outside your destiny   **146 precepts** instructions **147 resort** visits   **152 a watch** sleeplessness   **153 lightness** light-headedness   **declension** decline (plays on the grammatical sense)   **163 circumstances** circumstantial evidence   **165 centre** i.e. of the earth **166 try** test   **170 loose** set loose (often used of an animal; sometimes with the sense of releasing the female to the male for sex, which would lend sexual connotations to **encounter**)   **171 arras** large tapestry wall-hanging   **173 thereon** on that account

Let me be no assistant for a state,
175 But keep a farm and carters.

KING We will try it.

Enter Hamlet reading on a book

GERTRUDE But look where sadly the poor wretch
comes reading.

POLONIUS Away, I do beseech you both away:
I'll board him presently. O, give me leave.—

Exeunt King and Queen

180 How does my good lord Hamlet?

HAMLET Well, God-a-mercy.

POLONIUS Do you know me, my lord?

HAMLET Excellent, excellent well: you're a fishmonger.

POLONIUS Not I, my lord.

185 HAMLET Then I would you were so honest a man.

POLONIUS Honest, my lord?

HAMLET Ay, sir: to be honest, as this world goes, is to be
one man picked out of two thousand.

POLONIUS That's very true, my lord.

190 HAMLET For if the sun breed maggots in a dead dog, being
a good kissing carrion— Have you a daughter?

POLONIUS I have, my lord.

HAMLET Let her not walk i'th'sun: conception is a
blessing, but not as your daughter may conceive.
195 Friend, look to't.

POLONIUS How say you by that? Still harping on my   *Aside*
daughter: yet he knew me not at first; he said I was a
fishmonger. He is far gone, far gone: and truly in my
youth I suffered much extremity for love, very near
200 this. I'll speak to him again.— What do you read, my
lord?

HAMLET Words, words, words.

POLONIUS What is the matter, my lord?

HAMLET Between who?

205 POLONIUS I mean, the matter that you read, my lord.

HAMLET Slanders, sir, for the satirical slave says here
that old men have grey beards, that their faces are
wrinkled,   their   eyes   purging   thick   amber   or

174 **assistant ... state** policy adviser   175 **carters** cart drivers   177 **sadly** solemnly   179 **board** accost **presently** immediately   **give me leave** a polite way of asking to be left alone   181 **God-a-mercy** God have mercy (i.e. thank you)   183 **fishmonger** plays on slang senses of 'lecher' and 'pimp'   191 **good kissing carrion** good piece of rotting flesh to kiss (**carrion** also suggests 'whore')   193 **i'th'sun** in public/in the sun (or 'son') that causes breeding   **conception** understanding/becoming pregnant   203 **matter** content (Hamlet plays on sense of 'cause of a dispute')   208 **purging** discharging   **amber ... gum** tree resin

plum-tree gum and that they have a plentiful lack of
210 wit, together with weak hams: all which, sir, though
I most powerfully and potently believe, yet I hold it
not honesty to have it thus set down, for you
yourself, sir, should be old as I am, if like a crab you
could go backward.

215 POLONIUS Though this be madness, yet there is method   *Aside*
in't.— Will you walk out of the air, my lord?
HAMLET Into my grave?
POLONIUS Indeed, that is out o'th'air.— How pregnant   *Aside*
sometimes his replies are! A happiness that often
220 madness hits on, which reason and sanity could not
so prosperously be delivered of. I will leave him and
suddenly contrive the means of meeting between him
and my daughter.— My honourable lord, I will most
humbly take my leave of you.

225 HAMLET You cannot, sir, take from me anything that I
will more willingly part withal: except my life, my
life.
POLONIUS Fare you well, my lord.
HAMLET These tedious old fools.
Enter Rosencrantz and Guildenstern
230 POLONIUS You go to seek my lord Hamlet; there he is.
ROSENCRANTZ God save you, sir!   *To Polonius*
GUILDENSTERN Mine honoured lord!   [*Exit Polonius*]
ROSENCRANTZ My most dear lord!
HAMLET My excellent good friends! How dost thou,
235 Guildenstern? O, Rosencrantz! Good lads, how do ye
both?
ROSENCRANTZ As the indifferent children of the earth.
GUILDENSTERN Happy, in that we are not over-happy:
On fortune's cap we are not the very button.
240 HAMLET Nor the soles of her shoe?
ROSENCRANTZ Neither, my lord.
HAMLET Then you live about her waist, or in the middle
of her favours?
GUILDENSTERN Faith, her privates we.
245 HAMLET In the secret parts of fortune? O, most true: she
is a strumpet. What's the news?

210 **hams** legs   212 **honesty** decent/honourable   213 **old** as old   218 **pregnant** meaningful/
quick-witted (with childbearing connotations, continued in **delivered of**)   219 **happiness** fortuitousness
222 **suddenly** immediately   226 **withal** with   237 **indifferent** ordinary, average   238 **Happy** fortunate
239 **button** i.e. point at the very top of the cap   243 **favours** sexual favours (**middle** has vaginal
connotations)   244 **privates** ordinary citizens/genitals   246 **strumpet** prostitute

ROSENCRANTZ None, my lord, but that the world's grown honest.

HAMLET Then is doomsday near. But your news is not
250 true. Let me question more in particular: what have you, my good friends, deserved at the hands of fortune that she sends you to prison hither?

GUILDENSTERN Prison, my lord?

HAMLET Denmark's a prison.

255 **ROSENCRANTZ** Then is the world one.

HAMLET A goodly one, in which there are many confines, wards and dungeons, Denmark being one o'th'worst.

ROSENCRANTZ We think not so, my lord.

260 **HAMLET** Why, then, 'tis none to you; for there is nothing either good or bad but thinking makes it so: to me it is a prison.

ROSENCRANTZ Why then, your ambition makes it one: 'tis too narrow for your mind.

265 **HAMLET** O God, I could be bounded in a nutshell and count myself a king of infinite space, were it not that I have bad dreams.

GUILDENSTERN Which dreams indeed are ambition, for the very substance of the ambitious is merely the
270 shadow of a dream.

HAMLET A dream itself is but a shadow.

ROSENCRANTZ Truly, and I hold ambition of so airy and light a quality that it is but a shadow's shadow.

HAMLET Then are our beggars bodies, and our monarchs
275 and outstretched heroes the beggars' shadows. Shall we to th'court? For, by my fay, I cannot reason.

BOTH We'll wait upon you.

HAMLET No such matter: I will not sort you with the rest of my servants, for, to speak to you like an honest
280 man, I am most dreadfully attended. But, in the beaten way of friendship, what make you at Elsinore?

ROSENCRANTZ To visit you, my lord, no other occasion.

---

250 **particular** detail   257 **confines** places of confinement   **wards** prison cells   269 **substance** . . .
ambitious material that fuels ambition/stuff ambitious men are made of   274 **Then** . . . **shadows** i.e. if
ambition is nothing but shadow, then only unambitious beggars have bodily substance; their shadows must
then be made up of ambitious people such as **monarchs** and **heroes**   275 **outstretched** reaching out
ambitiously/elongated like shadows   276 **fay** faith   277 **wait upon** accompany (Hamlet emphasizes the
sense of 'serve')   278 **No such matter** i.e. I'll have no such thing   **sort** class   280 **dreadfully attended**
poorly waited upon (with possible play on sense of 'haunted by dire visions')   281 **beaten way** well-trodden
path

HAMLET Beggar that I am, I am even poor in thanks; but
I thank you, and sure, dear friends, my thanks are
285   too dear a halfpenny. Were you not sent for? Is it
your own inclining? Is it a free visitation? Come, deal
justly with me: come, come; nay, speak.

GUILDENSTERN What should we say, my lord?

HAMLET Why, anything, but to the purpose. You were
290   sent for, and there is a kind of confession in your
looks which your modesties have not craft enough
to colour: I know the good king and queen have sent
for you.

ROSENCRANTZ To what end, my lord?

295 **HAMLET** That you must teach me. But let me conjure
you, by the rights of our fellowship, by the
consonancy of our youth, by the obligation of our
ever-preserved love, and by what more dear a better
proposer could charge you withal, be even and direct
300   with me whether you were sent for or no?

ROSENCRANTZ What say you?   *Aside to Guildenstern?*

HAMLET Nay, then, I have an eye of you.— If you love   *Aside?*
me, hold not off.

GUILDENSTERN My lord, we were sent for.

305 **HAMLET** I will tell you why; so shall my anticipation
prevent your discovery, and your secrecy to the king
and queen moult no feather. I have of late — but
wherefore I know not — lost all my mirth, forgone all
custom of exercise; and indeed it goes so heavily with
310   my disposition that this goodly frame, the earth,
seems to me a sterile promontory, this most excellent
canopy, the air, look you, this brave o'erhanging
firmament, this majestical roof fretted with golden
fire, why, it appears no other thing to me than a foul
315   and pestilent congregation of vapours. What a piece
of work is a man! How noble in reason, how infinite
in faculty, in form and moving how express and

---

285 **too...halfpenny** too expensive at a halfpenny (i.e. worthless)/too expensive by a halfpenny (if the
visitors are not being honest about the reason for their visit) 289 **anything...purpose** anything
irrelevant, any lie you wish 291 **modesties** decency/sense of shame 292 **colour** disguise, excuse
295 **conjure** entreat, appeal to 297 **consonancy** harmony, friendship 298 **what more dear** whatever
more precious thing 299 **proposer** questioner **charge** urge, entreat **even** level/honest 302 **of** on
305 **my...discovery** my saying it first mean that you are not forced to reveal anything 307 **moult no
feather** remain undiminished 309 **custom of exercise** usual pursuits/gentlemanly activities
heavily dejectedly 310 **frame** framework, structure (like **canopy**, may also evoke the physical structure of
the theatre building) 311 **sterile promontory** barren point of land jutting out into the sea
312 **brave** splendid 313 **firmament** sky **fretted** adorned 317 **express** well-designed/expressive/exact

admirable, in action how like an angel, in
apprehension how like a god! The beauty of the
320   world, the paragon of animals — and yet, to me,
what is this quintessence of dust? Man delights not
me — no, nor woman neither, though by your
smiling you seem to say so.

ROSENCRANTZ My lord, there was no such stuff in my
325   thoughts.

HAMLET Why did you laugh when I said 'Man delights
not me'?

ROSENCRANTZ To think, my lord, if you delight not in
man, what Lenten entertainment the players shall
330   receive from you: we coted them on the way, and
hither are they coming to offer you service.

HAMLET He that plays the king shall be welcome; his
majesty shall have tribute of me: the adventurous
knight shall use his foil and target: the lover shall not
335   sigh *gratis*: the humorous man shall end his part in
peace: the clown shall make those laugh whose lungs
are tickled o'th'sear: and the lady shall say her mind
freely, or the blank verse shall halt for't. What
players are they?

340   ROSENCRANTZ Even those you were wont to take delight
in, the tragedians of the city.

HAMLET How chances it they travel? Their residence,
both in reputation and profit, was better both ways.

ROSENCRANTZ I think their inhibition comes by the
345   means of the late innovation.

HAMLET Do they hold the same estimation they did when
I was in the city? Are they so followed?

ROSENCRANTZ No, indeed, they are not.

HAMLET How comes it? Do they grow rusty?

350   ROSENCRANTZ Nay, their endeavour keeps in the
wonted pace. But there is, sir, an eyrie of children,

---

319 apprehension understanding   **321 quintessence** essence/purest form (literally the 'fifth essence', of which heavenly bodies were composed and supposedly present in all matter)   **329 Lenten entertainment** poor reception/meagre employment, i.e. appropriate to Lent   **330 coted** overtook   **333 tribute** homage/payment   **334 foil and target** sword and shield   **335 *gratis*** 'for nothing' (Latin)   **humorous** moody or ill-tempered (with an imbalance of the four bodily 'humours', fluids thought to control mood)
337 tickled o'th'sear easily triggered (to laughter)   **sear** part of the mechanism involved in firing a gun
338 halt limp (if the actor playing the **lady** is interrupted by heckling from the audience the rhythm of his speech will be lost)   **340 wont** accustomed   **342 residence** remaining in their usual home
344 inhibition (city) ban on performing plays   **345 late innovation** recent political insurrection/new fashion for boy-actors   **346 estimation** reputation   **351 eyrie** nest/brood

little eyases, that cry out on the top of question and
are most tyrannically clapped for't: these are now the
fashion, and so berattle the common stages — so
355   they call them — that many wearing rapiers are
afraid of goose-quills and dare scarce come thither.

HAMLET What, are they children? Who maintains 'em?
How are they escoted? Will they pursue the quality
no longer than they can sing? Will they not say
360   afterwards, if they should grow themselves to
common players — as it is most like, if their means
are no better — their writers do them wrong, to
make them exclaim against their own succession?

ROSENCRANTZ Faith, there has been much to-do on both
365   sides, and the nation holds it no sin to tar them to
controversy. There was for a while no money bid for
argument unless the poet and the player went to
cuffs in the question.

HAMLET Is't possible?

370 **GUILDENSTERN** O, there has been much throwing about
of brains.

HAMLET Do the boys carry it away?

ROSENCRANTZ Ay, that they do, my lord: Hercules and
his load too.

375 **HAMLET** It is not strange, for mine uncle is King of
Denmark, and those that would make mows at him
while my father lived, give twenty, forty, an hundred
ducats a-piece for his picture in little. There is
something in this more than natural, if philosophy
380   could find it out.

Flourish for the Players

GUILDENSTERN There are the players.

HAMLET Gentlemen, you are welcome to Elsinore. Your
hands, come: the appurtenance of welcome is fashion

---

352 eyases young hawks **cry … question** shrilly dominate the debate (i.e. the rivalry between child and
adult acting companies)   **353 tyrannically** outrageously/vehemently   **354 berattle … stages** clamour
against the public theatres (where the adult acting companies perform)   **355 many … thither** many
fashionable young men hardly dare attend the public theatres as they are so afraid of being mocked by the
playwrights working for the boy-actors   **358 escoted** supported   **quality** (acting) profession   **359 no …
sing** i.e. only until their voices break   **361 common** i.e. adult   **like** likely   **means** financial resources
363 succession future professions   **365 tar** incite   **366 no … question** the acting companies paid for the
plots of no new plays unless they featured the quarrel between the children's dramatists and the adult actors
(or 'without the playwright and the adult acting company coming to blows over the controversy')
372 carry it away win the day   **374 his load** i.e. the world, carried on Hercules' shoulders (possibly a
reference to the emblem of the Globe theatre)   **376 mows** mouths, grimaces   **378 ducats** gold coins
picture in little miniature portrait   **379 more than natural** i.e. unnatural   **philosophy** science
Flourish trumpet fanfare   **383 appurtenance** appropriate accompaniment

and ceremony: let me comply with you in the garb,
385   lest my extent to the players — which, I tell you,
must show fairly outward — should more appear like
entertainment than yours. You are welcome: but my
uncle-father and aunt-mother are deceived.

GUILDENSTERN In what, my dear lord?

390   HAMLET I am but mad north-north-west: when the wind
is southerly I know a hawk from a handsaw.

Enter Polonius

POLONIUS Well be with you, gentlemen.

HAMLET Hark you, Guildenstern, and you too — at each
ear a hearer: that great baby you see there is not yet
395   out of his swathing-clouts.

ROSENCRANTZ Happily he's the second time come to
them, for they say an old man is twice a child.

HAMLET I will prophesy: he comes to tell me of the
players, mark it.— You say right, sir: for a Monday
400   morning, 'twas so indeed.

POLONIUS My lord, I have news to tell you.

HAMLET My lord, I have news to tell you.
When Roscius, an actor in Rome—

POLONIUS The actors are come hither, my lord.

405   HAMLET Buzz, buzz!

POLONIUS Upon mine honour—

HAMLET Then came each actor on his ass—

POLONIUS The best actors in the world, either for
tragedy, comedy, history, pastoral, pastorical-comical,
410   historical-pastoral, tragical-historical, tragical-comical-
historical-pastoral, scene individable, or poem
unlimited. Seneca cannot be too heavy, nor Plautus
too light. For the law of writ and the liberty, these are
the only men.

---

384 comply observe proper courtesies   **garb** appropriate manner   **385 my extent** the behaviour I extend
386 fairly courteously   **387 entertainment** welcome   **390 but mad north-north-west** only mad when
the wind is in the north-north-west/only slightly mad (like a faulty compass that points north-north-west
rather than north)   **391 handsaw** hand-held saw (some editors emend to 'hernshaw', a type of heron)
395 swathing-clouts swaddling-clothes in which a newborn **baby** was wrapped   **396 Happily** perhaps
399 You . . . indeed Hamlet pretends to Polonius that he is mid-conversation with his friends   **403 Roscius**
a famous Roman actor   **405 Buzz, buzz!** dismissive exclamation made in response to idle gossip or old
news   **407 ass** may pun on 'arse'   **411 scene individable** a play observing the unities of time, place and
action/a play whose genre is unclassifiable   **poem unlimited** dramatic verse (a play) that does not observe
the unities of time, place and action/a play whose genre is all-inclusive/a play that explores a general rather
than a specific question (a rhetorical application of **unlimited**)   **412 Seneca** Roman writer of tragedies
heavy sorrowful/weighty   **Plautus** Roman writer of comedies   **413 For . . . liberty** for plays written
according to the rules and for those that disregard all prescriptions

415 **HAMLET** O Jephthah, judge of Israel, what a treasure
hadst thou!

POLONIUS What a treasure had he, my lord?

HAMLET Why,

'One fair daughter and no more,

420 The which he loved passing well.'

POLONIUS Still on my daughter.   *Aside*

HAMLET Am I not i'th'right, old Jephthah?

POLONIUS If you call me Jephthah, my lord, I have a
daughter that I love passing well.

425 **HAMLET** Nay, that follows not.

POLONIUS What follows, then, my lord?

HAMLET Why,

'As by lot, God wot',

and then, you know,

430 'It came to pass, as most like it was' —

the first row of the pious chanson will show you
more, for look where my abridgements come.—

Enter four or five Players

You're welcome, masters, welcome all.— I am glad to
see thee well.— Welcome, good friends.— O, my old

435 friend! Thy face is valanced since I saw thee last:
com'st thou to beard me in Denmark?— What, my
young lady and mistress! By'r lady, your ladyship is
nearer heaven than when I saw you last, by the
altitude of a chopine. Pray God your voice, like a

440 piece of uncurrent gold, be not cracked within the
ring. Masters, you are all welcome. We'll e'en to't like
French falconers, fly at anything we see. We'll have a
speech straight: come, give us a taste of your quality:
come, a passionate speech.

445 **FIRST PLAYER** What speech, my lord?

HAMLET I heard thee speak me a speech once, but it was
never acted, or if it was, not above once, for the play,

415 O . . . thou! In the Bible, Jephthah vowed to God that if he was successful in war he would sacrifice the
first creature he met on his return home; he encountered his daughter but kept his word   419 'One . . . well.'
lines from a well-known ballad   420 passing surpassingly, exceedingly   425 follows not is not logical/is not
the next line   428 lot chance   wot knows   430 like likely   431 row line   chanson song   432 my
abridgements things that cut me short/entertainment (in either case, the arrival of the players)
435 valanced fringed (with a beard)   436 beard defy, affront (plays on the usual sense)   437 By'r lady by
Our Lady (the Virgin Mary)   your ladyship addressed to a teenage apprentice actor who plays women's
parts   439 chopine high woman's shoe with a very thick platform sole   440 uncurrent not legal tender
cracked . . . ring i.e. broken, and therefore unfit for women's roles, with play on the sense of 'deflowered'
(coins featured the monarch's head within a ring; if the coin was damaged within the ring it was no longer
valid)   441 e'en to't go straight to it   443 straight straight away   quality skill

I remember, pleased not the million: 'twas caviar to
the general. But it was — as I received it, and others,
whose judgement in such matters cried in the top of
mine — an excellent play, well digested in the scenes,
set down with as much modesty as cunning. I
remember one said there was no sallets in the lines to
make the matter savoury, nor no matter in the
phrase that might indict the author of affectation, but
called it an honest method, as wholesome as sweet,
and by very much more handsome than fine. One
speech in it I chiefly loved: 'twas Aeneas' tale to Dido,
and thereabout of it especially where he speaks of
Priam's slaughter: if it live in your memory, begin at
this line — let me see, let me see —
          'The rugged Pyrrhus, like th'Hyrcanian beast'—
It is not so: it begins with Pyrrhus:
          'The rugged Pyrrhus, he whose sable arms,
          Black as his purpose, did the night resemble
          When he lay couchèd in the ominous horse,
          Hath now this dread and black complexion
                    smeared
          With heraldry more dismal: head to foot
          Now is he total gules, horridly tricked
          With blood of fathers, mothers, daughters,
                    sons,
          Baked and impasted with the parching streets
          That lend a tyrannous and damnèd light
          To their vile murders: roasted in wrath and fire,
          And thus o'er-sizèd with coagulate gore,
          With eyes like carbuncles, the hellish Pyrrhus

450
455
460
465
470
475

---

448 caviar ... general i.e. wasted on the unappreciative multitude   **450 cried ... of** was superior to
451 digested arranged   **452 modesty** restraint/propriety   **cunning** skill, artistry   **453 sallets** salads or
their components (i.e. spicy parts, vulgar phrases)   **454 savoury** highly flavoured   **455 indict** accuse
456 as ... fine this line is missing from the Folio text, probably due to printer's error (the same goes for the
short line at the end of Hamlet's speech)   **457 handsome than fine** seemly and graceful rather than
showy   **458 Aeneas' ... Dido** after the Trojan war Aeneas landed at Carthage, where Dido was queen; he
told of his experiences and she fell in love with him   **460 Priam** King of Troy, killed by **Pyrrhus** during the
attack on his city   **462 rugged** harsh, severe   **Pyrrhus** Achilles' son; after the death of his father in the
Trojan war, he took part in the conflict and was noted for his vengeful savagery   **th'Hyrcanian beast** the
tiger of Hyrcania (land bordering the Caspian Sea), known for its ferocity   **464 sable** black   **466 couchèd**
hidden   **ominous horse** fateful wooden horse by which the Greeks gained access to Troy   **468 heraldry**
more dismal i.e. blood, imaged as heraldic markings   **dismal** ominous, fatal   **469 total gules** entirely red
(**gules** is a heraldic term)   **tricked** adorned/delineated (heraldic term for the sketching of a coat of arms)
471 impasted dried into a crust   **parching** scorching (because burning)   **472 tyrannous** harsh
474 o'er-sizèd covered, as if with size (a sticky substance used to treat paper)/rendered larger (through a
thick covering of blood)   **coagulate** coagulated, congealed   **475 carbuncles** red gems supposed to emit
light in the dark

Old grandsire Priam seeks.'
So, proceed you.

POLONIUS Fore God, my lord, well spoken, with good
accent and good discretion.

480 **FIRST PLAYER** 'Anon he finds him
Striking too short at Greeks: his antique sword,
Rebellious to his arm, lies where it falls,
Repugnant to command. Unequal matched,
Pyrrhus at Priam drives, in rage strikes wide,
485 But with the whiff and wind of his fell sword
Th'unnervèd father falls. Then senseless Ilium,
Seeming to feel this blow, with flaming top
Stoops to his base, and with a hideous crash
Takes prisoner Pyrrhus' ear, for, lo, his sword,
490 Which was declining on the milky head
Of reverend Priam, seemed i'th'air to stick:
So as a painted tyrant Pyrrhus stood,
And, like a neutral to his will and matter,
Did nothing.
495 But as we often see against some storm
A silence in the heavens, the rack stand still,
The bold winds speechless and the orb below
As hush as death, anon the dreadful thunder
Doth rend the region, so, after Pyrrhus' pause,
500 Arousèd vengeance sets him new a-work,
And never did the Cyclops' hammers fall
On Mars his armours forged for proof eterne
With less remorse than Pyrrhus' bleeding sword
Now falls on Priam.
505 Out, out, thou strumpet Fortune! All you gods
In general synod take away her power,
Break all the spokes and fellies from her wheel,
And bowl the round nave down the hill of heaven,
As low as to the fiends!'

476 **grandsire** grandfather (Priam had fifty sons and numerous grandchildren)   479 **discretion** judgement
480 **Anon** shortly   481 **too short** inadequately (presumably because of his old age)   **antique** old
483 **Repugnant** resistant   485 **whiff and wind** i.e. mere slicing through the air   **fell** fierce
486 **Th'unnervèd** the weakened   **senseless** incapable of feeling   **Ilium** Troy/the royal palace at Troy
489 **Takes . . . ear** i.e. the noise arrests him in mid-action   490 **declining** descending   **milky** white with
age   492 **painted** motionless as if in a painting/blood-covered   493 **like . . . matter** suspended between his
will and its effect   495 **against** in anticipation of/before   496 **rack** clouds   497 **orb** i.e. earth
499 **region** sky   501 **Cyclops** one-eyed giants who worked for the blacksmith god Vulcan making armour
for the gods   502 **Mars his** Mars' (Roman god of war)   **proof eterne** eternal impenetrability
503 **remorse** pity   506 **synod** assembly   507 **fellies** pieces of wood that form the rim of a wheel   **wheel**
the wheel of **Fortune**, according to the turns of which men rose or fell   508 **nave** central part of the wheel,
the hub

510   **POLONIUS** This is too long.

     HAMLET It shall to th'barber's, with your beard.—
        Prithee, say on: he's for a jig or a tale of bawdry, or
        he sleeps: say on; come to Hecuba.

     FIRST PLAYER 'But who, O, who had seen the mobled
        queen—'

515   **HAMLET** 'The mobled queen.'

     POLONIUS That's good: 'mobled queen' is good.

     FIRST PLAYER 'Run barefoot up and down, threat'ning
          the flame
        With bisson rheum, a clout about that head
        Where late the diadem stood, and for a robe,
520   About her lank and all o'er-teemèd loins
        A blanket, in th'alarm of fear caught up.
        Who this had seen, with tongue in venom steeped,
        Gainst Fortune's state would treason have
          pronounced:
        But if the gods themselves did see her then
525   When she saw Pyrrhus make malicious sport
        In mincing with his sword her husband's limbs,
        The instant burst of clamour that she made —
        Unless things mortal move them not at all —
        Would have made milch the burning eyes of
          heaven,
530   And passion in the gods.'

     POLONIUS Look, whe'er he has not turned his colour and
        has tears in's eyes. Pray you no more.

     HAMLET 'Tis well: I'll have thee speak out the rest
        soon.— Good my lord, will you see the players well
535   bestowed? Do ye hear, let them be well used, for they
        are the abstracts and brief chronicles of the time:
        after your death you were better have a bad epitaph
        than their ill report while you lived.

     POLONIUS My lord, I will use them according to their
540   desert.

     HAMLET God's bodikins, man, better: use every man after
        his desert, and who should scape whipping? Use
        them after your own honour and dignity: the less

---

512 jig a light, often bawdy, entertainment that took place after the main play and involved singing and dancing   **513 Hecuba** wife of King Priam   **514 who** whoever   **515 mobled** muffled/veiled   **518 bisson rheum** blinding tears   **clout** cloth   **519 late** recently   **diadem** crown   **520 lank** shrunken, empty   **o'er-teemèd** exhausted with childbearing   **522 Who . . . seen** whoever had seen this   **523 state** rule, government   **pronounced** spoken   **529 milch** milk-producing, i.e. tearful   **530 passion** (produced) grief   **531 whe'er** whether   **535 bestowed** lodged   **used** treated   **536 abstracts** summaries, epitomes   **540 desert** merit, worth   **541 God's bodikins** by God's little body   **after** according to

they deserve, the more merit is in your bounty. Take
545   them in.

POLONIUS Come, sirs.   *Exit Polonius*

HAMLET Follow him, friends: we'll hear a play tomorrow.—
Dost thou hear me, old friend? Can you play *The*   *To a Player*
Murder of Gonzago?

550   **A PLAYER** Ay, my lord.

HAMLET We'll ha't tomorrow night. You could, for a
need, study a speech of some dozen or sixteen lines
which I would set down and insert in't, could ye not?

A PLAYER Ay, my lord.

555   **HAMLET** Very well. Follow that lord, and look you mock
him not.—   [*Exeunt Players*]
My good friends, I'll leave you till night. You are
welcome to Elsinore.

ROSENCRANTZ Good my lord.

Exeunt [*Rosencrantz and*
Guildenstern]. *Hamlet remains*

560   **HAMLET** Ay, so, God buy ye.— Now I am alone.
O, what a rogue and peasant slave am I!
Is it not monstrous that this player here,
But in a fiction, in a dream of passion,
Could force his soul so to his whole conceit
565   That from her working all his visage wanned,
Tears in his eyes, distraction in's aspect,
A broken voice, and his whole function suiting
With forms to his conceit? And all for nothing!
For Hecuba!
570   What's Hecuba to him, or he to Hecuba,
That he should weep for her? What would he do
Had he the motive and the cue for passion
That I have? He would drown the stage with tears
And cleave the general ear with horrid speech,
575   Make mad the guilty and appal the free,
Confound the ignorant and amaze indeed
The very faculty of eyes and ears. Yet I,

---

544 **bounty** generosity   551 **ha't** have it   **for a need** if necessary   552 **study** memorize   563 **But**
merely   564 **conceit** imagination   565 **her** i.e. conceit's, imagination's   **wanned** paled   566 **distraction**
distress, agitation   **aspect** expression/glance   567 **his . . . conceit** all of his natural powers furnishing
actions to match his imaginings   572 **motive** provocation (modern sense of 'motivation' of a dramatic
character did not yet exist, though **cue** is clearly an actor's term)   574 **horrid** terrifying, horrifying
575 **appal** make pale/shock   **free** innocent   576 **Confound** stun/confuse   **the ignorant** those who know
nothing of the crime   **amaze** bewilder/terrify/stun

A dull and muddy-mettled rascal, peak
Like John-a-dreams, unpregnant of my cause,
580   And can say nothing: no, not for a king
Upon whose property and most dear life
A damned defeat was made. Am I a coward?
Who calls me villain? Breaks my pate across?
Plucks off my beard and blows it in my face?
585   Tweaks me by th'nose? Gives me the lie i'th'throat,
As deep as to the lungs? Who does me this?
Ha!
Why, I should take it, for it cannot be
But I am pigeon-livered and lack gall
590   To make oppression bitter, or ere this
I should have fatted all the region kites
With this slave's offal: bloody, bawdy villain!
Remorseless, treacherous, lecherous, kindless villain!
O, vengeance!
595   Why, what an ass am I! Ay, sure, this is most brave,
That I, the son of the dear murderèd,
Prompted to my revenge by heaven and hell,
Must like a whore unpack my heart with words
And fall a-cursing, like a very drab, a scullion!
600   Fie upon't, foh! About, my brain! I have heard
That guilty creatures sitting at a play
Have by the very cunning of the scene
Been struck so to the soul that presently
They have proclaimed their malefactions:
605   For murder, though it have no tongue, will speak
With most miraculous organ. I'll have these players
Play something like the murder of my father
Before mine uncle: I'll observe his looks,
I'll tent him to the quick: if he but blench,
610   I know my course. The spirit that I have seen
May be the devil, and the devil hath power
T'assume a pleasing shape, yea, and perhaps,
Out of my weakness and my melancholy,

578 muddy-mettled dull-spirited   peak mope, languish   579 John-a-dreams general name for a
dreamy person   unpregnant of sluggish towards, not prompted by   581 property regal identity/
kingdom   582 defeat destruction   583 pate head   584 Plucks off pulls a tuft from   585 Gives...
lungs? Calls me an outrageous liar?   586 me this this to me   589 pigeon-livered pigeons were
proverbially gentle birds, supposed to lack gall (bitterness/anger)   591 region kites sky's birds of prey
592 offal intestines/remains   593 Remorseless pitiless   kindless unnatural   595 brave fine/bold
599 drab prostitute/slut   scullion lowest domestic servant   600 About about it, to work
602 cunning skill   603 presently immediately   604 malefactions wrongdoings, crimes   609 tent probe
(as one would a wound)   blench flinch/turn pale

As he is very potent with such spirits,
615 Abuses me to damn me. I'll have grounds
More relative than this: the play's the thing
Wherein I'll catch the conscience of the king.   *Exit*

[Act 3 Scene 1]   *running scene 7*

Enter King, Queen, Polonius, Ophelia, Rosencrantz,
Guildenstern and Lords

KING And can you by no drift of circumstance
Get from him why he puts on this confusion,
Grating so harshly all his days of quiet
With turbulent and dangerous lunacy?
5 ROSENCRANTZ He does confess he feels himself
distracted,
But from what cause he will by no means speak.
GUILDENSTERN Nor do we find him forward to be
sounded,
But with a crafty madness keeps aloof
When we would bring him on to some confession
10 Of his true state.
GERTRUDE Did he receive you well?
ROSENCRANTZ Most like a gentleman.
GUILDENSTERN But with much forcing of his disposition.
ROSENCRANTZ Niggard of question, but of our demands
15 Most free in his reply.
GERTRUDE Did you assay him to any pastime?
ROSENCRANTZ Madam, it so fell out that certain players
We o'erraught on the way: of these we told him,
And there did seem in him a kind of joy
20 To hear of it: they are about the court,
And, as I think, they have already order
This night to play before him.
POLONIUS 'Tis most true:
And he beseeched me to entreat your majesties
25 To hear and see the matter.
KING With all my heart, and it doth much content me
To hear him so inclined.

614 spirits i.e. melancholy   616 relative relevant/cogent/substantial   3.1   1 drift of circumstance
course of roundabout talk   3 Grating fretting/harping, dwelling querulously upon/wearing away
7 forward ready, inclined   sounded questioned, probed   13 disposition inclination   14 Niggard of
question sparing in his questions/reluctant to initiate conversation   demands questions   16 assay try to
tempt   18 o'erraught overtook

Good gentlemen, give him a further edge
And drive his purpose on to these delights.

30 ROSENCRANTZ We shall, my lord.

Exeunt [Rosencrantz and Guildenstern]

KING Sweet Gertrude, leave us too.   ↓*Exit Lords*↓
For we have closely sent for Hamlet hither,
That he, as 'twere by accident, may here
Affront Ophelia:

35 Her father and myself, lawful espials,
Will so bestow ourselves that, seeing unseen,
We may of their encounter frankly judge,
And gather by him, as he is behaved,
If't be th'affliction of his love or no

40 That thus he suffers for.

GERTRUDE I shall obey you.—
And for your part, Ophelia, I do wish
That your good beauties be the happy cause
Of Hamlet's wildness: so shall I hope your virtues

45 Will bring him to his wonted way again,
To both your honours.

OPHELIA Madam, I wish it may.   [*Exit Gertrude*]

POLONIUS Ophelia, walk you here.— Gracious, so please
  you,
We will bestow ourselves.— Read on this book,   *To Ophelia*

50 That show of such an exercise may colour   *Gives a book*
Your loneliness. We are oft to blame in this —
'Tis too much proved — that with devotion's visage
And pious action we do sugar o'er
The devil himself.

55 KING O, 'tis true!   *Aside*
How smart a lash that speech doth give my
  conscience!
The harlot's cheek, beautied with plast'ring art,
Is not more ugly to the thing that helps it
Than is my deed to my most painted word.

60 O, heavy burden!

POLONIUS I hear him coming: let's withdraw, my lord.

Exeunt [King and Polonius]

To a place from where they eavesdrop,
while Ophelia pretends to read

---

28 **edge** sharpness of inclination/incitement   32 **closely** secretly/privately   34 **Affront** come face to face with   35 **espials** spies   48 **Gracious** your grace (addressed to the king)   50 **exercise** devout practice (the book is presumably of a religious nature)   **colour Your loneliness** account for the fact that you are alone   52 **visage** face, appearance   57 **plast'ring art** i.e. cosmetics   58 **to . . . it** compared to the cosmetics that improve it

Enter Hamlet

HAMLET To be, or not to be, that is the question:
Whether 'tis nobler in the mind to suffer
The slings and arrows of outrageous fortune,
65   Or to take arms against a sea of troubles,
And by opposing end them? To die, to sleep —
No more — and by a sleep to say we end
The heartache and the thousand natural shocks
That flesh is heir to: 'tis a consummation
70   Devoutly to be wished. To die, to sleep:
To sleep, perchance to dream: ay, there's the rub,
For in that sleep of death what dreams may come
When we have shuffled off this mortal coil,
Must give us pause: there's the respect
75   That makes calamity of so long life,
For who would bear the whips and scorns of time,
The oppressor's wrong, the proud man's contumely,
The pangs of disprized love, the law's delay,
The insolence of office and the spurns
80   That patient merit of the unworthy takes,
When he himself might his quietus make
With a bare bodkin? Who would these fardels bear,
To grunt and sweat under a weary life,
But that the dread of something after death,
85   The undiscovered country from whose bourn
No traveller returns, puzzles the will,
And makes us rather bear those ills we have
Than fly to others that we know not of?
Thus conscience does make cowards of us all:
90   And thus the native hue of resolution
Is sicklied o'er with the pale cast of thought,
And enterprises of great pith and moment
With this regard their currents turn away,
And lose the name of action. Soft you now,

---

64 **slings** catapults, ballista, cannons or the missiles hurled by them   **outrageous** excessively wicked/
violent, cruel   68 **shocks** violent blows/clashes with the enemy   69 **consummation** ending   71 **rub**
obstacle (a bowling term)   73 **shuffled off** cast off/evaded/got rid of in a perfunctory or unsatisfactory
manner   **mortal coil** bustle or turmoil of this mortal life   74 **respect** consideration   75 **of . . . life** continue
for so long   76 **scorns** insults, mockeries   77 **contumely** insolence, contempt, insulting language or
behaviour   78 **disprized** undervalued/dishonoured   79 **office** office-holders   **spurns** kicks
80 **of . . . takes** receives from those who are unworthy   81 **quietus** discharge of debts (i.e. death)   82 **bare**
mere/unsheathed   **bodkin** dagger/awl/pointed instrument   **fardels** burdens   85 **bourn** boundary
86 **puzzles** bewilders, confounds   89 **conscience** consciousness/introspection/awareness of right and
wrong   90 **native hue** natural colour   91 **cast** tinge, shade   92 **pith and moment** substance and
importance   94 **Soft you** wait a moment

95   The fair Ophelia.— Nymph, in thy orisons
        Be all my sins remembered.
        OPHELIA Good my lord,
        How does your honour for this many a day?
        HAMLET I humbly thank you: well, well, well.
100   OPHELIA My lord, I have remembrances of yours,
        That I have longèd long to re-deliver:
        I pray you now receive them.   *Offers love tokens*
        HAMLET No, no: I never gave you aught.
        OPHELIA My honoured lord, I know right well you did,
105   And with them words of so sweet breath composed
        As made the things more rich: their perfume lost,
        Take these again, for to the noble mind
        Rich gifts wax poor when givers prove unkind.
        There, my lord.   *Tries to hand over tokens*
110   HAMLET Ha, ha! Are you honest?
        OPHELIA My lord?
        HAMLET Are you fair?
        OPHELIA What means your lordship?
        HAMLET That if you be honest and fair, your honesty
115   should admit no discourse to your beauty.
        OPHELIA Could beauty, my lord, have better commerce
        than with honesty?
        HAMLET Ay, truly, for the power of beauty will sooner
        transform honesty from what it is to a bawd than the
120   force of honesty can translate beauty into his
        likeness: this was sometime a paradox, but now the
        time gives it proof. I did love you once.
        OPHELIA Indeed, my lord, you made me believe so.
        HAMLET You should not have believed me, for virtue
125   cannot so inoculate our old stock but we shall relish
        of it: I loved you not.
        OPHELIA I was the more deceived.
        HAMLET Get thee to a nunnery. Why wouldst thou be a
        breeder of sinners? I am myself indifferent honest, but
130   yet I could accuse me of such things that it were
        better my mother had not borne me: I am very

95 orisons prayers   100 remembrances keepsakes, love tokens   110 honest chaste   112 fair
beautiful   114 your . . . beauty your chastity should hold no dealings with your beauty/your chastity
should not permit anyone to converse with your beauty   116 commerce interaction (Hamlet picks up on
the sense of 'sexual dealings')   120 his its (i.e. honesty's)   121 sometime once   paradox seemingly
absurd statement/observation that contradicts commonly held beliefs   124 virtue . . . it virtue cannot be so
successfully grafted onto an old sinful tree without some flavour of sin being retained   128 nunnery
convent, playing on slang sense of 'brothel'   129 indifferent honest moderately virtuous

proud, revengeful, ambitious, with more offences at
my beck than I have thoughts to put them in,
imagination to give them shape, or time to act them
135   in. What should such fellows as I do crawling
between heaven and earth? We are arrant knaves all:
believe none of us. Go thy ways to a nunnery.
Where's your father?

OPHELIA At home, my lord.

140 **HAMLET** Let the doors be shut upon him, that he may play
the fool nowhere but in's own house. Farewell.

OPHELIA O, help him, you sweet heavens!

HAMLET If thou dost marry, I'll give thee this plague for
thy dowry: be thou as chaste as ice, as pure as snow,
145   thou shalt not escape calumny. Get thee to a nunnery:
go, farewell. Or, if thou wilt needs marry, marry a fool,
for wise men know well enough what monsters you
make of them. To a nunnery, go, and quickly too.
Farewell.

150 **OPHELIA** O heavenly powers, restore him!

HAMLET I have heard of your paintings too, well enough.
God has given you one face and you make yourself
another: you jig, you amble and you lisp, and nickname
God's creatures, and make your wantonness your
155   ignorance. Go to, I'll no more on't: it hath made me mad.
I say we will have no more marriages: those that are
married already, all but one shall live: the rest shall keep
as they are. To a nunnery, go.   *Exit Hamlet*

OPHELIA O, what a noble mind is here o'erthrown!
160   The courtier's, soldier's, scholar's, eye, tongue,
       sword,
    Th'expectancy and rose of the fair state,
    The glass of fashion and the mould of form,
    Th'observed of all observers, quite, quite down!
    And I, of ladies most deject and wretched,
165   That sucked the honey of his music vows,
    Now see that noble and most sovereign reason
    Like sweet bells jangled out of tune and harsh,

---

133 beck command   **145 calumny** slander   **147 monsters** men with unfaithful wives were traditionally
supposed to grow horns   **151 paintings** use of cosmetics   **153 amble** walk with an easy (or an
exaggerated) motion **lisp** speak in an affected manner   **154 make…ignorance** use innocence as an
excuse for behaviour that is wilful/affected/promiscuous   **155 on't** of it   **161 Th'expectancy** the hope
162 glass of fashion mirror on whose image men model themselves **form** etiquette/ideal pattern

That unmatched form and feature of blown youth
Blasted with ecstasy. O, woe is me,
170 T'have seen what I have seen, see what I see!

Enter King and Polonius   *From their hiding place*

KING Love? His affections do not that way tend,
Nor what he spake, though it lacked form a little,
Was not like madness. There's something in his soul
O'er which his melancholy sits on brood,
175 And I do doubt the hatch and the disclose
Will be some danger, which to prevent,
I have in quick determination
Thus set it down: he shall with speed to England
For the demand of our neglected tribute.
180 Haply the seas and countries different
With variable objects shall expel
This something-settled matter in his heart,
Whereon his brains still beating puts him thus
From fashion of himself. What think you on't?
185 POLONIUS It shall do well. But yet do I believe
The origin and commencement of this grief
Sprung from neglected love.— How now, Ophelia?
You need not tell us what Lord Hamlet said:
We heard it all. My lord, do as you please,
190 But, if you hold it fit, after the play
Let his queen mother all alone entreat him
To show his griefs: let her be round with him,
And I'll be placed, so please you, in the ear
Of all their conference. If she find him not,
195 To England send him, or confine him where
Your wisdom best shall think.
KING It shall be so:
Madness in great ones must not unwatched go.

Exeunt

168 **blown** blooming   169 **Blasted with ecstasy** destroyed by madness   171 **affections** emotions
174 **on brood** brooding, like a bird sitting on eggs   175 **doubt** fear   **disclose** disclosure/hatching
178 **set it down** decided   179 **tribute** regular amount paid by one state to another, usually in return for
peace   180 **Haply** perhaps/with luck   181 **objects** sights   182 **something-settled matter** somewhat
fixed preoccupation (perhaps with medical sense 'festering pus' or, sinisterly, 'stagnant blood')   184 **fashion
of himself** his usual behaviour, his old self   192 **round** blunt/severe   194 **find him not** fails to find the
cause of his unhappiness

[Act 3 Scene 2]   *running scene 8*

Enter Hamlet and two or three of the Players

HAMLET Speak the speech, I pray you, as I pronounced it
to you, trippingly on the tongue: but if you mouth it,
as many of your players do, I had as lief the town-
crier had spoke my lines. Nor do not saw the air too
5   much with your hand, thus, but use all gently; for in
the very torrent, tempest, and, as I may say, the
whirlwind of passion, you must acquire and beget a
temperance that may give it smoothness. O, it offends
me to the soul to see a robustious periwig-pated
10   fellow tear a passion to tatters, to very rags, to split
the ears of the groundlings, who for the most part are
capable of nothing but inexplicable dumb shows and
noise: I could have such a fellow whipped for
o'erdoing Termagant: it out-Herods Herod. Pray
15   you avoid it.

A PLAYER I warrant your honour.

HAMLET Be not too tame neither, but let your own
discretion be your tutor: suit the action to the word,
the word to the action, with this special observance:
20   that you o'erstep not the modesty of nature; for
anything so overdone is from the purpose of playing,
whose end, both at the first and now, was and is to
hold as 'twere the mirror up to nature, to show virtue
her own feature, scorn her own image, and the very
25   age and body of the time his form and pressure. Now
this overdone or come tardy off, though it make
the unskilful laugh, cannot but make the judicious
grieve; the censure of the which one must in your
allowance o'erweigh a whole theatre of others. O,
30   there be players that I have seen play, and heard
others praise, and that highly — not to speak it
profanely — that, neither having the accent of
Christians nor the gait of Christian, pagan, nor no

3.2   **2 trippingly** nimbly   **mouth** declaim, speak pompously   **3 as lief** as soon, rather   **9 robustious** boisterous/unruly   **periwig-pated** wig-wearing   **11 groundlings** members of the audience standing in the yard in front of the stage, the cheapest place from which to watch   **are capable of** can understand   **12 dumb shows** mimes/unsophisticated spectacles   **14 Termagant** imaginary deity believed to have been worshipped by Muslims and represented in the old mystery plays as a raging tyrant   **Herod** biblical king who featured in the mystery plays as a raging tyrant   **16 warrant** assure   **18 discretion** judgement   **20 modesty** restraints   **21 from** i.e. far from   **25 pressure** stamp, impression   **26 come tardy off** performed inadequately   **27 unskilful** ignorant, unsophisticated   **28 censure** judgement/criticism   **the which one** one of whom   **29 allowance** admission, acknowledgement

man, have so strutted and bellowed that I have
35   thought some of nature's journeymen had made men
and not made them well, they imitated humanity so
abominably .

A PLAYER I hope we have reformed that indifferently
with us, sir.

40   HAMLET O, reform it altogether. And let those that play
your clowns speak no more than is set down for
them, for there be of them that will themselves laugh,
to set on some quantity of barren spectators to laugh
too, though in the meantime some necessary
45   question of the play be then to be considered: that's
villainous, and shows a most pitiful ambition in the
fool that uses it. Go, make you ready.—

Exeunt Players

Enter Polonius, Rosencrantz and Guildenstern

How now, my lord, will the king hear this piece of
work?

50   POLONIUS And the queen too, and that presently.

HAMLET Bid the players make haste.—   *Exit Polonius*
Will you two help to hasten them?

BOTH We will, my lord.

Exeunt [Rosencrantz and Guildenstern]

Enter Horatio

HAMLET What ho, Horatio!

55   HORATIO Here, sweet lord, at your service.

HAMLET Horatio, thou art e'en as just a man
As e'er my conversation coped withal.

HORATIO O, my dear lord—

HAMLET Nay, do not think I flatter,
60   For what advancement may I hope from thee
That no revenue hast but thy good spirits
To feed and clothe thee? Why should the poor be
flattered?
No, let the candied tongue lick absurd pomp,
And crook the pregnant hinges of the knee
65   Where thrift may follow fawning. Dost thou hear?
Since my dear soul was mistress of her choice

---

35 journeymen labourers   **37 abominably** plays on the popular misconception that the word was derived from Latin *ab homine*, i.e. 'away from man, unnatural' (previously spelled 'abhominably')   **38 indifferently** moderately well   **42 of** some amongst   **43 barren** apathetic/dull-witted   **44 necessary question** important aspect   **47 uses** does, practises   **50 presently** imminently   **57 As ... withal** as ever my dealings with people brought me into contact with   **63 candied** sugared (i.e. flattering)   **64 crook** bend **pregnant** ready   **65 thrift** profit

And could of men distinguish, her election
Hath sealed thee for herself, for thou hast been
As one, in suffering all, that suffers nothing,
70 A man that fortune's buffets and rewards
Hath ta'en with equal thanks: and blest are those
Whose blood and judgement are so well commingled
That they are not a pipe for fortune's finger
To sound what stop she please. Give me that man
75 That is not passion's slave, and I will wear him
In my heart's core, ay, in my heart of heart,
As I do thee. Something too much of this.
There is a play tonight before the king:
One scene of it comes near the circumstance
80 Which I have told thee of my father's death:
I prithee, when thou see'st that act afoot,
Even with the very comment of thy soul
Observe mine uncle: if his occulted guilt
Do not itself unkennel in one speech,
85 It is a damnèd ghost that we have seen,
And my imaginations are as foul
As Vulcan's stithy. Give him heedful note,
For I mine eyes will rivet to his face,
And after we will both our judgements join
90 In censure of his seeming.
HORATIO Well, my lord.
If he steal aught the whilst this play is playing
And scape detecting, I will pay the theft.
Enter King, Queen, Polonius, Ophelia, Rosencrantz,
Guildenstern and other Lords Attendant with his Guard
carrying torches. Danish march. Sound a flourish
HAMLET They are coming to the play: I must be idle.
95 Get you a place.
KING How fares our cousin Hamlet?

---

67 **election** choice   68 **sealed** designated (literally, placed a legally binding seal upon)   69 **As . . . nothing**
like one who endures everything with fortitude and is not wounded by any of it   **suffering** undergoing/
enduring (the sense then shifts to 'is hurt by')   70 **buffets** blows   72 **blood** passion   74 **stop** note
produced by placing the finger over a hole in a wind instrument   76 **core** puns on the Latin *cor* meaning
'heart'   82 **the . . . soul** your most insightful, penetrating consideration   83 **occulted** hidden
84 **unkennel** reveal (as a fox is driven out of its hole)   85 **damnèd** i.e. evil, devilish   86 **foul** black, grimy
87 **Vulcan's stithy** the forge of Vulcan, Roman god of fire and blacksmiths   **heedful note** careful attention
90 **censure . . . seeming** forming an opinion of his appearance   92 **steal aught** gets away with anything
march i.e. march played on drums   94 **idle** unoccupied/mad   96 **fares** is (but Hamlet responds to the
sense of 'feeds')

HAMLET Excellent, i'faith, of the chameleon's dish: I eat the
    air, promise-crammed: you cannot feed capons so.

KING I have nothing with this answer, Hamlet: these
100   words are not mine.

HAMLET No, nor mine now.— My lord, you played once   *To Polonius*
    i'th'university, you say?

POLONIUS That I did, my lord, and was accounted a good
    actor.

105 HAMLET And what did you enact?

POLONIUS I did enact Julius Caesar: I was killed
    i'th'Capitol: Brutus killed me.

HAMLET It was a brute part of him to kill so capital a calf
    there.— Be the players ready?

110 ROSENCRANTZ Ay, my lord: they stay upon your
    patience.

GERTRUDE Come hither, my good Hamlet, sit by me.

HAMLET No, good mother, here's metal more attractive.

POLONIUS O, ho! Do you mark that?   *To King*

115 HAMLET Lady, shall I lie in your lap?

OPHELIA No, my lord.

HAMLET I mean, my head upon your lap?

OPHELIA Ay, my lord.

HAMLET Do you think I meant country matters?

120 OPHELIA I think nothing, my lord.

HAMLET That's a fair thought to lie between maids' legs.

OPHELIA What is, my lord?

HAMLET Nothing.

OPHELIA You are merry, my lord.

125 HAMLET Who, I?

OPHELIA Ay, my lord.

HAMLET O, God, your only jig-maker. What should a
    man do but be merry? For look you how cheerfully
    my mother looks, and my father died within's two
130 hours.

OPHELIA Nay, 'tis twice two months, my lord.

---

97 chameleon's dish supposedly these reptiles fed on air   98 capons castrated cockerels fattened to make
their meat more flavoursome   99 have nothing with gain nothing from   100 not mine nothing to do with
my question (Hamlet responds to the sense of 'do not belong to me')   107 i'th'Capitol at Capitoline Hill, site
of the temple of supreme Roman god Jupiter   108 brute brutal/stupid/animal (with obvious pun on Brutus)
part deed/role   calf fool   110 stay . . . patience await your permission (to start)   113 metal more
attractive more magnetic metal (metal puns on 'mettle' for an additional sense of 'one of a more pleasing
disposition')   115 lie . . . lap recline upon your lap/have sex with you   119 country matters sex (country
puns on 'cunt')   123 Nothing i.e. 'no thing' (vagina)   127 your only jig-maker I'm your unrivalled
composer of jigs (bawdy playlets)

HAMLET So long? Nay then, let the devil wear black, for
I'll have a suit of sables. O heavens! Die two months
ago, and not forgotten yet? Then there's hope a great
135 man's memory may outlive his life half a year: but,
by'r lady, he must build churches, then, or else shall
he suffer not thinking on, with the hobby-horse,
whose epitaph is 'For, O, for, O, the hobby-horse is
forgot.'

Hautboys play. The dumb show enters
Enter a King and Queen very lovingly, the Queen embracing
him. She kneels, and makes show of protestation unto him.
He takes her up, and declines his head upon her neck: lays
him down upon a bank of flowers: she, seeing him asleep,
leaves him. Anon comes in a fellow, takes off his crown, kisses
it, and pours poison in the King's ears, and exits. The Queen
returns, finds the King dead, and makes passionate action.
The Poisoner, with some two or three Mutes, comes in again,
seeming to lament with her. The dead body is carried away.
The Poisoner woos the Queen with gifts: she seems loath and
unwilling awhile, but in the end accepts his love.   Exeunt

140 **OPHELIA** What means this, my lord?

HAMLET Marry, this is miching malicho: that means
mischief.

OPHELIA Belike this show imports the argument of the
play.

145 **HAMLET** We shall know by these fellows: the players
cannot keep counsel, they'll tell all.

OPHELIA Will they tell us what this show meant?

HAMLET Ay, or any show that you'll show him: be not
you ashamed to show, he'll not shame to tell you
150 what it means.

OPHELIA You are naught, you are naught: I'll mark the
play.

Enter Prologue

PROLOGUE For us, and for our tragedy,
    Here stooping to your clemency,
155   We beg your hearing patiently.   *[Exit]*

HAMLET Is this a prologue, or the posy of a ring?

---

133 **suit of sables** luxurious suit trimmed with dark-coloured sable fur   137 **suffer...on** be forgotten **hobby-horse** artificial horse fastened around the waist of one of the participants in a morris dance; **the hobby-horse is forgot** was a popular phrase   *Hautboys* oboe-like instruments   *protestation* solemn declaration (of love)   *passionate action* gestures of extreme grief   *Mutes* i.e. other actors   141 **miching malicho** lurking iniquity, skulking mischief   143 **Belike** presumably   **argument** plot   146 **counsel** a secret   148 **show** sexual display   **be not you** if you are not   151 **naught** indecent/offensive   156 **posy of a ring** short (usually clichéd) verse motto engraved on a ring

OPHELIA 'Tis brief, my lord.

HAMLET As woman's love.

Enter [two Players as] King and his Queen [Baptista]

PLAYER KING   Full thirty times hath Phoebus' cart gone
            round

160   Neptune's salt wash and Tellus' orbèd ground,
            And thirty dozen moons with borrowed sheen
            About the world have times twelve thirties been,
            Since love our hearts and Hymen did our hands
            Unite commutual in most sacred bands.

165 **BAPTISTA** So many journeys may the sun and moon
            Make us again count o'er ere love be done!
            But, woe is me, you are so sick of late,
            So far from cheer and from your former state,
            That I distrust you: yet, though I distrust,

170   Discomfort you, my lord, it nothing must,
            For women's fear and love holds quantity,
            In neither aught, or in extremity.
            Now, what my love is, proof hath made you know,
            And as my love is sized, my fear is so.

175 **PLAYER KING** Faith, I must leave thee, love, and shortly
            too:
            My operant powers my functions leave to do.
            And thou shalt live in this fair world behind,
            Honoured, beloved: and haply one as kind
            For husband shalt thou—

BAPTISTA   O, confound the rest!

180   Such love must needs be treason in my breast:
            In second husband let me be accurst!
            None wed the second but who killed the first.

HAMLET Wormwood, wormwood.   *Aside?*

BAPTISTA The instances that second marriage move

185   Are base respects of thrift, but none of love:
            A second time I kill my husband dead,
            When second husband kisses me in bed.

---

159 **Phoebus' cart** the sun god's chariot   160 **Neptune's salt wash** i.e. the sea (of which Neptune was god)   **Tellus' orbèd ground** i.e. the earth (of which Tellus was goddess)   161 **borrowed sheen** reflected radiance   163 **Hymen** god of marriage   164 **bands** bonds   169 **distrust** fear for   170 **Discomfort** dismay, discourage   171 **holds quantity** are to be found in the same proportions   172 **In … extremity** they are either non-existent or excessive   173 **proof** tried and tested experience   174 **as … so** my fear is just as great as my love   176 **operant** vital/active   **leave to do** cease to perform   179 **confound** destroy (i.e. do not say)   182 **None** no woman   183 **Wormwood** i.e. that's bitter (the sharp-tasting plant was also used to purge the digestive tract of worms, so there may also be a suggestion of bringing forth gnawing guilt)   184 **instances** motives   **move** prompt   185 **respects of thrift** considerations of personal profit

PLAYER KING I do believe you think what now you
            speak,
            But what we do determine oft we break.
190   Purpose is but the slave to memory,
            Of violent birth, but poor validity,
            Which now, like fruit unripe, sticks on the tree,
            But fall unshaken when they mellow be.
            Most necessary 'tis that we forget
195   To pay ourselves what to ourselves is debt:
            What to ourselves in passion we propose,
            The passion ending, doth the purpose lose.
            The violence of either grief or joy
            Their own enactures with themselves destroy:
200   Where joy most revels, grief doth most lament;
            Grief joys, joy grieves, on slender accident.
            This world is not for aye, nor 'tis not strange
            That even our loves should with our fortunes
                change,
            For 'tis a question left us yet to prove,
205   Whether love lead fortune, or else fortune love.
            The great man down, you mark his favourites flies:
            The poor advanced makes friends of enemies.
            And hitherto doth love on fortune tend,
            For who not needs shall never lack a friend,
210   And who in want a hollow friend doth try,
            Directly seasons him his enemy.
            But, orderly to end where I begun,
            Our wills and fates do so contrary run
            That our devices still are overthrown:
215   Our thoughts are ours, their ends none of our own.
            So think thou wilt no second husband wed,
            But die thy thoughts when thy first lord is dead.
BAPTISTA Nor earth to me give food, nor heaven light,
            Sport and repose lock from me day and night,
220   Each opposite that blanks the face of joy

---

190 Purpose . . . validity our intentions are subject to the weakness of memory, being passionate at the
outset, but lacking in endurance   **192 Which** i.e. purpose   **194 Most . . . debt** it is inevitable that we
should forget to fulfil our obligations to ourselves   **199 enactures** fulfilments, performances   **201 Grief . . .
accident** i.e. one extreme of emotion turns to its opposite at the slightest event   **202 aye** ever   **206 down**
fallen in fortune   **207 poor advanced** poor man who improves his station in life   **208 hitherto** up to this
point (in the argument)   **tend** attend/serve   **209 who not needs** he who does not lack fortune
210 who in want he who, being in need   **try** test   **211 seasons him** ripens him into   **214 devices**
plans   **still** continually   **215 ends** outcomes   **218 Nor** let neither   **219 Sport . . . night** let me be barred
from recreation during the day and rest at night   **220 opposite** opposing force   **blanks** makes pale

Meet what I would have well and it destroy!
Both here and hence pursue me lasting strife,
If, once a widow, ever I be wife!

HAMLET If she should break it now!

225 **PLAYER KING** 'Tis deeply sworn. Sweet, leave me here
  awhile:
  My spirits grow dull, and fain I would beguile
  The tedious day with sleep.

BAPTISTA Sleep rock thy brain,   [*He*] *sleeps*
And never come mischance between us twain. *Exit*

230 **HAMLET** Madam, how like you this play?

GERTRUDE The lady protests too much, methinks.

HAMLET O, but she'll keep her word.

KING Have you heard the argument? Is there no offence
  in't?

235 **HAMLET** No, no, they do but jest, poison in jest: no
  offence i'th'world.

KING What do you call the play?

HAMLET *The Mousetrap.* Marry, how? Tropically. This
  play is the image of a murder done in Vienna:
240 Gonzago is the duke's name, his wife, Baptista. You
  shall see anon: 'tis a knavish piece of work, but what
  o'that? Your majesty and we that have free souls, it
  touches us not: let the galled jade wince, our withers
  are unwrung .

Enter Lucianus

245 This is one Lucianus, nephew to the king.

OPHELIA You are a good chorus, my lord.

HAMLET I could interpret between you and your love, if I
  could see the puppets dallying.

OPHELIA You are keen, my lord, you are keen.

250 **HAMLET** It would cost you a groaning to take off my
  edge.

OPHELIA Still better, and worse.

---

221 **Meet . . . destroy** (may it) encounter and destroy everything that I would like to see prosper   222 **here
and hence** in this and in the next world   226 **fain** willingly   **beguile** while away   231 **protests** makes
declarations, vows   233 **offence** offensive matter (Hamlet shifts the sense to 'actual injury/real crime')
235 **jest** pretend, act   238 **Tropically** figuratively   240 **duke's** i.e. king's   243 **galled jade** saddle-sore
old horse   **wince** kick out from pain   **withers** part of the horse's back between the shoulder blades
244 **unwrung** not pinched or chafed   246 **chorus** actor who narrated or interpreted parts of a play
247 **interpret** provide dialogue as an actor does in a puppet show/act as a go-between   248 **puppets**
possibly plays on a sense of 'breasts/genitals'   **dallying** spending idle time together/flirting/having sex
249 **keen** quick/cutting   250 **groaning** the moans of a woman losing her virginity (or possibly
subsequently, in labour)   **take . . . edge** deter my sharp wit/blunt my sexual appetite/cause me to lose my
erection   252 **better, and worse** i.e. wittier, yet more insulting

HAMLET So you mis-take your husbands.— Begin, murderer: pox, leave thy damnable faces, and begin.

255   Come, the croaking raven doth bellow for revenge.

LUCIANUS Thoughts black, hands apt, drugs fit and time agreeing,

    Confederate season, else no creature seeing,

    Thou mixture rank, of midnight weeds collected,

    With Hecate's ban thrice blasted, thrice infected,

260   Thy natural magic and dire property,

    On wholesome life usurp immediately.

Pours the poison in his ears

HAMLET He poisons him i'th'garden for's estate. His name's Gonzago: the story is extant and writ in choice Italian. You shall see anon how the murderer

265   gets the love of Gonzago's wife.   *King stands*

OPHELIA The king rises.

HAMLET What, frighted with false fire?

GERTRUDE How fares my lord?

POLONIUS Give o'er the play.

270 **KING** Give me some light. Away!

ALL Lights, lights, lights!

                Exeunt. Hamlet and Horatio remain

HAMLET Why, let the strucken deer go weep,

    The hart ungallèd play,

    For some must watch, while some must sleep:

275   So runs the world away.

    Would not this, sir, and a forest of feathers — if the rest of my fortunes turn Turk with me — with two Provincial roses on my razed shoes, get me a fellowship in a cry of players, sir?

280 **HORATIO** Half a share.

---

253 So in just such a manner   **mis-take your husbands** swear insincerely to love and be faithful to your husbands (according to the marriage vow 'for better or for worse'); plays on the idea of 'mistaking' another man for one's true husband, as Hamlet deems Gertrude to have done   **254 pox** i.e. a plague on it

255 the . . . revenge refers to lines from the anonymous *True Tragedy of Richard III*   **raven** considered a bird of ill omen whose cry heralded death   **257 Confederate . . . seeing** the occasion itself an ally, there being no one else to see me   **258 rank** virulent/pungent/foul   **259 Hecate's ban** the curse of Hecate, goddess of witchcraft   **260 dire property** dreadful nature   **261 wholesome** healthy   **262 for's** for his   **His** i.e. the king's   **267 false fire** the discharge of blank cartridges from a firearm   **272 strucken** wounded   **273 hart ungallèd** uninjured male deer   **274 watch** remain awake   **276 this** the play/the verse just uttered

feathers i.e. elaborate plumes on a hat   **277 turn Turk with** abandon (like one renouncing Christianity to become a Muslim)   **278 Provincial roses** French roses from Provence (here rosettes, worn to hide the shoe fastenings and, like the **feathers**, a feature of the actor's garb)   **razed shoes** shoes with ornamental cuts in the leather   **fellowship . . . cry** partnership in a pack   **280 share** the major players in the Chamberlain's Men had shares in the company's assets

HAMLET A whole one, I.
For thou dost know, O Damon dear,
This realm dismantled was
Of Jove himself, and now reigns here
285   A very, very — pajock.

HORATIO You might have rhymed.

HAMLET O, good Horatio, I'll take the ghost's word for a
thousand pound. Didst perceive?

HORATIO Very well, my lord.

290   **HAMLET** Upon the talk of the poisoning?

HORATIO I did very well note him.

HAMLET O, ha! Come, some music. Come, the recorders.
For if the king like not the comedy,
Why then, belike, he likes it not, perdy.
295   Come, some music!

Enter Rosencrantz and Guildenstern

GUILDENSTERN Good my lord, vouchsafe me a word with
you.

HAMLET Sir, a whole history.

GUILDENSTERN The king, sir—

300   **HAMLET** Ay, sir, what of him?

GUILDENSTERN Is in his retirement marvellous
distempered.

HAMLET With drink, sir?

GUILDENSTERN No, my lord, rather with choler.

305   **HAMLET** Your wisdom should show itself more richer to
signify this to his doctor, for for me to put him to his
purgation would perhaps plunge him into far more
choler.

GUILDENSTERN Good my lord, put your discourse into
310   some frame and start not so wildly from my affair.

HAMLET I am tame, sir: pronounce.

GUILDENSTERN The queen, your mother, in most great
affliction of spirit, hath sent me to you.

HAMLET You are welcome.

---

282 Damon either an allusion to the Greek tale of Damon and Pythias, famous for their great friendship, or used as a traditional pastoral name   **283 dismantled** stripped/deprived   **284 Jove** supreme Roman god   **285 pajock** either 'patchock' (i.e. base, ragged fellow) or 'peacock'   **286 rhymed** the word that might be expected to rhyme with **was** is 'ass'   **294 perdy** corruption of the French *par dieu* ('by God')
296 vouchsafe permit   **301 retirement** withdrawal to his rooms   **302 distempered** out of humour (Hamlet chooses to understand the sense of 'drunk')   **304 choler** anger (provoked by an excess of bile, one of the four bodily humours)   **306 signify** communicate   **307 purgation** cleansing the body through bloodletting or the use of emetics or laxatives (Hamlet plays on the idea of eliciting confession; the senses of legal and spiritual purging are also relevant)   **310 frame** order   **start** swerve/recoil

315   GUILDENSTERN Nay, good my lord, this courtesy is not of the right breed. If it shall please you to make me a wholesome answer, I will do your mother's commandment: if not, your pardon and my return shall be the end of my business.

320   HAMLET Sir, I cannot.

GUILDENSTERN What, my lord?

HAMLET Make you a wholesome answer: my wit's diseased. But, sir, such answers as I can make, you shall command, or rather, as you say, my mother: 325 therefore no more, but to the matter: my mother, you say—

ROSENCRANTZ Then thus she says: your behaviour hath struck her into amazement and admiration.

HAMLET O, wonderful son, that can so astonish a 330 mother! But is there no sequel at the heels of this mother's admiration?

ROSENCRANTZ She desires to speak with you in her closet ere you go to bed.

HAMLET We shall obey, were she ten times our mother. 335 Have you any further trade with us?

ROSENCRANTZ My lord, you once did love me.

HAMLET So I do still, by these pickers and stealers.

ROSENCRANTZ Good my lord, what is your cause of distemper? You do freely bar the door of your own 340 liberty, if you deny your griefs to your friend.

HAMLET Sir, I lack advancement.

ROSENCRANTZ How can that be, when you have the voice of the king himself for your succession in Denmark?

345   HAMLET Ay, but 'While the grass grows' — the proverb is something musty.

Enter one with a recorder

O, the recorder! Let me see.   *Takes the recorder*
To withdraw with you: why do you go about to   *to Ros.*
recover the wind of me, as if you would drive me into   *and Guild.*
350   a toil?

---

316 breed kind/courtly breeding   **317 wholesome** healthy, sane   **318 pardon** permission (to leave)
328 amazement bewilderment/alarm   **admiration** astonishment, wonder   **329 wonderful**
astonishing/excellent   **333 closet** private room   **335 trade** dealings (a deliberately derogatory term here)
337 pickers and stealers hands   **340 liberty** freedom from mental anguish (but a suggestive image of
literal imprisonment)   **deny** refuse to tell   **345 'While . . . grows'** the rest of the proverb is 'the horse
starves'   **348 withdraw** speak privately   **349 recover . . . toil** a hunting metaphor: the hunter would get to
the windward side of the prey (**recover the wind**), allowing it to scent him and thus driving the animal in the
opposite direction and into a net (**toil**)

GUILDENSTERN O, my lord, if my duty be too bold, my
love is too unmannerly.

HAMLET I do not well understand that. Will you play
upon this pipe?

355 **GUILDENSTERN** My lord, I cannot.

HAMLET I pray you.

GUILDENSTERN Believe me, I cannot.

HAMLET I do beseech you.

GUILDENSTERN I know no touch of it, my lord.

360 **HAMLET** 'Tis as easy as lying: govern these ventages with
your finger and thumb, give it breath with your
mouth and it will discourse most excellent music.
Look you, these are the stops.

GUILDENSTERN But these cannot I command to any
365 utterance of harmony: I have not the skill.

HAMLET Why, look you now, how unworthy a thing you
make of me! You would play upon me; you would
seem to know my stops, you would pluck out the
heart of my mystery, you would sound me from my
370 lowest note to the top of my compass, and there is
much music, excellent voice, in this little organ, yet
cannot you make it speak. Why, do you think that I
am easier to be played on than a pipe? Call me what
instrument you will, though you can fret me, you
375 cannot play upon me.— God bless you, sir!   *To the entering*
Enter Polonius   *Polonius*

POLONIUS My lord, the queen would speak with you,
and presently.

HAMLET Do you see that cloud that's almost in shape like
a camel?

380 **POLONIUS** By th'mass, and it's like a camel indeed.

HAMLET Methinks it is like a weasel.

POLONIUS It is backed like a weasel.

HAMLET Or like a whale?

POLONIUS Very like a whale.

385 **HAMLET** Then will I will come to my mother by and
by.— They fool me to the top of my bent.— I will come   *Aside*
by and by.

POLONIUS I will say so.   *Exit*

---

351 if…unmannerly i.e. if I am overly bold in my behaviour it is my love for you that is to blame
360 ventages holes (or **stops**) **369 mystery** secret/craft, skill (playing an instrument)   **sound** question/
produce music from   **370 compass** range   **374 fret** irritate/provide with frets (ridges for fingering on a
lute)   **377 presently** straight away   **380 By th'mass** by the Mass (a common oath)   **386 fool…bent**
indulge me in my foolishness to the limit/force me to play the fool to the limit of my ability (or endurance)

HAMLET 'By and by' is easily said.
390   Leave me, friends.   [*Exeunt all but Hamlet*]
'Tis now the very witching time of night,
When churchyards yawn and hell itself breathes out
Contagion to this world: now could I drink hot blood
And do such bitter business as the day
395   Would quake to look on. Soft, now to my mother.
O heart, lose not thy nature; let not ever
The soul of Nero enter this firm bosom:
Let me be cruel, not unnatural.
I will speak daggers to her, but use none.
400   My tongue and soul in this be hypocrites:
How in my words somever she be shent,
To give them seals never my soul consent!   [*Exit*]

[Act 3 Scene 3]   *running scene 9*

Enter King, Rosencrantz and Guildenstern

KING I like him not, nor stands it safe with us
To let his madness range. Therefore prepare you:
I your commission will forthwith dispatch,
And he to England shall along with you.
5   The terms of our estate may not endure
Hazard so dangerous as doth hourly grow
Out of his lunacies.
GUILDENSTERN We will ourselves provide:
Most holy and religious fear it is
10   To keep those many many bodies safe
That live and feed upon your majesty.
ROSENCRANTZ The single and peculiar life is bound
With all the strength and armour of the mind
To keep itself from noyance, but much more
15   That spirit upon whose weal depends and rests
The lives of many. The cease of majesty
Dies not alone, but like a gulf doth draw
What's near it with it: it is a massy wheel
Fixed on the summit of the highest mount,
20   To whose huge spokes ten thousand lesser things

396 **nature** natural feelings   397 **Nero** Roman emperor who murdered his mother   401 **How . . . shent**
however much I rebuke and punish her verbally   **somever** to whatever extent   402 **give them seals** i.e.
by acting upon them   3.3   1 **him** i.e. his behaviour   3 **dispatch** make ready/deal with promptly
5 **terms . . . estate** conditions or responsibilities of my position as king   8 **provide** prepare, equip
9 **fear** concern, responsibility   12 **single and peculiar** individual and private   14 **noyance** vexation/
harm   15 **weal** welfare   16 **cease** cessation/decease   17 **gulf** whirlpool   18 **massy** massive/weighty

Are mortised and adjoined, which, when it falls,
Each small annexment, petty consequence,
Attends the boist'rous ruin. Never alone
Did the king sigh, but with a general groan.

25 KING Arm you, I pray you, to this speedy voyage,
For we will fetters put upon this fear,
Which now goes too free-footed.

BOTH We will haste us.

Exeunt Gentlemen [Rosencrantz and Guildenstern]
Enter Polonius

POLONIUS My lord, he's going to his mother's closet:
30 Behind the arras I'll convey myself
To hear the process. I'll warrant she'll tax him home,
And, as you said, and wisely was it said,
'Tis meet that some more audience than a mother,
Since nature makes them partial, should o'erhear
35 The speech, of vantage. Fare you well, my liege:
I'll call upon you ere you go to bed,
And tell you what I know.

KING Thanks, dear my lord.—   [*Exit Polonius*]
O, my offence is rank, it smells to heaven:
40 It hath the primal eldest curse upon't,
A brother's murder. Pray can I not,
Though inclination be as sharp as will:
My stronger guilt defeats my strong intent,
And like a man to double business bound,
45 I stand in pause where I shall first begin,
And both neglect. What if this cursèd hand
Were thicker than itself with brother's blood,
Is there not rain enough in the sweet heavens
To wash it white as snow? Whereto serves mercy
50 But to confront the visage of offence?
And what's in prayer but this two-fold force,
To be forestallèd ere we come to fall,
Or pardoned being down? Then I'll look up:
My fault is past. But, O, what form of prayer
55 Can serve my turn? 'Forgive me my foul murder'?
That cannot be, since I am still possessed

21 **mortised** fastened securely   22 **annexment** adjunct, hanger-on   **petty consequence** trivial
attachment   23 **attends** accompanies   **boist'rous** massive/turbulent   25 **Arm you** prepare yourselves
31 **process** proceedings   **tax him home** reprove him thoroughly   33 **meet** fitting   35 **of vantage** in
addition/from an advantageous position   39 **rank** foul-smelling/rotten   40 **primal eldest curse** God's
curse on Cain, the first murderer, who killed his brother Abel (biblical)   42 **inclination...will** my urge and
determination to pray are equally strong   44 **bound** directed/tied/sworn   49 **Whereto...offence?** What
is the point of mercy if not to confront sin face to face?   52 **forestallèd** prevented   55 **turn** need, purpose

Of those effects for which I did the murder:
My crown, mine own ambition and my queen.
May one be pardoned and retain th'offence?
60   In the corrupted currents of this world
Offence's gilded hand may shove by justice,
And oft 'tis seen the wicked prize itself
Buys out the law. But 'tis not so above:
There is no shuffling, there the action lies
65   In his true nature, and we ourselves compelled,
Even to the teeth and forehead of our faults,
To give in evidence. What then? What rests?
Try what repentance can. What can it not?
Yet what can it, when one cannot repent?
70   O, wretched state! O, bosom black as death!
O, limèd soul that, struggling to be free,
Art more engaged! Help, angels, make assay!
Bow, stubborn knees, and heart with strings of steel,   *Kneels*
Be soft as sinews of the newborn babe!
75   All may be well.
Enter Hamlet
HAMLET Now might I do it pat, now he is praying: *Draws*
And now I'll do't. And so he goes to heaven,
And so am I revenged. That would be scanned:
A villain kills my father, and for that,
80   I, his foul son, do this same villain send
To heaven.
O, this is hire and salary, not revenge.
He took my father grossly, full of bread,
With all his crimes broad blown, as fresh as May,
85   And how his audit stands who knows save heaven?
But in our circumstance and course of thought
'Tis heavy with him: and am I then revenged,
To take him in the purging of his soul,
When he is fit and seasoned for his passage?

---

57 effects benefits, acquisitions   **59 th'offence** i.e. the profits gained from committing the offence
60 currents courses, practices   **61 gilded** golden/bearing bribes   **by** to one side   **64 There** i.e. **above**, in
heaven   **shuffling** evasion, deceit   **the action lies** the sin is laid bare/the case is admissible (legal
metaphor, continued with **evidence**)   **66 to ... forehead** in the very face   **67 give in** give, submit   **rests**
remains   **71 limèd** caught as a bird is trapped by bird-lime (sticky substance spread on branches)
72 assay a great effort/an attempt   **76 pat** opportunely, conveniently   **78 would be scanned** needs to be
examined/would be interpreted as follows   **80 foul** sinful/treacherous/shameful; most editors prefer Quarto's
'sole'   **82 hire and salary** i.e. as if Hamlet had hired Claudius to do the murder and was now giving him his
wages   **83 grossly ... bread** i.e. in the grips of worldly pleasures, with no spiritual preparation (such as
fasting)   **84 broad blown** in full bloom   **85 audit** account   **86 circumstance ... thought** situation and
way of thinking/limited condition and way of thinking/indirect way of thinking   **87 heavy** grave/
gloomy   **88 take him** kill Claudius   **89 seasoned** prepared   **passage** journey into the next world

90   No.   *Puts up his sword*
        Up, sword, and know thou a more horrid hent:
        When he is drunk asleep, or in his rage,
        Or in th'incestuous pleasure of his bed,
        At gaming, swearing, or about some act
95   That has no relish of salvation in't,
        Then trip him, that his heels may kick at heaven,
        And that his soul may be as damned and black
        As hell, whereto it goes. My mother stays.
        This physic but prolongs thy sickly days.   *Exit*
100   **KING** My words fly up, my thoughts remain below:
        Words without thoughts never to heaven go.   *Exit*

[Act 3 Scene 4]   *running scene 10*

Enter Queen and Polonius

POLONIUS He will come straight. Look you lay home to
        him:
        Tell him his pranks have been too broad to bear with,
        And that your grace hath screened and stood
            between
        Much heat and him. I'll silence me e'en here.
5   Pray you, be round with him.
        HAMLET Mother, mother, mother!   *Within*
        GERTRUDE I'll warrant you,
        Fear me not: withdraw, I hear him coming.
        Enter Hamlet   **Polonius hides behind the arras**
        HAMLET Now, mother, what's the matter?
10   **GERTRUDE** Hamlet, thou hast thy father much offended.
        HAMLET Mother, you have my father much offended.
        GERTRUDE Come, come, you answer with an idle
            tongue.
        HAMLET Go, go, you question with a wicked tongue.
        GERTRUDE Why, how now, Hamlet?
15   **HAMLET** What's the matter now?
        GERTRUDE Have you forgot me?
        HAMLET No, by the rood, not so:
        You are the queen, your husband's brother's wife,
        But — would you were not so — you are my mother.

91 **hent** time to be seized at/opportunity   92 **drunk asleep** in a drunken stupor   95 **relish** trace, flavour
98 **stays** awaits   99 **physic** medicine (either Claudius' prayer or Hamlet's postponement of the murder)
3.4   1 **straight** straight away   **lay home** speak plainly, take to task   2 **broad** unrestrained   4 **heat** i.e.
Claudius' anger   5 **round** blunt/severe   17 **rood** Christian cross   18 **queen** perhaps this puns on 'quean'
(i.e. whore)

20   GERTRUDE Nay, then, I'll set those to you that can
          speak.
      HAMLET Come, come, and sit you down, you shall not
          budge:
          You go not till I set you up a glass
          Where you may see the inmost part of you.
      GERTRUDE What wilt thou do? Thou wilt not murder
          me?
25   Help, help, ho!
      POLONIUS What, ho? Help, help, help!   *Behind the arras*
      HAMLET How now? A rat? Dead, for a ducat, dead!   *Draws*
      POLONIUS O, I am slain!   [*Hamlet*] *kills Polonius*
      GERTRUDE O me, what hast thou done?
30   HAMLET Nay, I know not: is it the king?
      GERTRUDE O, what a rash and bloody deed is this!
      HAMLET A bloody deed: almost as bad, good mother,
          As kill a king and marry with his brother.
      GERTRUDE As kill a king?
35   HAMLET Ay, lady, 'twas my word.—   *Discovers Polonius*
          Thou wretched, rash, intruding fool, farewell.
          I took thee for thy better: take thy fortune;
          Thou find'st to be too busy is some danger.—
          Leave wringing of your hands. Peace. Sit you down,
40   And let me wring your heart, for so I shall,
          If it be made of penetrable stuff,
          If damnèd custom have not brazed it so
          That it is proof and bulwark against sense.
      GERTRUDE What have I done, that thou dar'st wag thy
          tongue
45   In noise so rude against me?
      HAMLET Such an act
          That blurs the grace and blush of modesty,
          Calls virtue hypocrite, takes off the rose
          From the fair forehead of an innocent love
50   And sets a blister there, makes marriage vows
          As false as dicers' oaths: O, such a deed
          As from the body of contraction plucks
          The very soul, and sweet religion makes
          A rhapsody of words. Heaven's face doth glow:

22 **glass** mirror   27 **Dead . . . ducat** i.e. I'll bet a ducat (gold coin) he'll soon be dead/I'll kill him for a mere ducat   38 **busy** interfering, prying   42 **brazed** covered with brass, hardened   43 **proof . . . sense** fortified against feeling   **proof** armour   45 **rude** violent/harsh/offensive   52 **contraction** binding agreement (specifically the marriage contract)   54 **rhapsody** confused mass   **glow** i.e. blush for shame

55   Yea, this solidity and compound mass
       With tristful visage, as against the doom,
       Is thought-sick at the act.
       GERTRUDE Ay me, what act,
       That roars so loud and thunders in the index?
60   **HAMLET** Look here, upon this picture, and on this,   *Shows her two*
       The counterfeit presentment of two brothers.   *pictures*
       See what a grace was seated on his brow:
       Hyperion's curls, the front of Jove himself,
       An eye like Mars to threaten or command,
65   A station like the herald Mercury
       New-lighted on a heaven-kissing hill,
       A combination and a form indeed
       Where every god did seem to set his seal
       To give the world assurance of a man:
70   This was your husband. Look you now, what follows:
       Here is your husband, like a mildewed ear,
       Blasting his wholesome brother. Have you eyes?
       Could you on this fair mountain leave to feed
       And batten on this moor? Ha! Have you eyes?
75   You cannot call it love, for at your age
       The heyday in the blood is tame, it's humble,
       And waits upon the judgement: and what judgement
       Would step from this to this? What devil was't
       That thus hath cozened you at hoodman-blind?
80   O, shame, where is thy blush? Rebellious hell,
       If thou canst mutine in a matron's bones,
       To flaming youth let virtue be as wax
       And melt in her own fire. Proclaim no shame
       When the compulsive ardour gives the charge,
85   Since frost itself as actively doth burn
       And reason panders will.
       GERTRUDE O Hamlet, speak no more:
       Thou turn'st mine eyes into my very soul,

---

55 this … mass i.e. the earth   **56 tristful** sorrowful   **as … doom** as if in anticipation of doomsday
59 index table of contents that prefaces the body of a book   **61 counterfeit presentment** painted
representation   **63 Hyperion** Greek god of the sun, and one of the Titans   **front** forehead/face   **64 Mars**
Roman god of war   **65 station** manner of standing   **Mercury** winged messenger of the Roman gods
66 New-lighted newly alighted   **68 seal** i.e. mark of approval   **71 ear** i.e. of corn   **72 Blasting**
withering   **73 leave** cease   **74 batten** feed greedily   **moor** marshland/waste ground (may play on the
sense of 'dark-skinned person' to contrast with the **fair mountain**)   **76 heyday … blood** (youthful) period
of sexual excitement   **79 cozened** cheated   **hoodman-blind** blind-man's-buff (Hamlet imagines a
blindfolded Gertrude being tricked into picking the wrong man)   **81 mutine** mutiny   **matron** mature
married woman   **84 compulsive … charge** compelling sexual passion (of youth) attacks   **85 frost** i.e. age
86 panders acts as a go-between for/ministers to the gratification of   **will** sexual desire

And there I see such black and grainèd spots
90   As will not leave their tint.

HAMLET   Nay, but to live
In the rank sweat of an enseamèd bed,
Stewed in corruption, honeying and making love
Over the nasty sty—

95   GERTRUDE   O, speak to me no more:
These words like daggers enter in mine ears.
No more, sweet Hamlet!

HAMLET   A murderer and a villain,
A slave that is not twentieth part the tithe
100   Of your precedent lord, a vice of kings,
A cutpurse of the empire and the rule,
That from a shelf the precious diadem stole,
And put it in his pocket!

GERTRUDE   No more!

Enter Ghost

105   HAMLET   A king of shreds and patches—
Save me, and hover o'er me with your wings,   *Sees the Ghost*
You heavenly guards!— What would you, gracious
    figure?

GERTRUDE   Alas, he's mad!

HAMLET   Do you not come your tardy son to chide,
110   That, lapsed in time and passion, lets go by
Th'important acting of your dread command? O, say!

GHOST   Do not forget: this visitation
Is but to whet thy almost blunted purpose.
But look, amazement on thy mother sits.
115   O, step between her and her fighting soul:
Conceit in weakest bodies strongest works:
Speak to her, Hamlet.

HAMLET   How is it with you, lady?

GERTRUDE   Alas, how is't with you,
120   That you do bend your eye on vacancy
And with th'incorporal air do hold discourse?
Forth at your eyes your spirits wildly peep,

89 grainèd engrained, indelible   90 leave their tint abandon their colour   92 enseamèd saturated with grease or pig's fat, i.e. soiled from sexual activity   93 Stewed soaked/slowly boiled (puns on 'stew' – i.e. brothel)   honeying exchanging endearments   making love talking amorously/having sex   94 nasty filthy/lewd/repellent   sty pigsty/place inhabited by whores and lustful people   99 tithe tenth part
100 precedent lord previous husband (precedent may have connotations of 'exemplary/higher ranking')
vice epitome of wickedness/buffoon or trickster from morality plays   101 cutpurse pickpocket
102 diadem crown   105 shreds and patches paltry bits and pieces/the multicoloured clothing of a fool or clown   111 important urgent, pressing   116 Conceit imagination   121 th'incorporal the insubstantial
122 spirits vital spirits, a bodily fluid thought to be vital for life

And, as the sleeping soldiers in th'alarm,
Your bedded hair, like life in excrements,
125   Start up and stand on end. O gentle son,
Upon the heat and flame of thy distemper
Sprinkle cool patience. Whereon do you look?
HAMLET On him, on him! Look you how pale he glares!
His form and cause conjoined, preaching to stones,
130   Would make them capable.— Do not look upon me,   *To the Ghost*
Lest with this piteous action you convert
My stern effects: then what I have to do
Will want true colour; tears perchance for blood.
GERTRUDE To who do you speak this?
135 HAMLET Do you see nothing there?
GERTRUDE Nothing at all, yet all that is I see.
HAMLET Nor did you nothing hear?
GERTRUDE No, nothing but ourselves.
HAMLET Why, look you there: look, how it steals away.
140   My father, in his habit as he lived!
Look where he goes even now out at the portal.
                                                                Exit [Ghost]
GERTRUDE This is the very coinage of your brain:
This bodiless creation ecstasy is very cunning in.
HAMLET Ecstasy?
145   My pulse as yours doth temperately keep time,
And makes as healthful music: it is not madness
That I have uttered. Bring me to the test,
And I the matter will reword, which madness
Would gambol from. Mother, for love of grace,
150   Lay not a flattering unction to your soul
That not your trespass, but my madness speaks:
It will but skin and film the ulcerous place,
Whilst rank corruption, mining all within,
Infects unseen. Confess yourself to heaven,
155   Repent what's past, avoid what is to come,
And do not spread the compost o'er the weeds
To make them ranker. Forgive me this my virtue,

---

123 as . . . th'alarm like soldiers awoken abruptly by a call to arms   124 like . . . excrements as if growths of hair had lives of their own   129 His . . . conjoined the combination of his appearance and his reason (for wanting revenge)   130 capable responsive   131 piteous pity-inspiring   convert . . . effects divert me from the grim deeds I intend to carry out   133 want lack   colour character, quality/motive, grounds/hue (colourless   tears rather than red blood)   140 habit clothing/demeanour   as as when/as if   142 coinage invention   143 cunning skilful/crafty   148 reword repeat   149 gambol spring away   150 unction ointment   151 trespass sin   152 skin and film form a thin skin over   153 mining corroding/undermining/sapping   157 ranker more abundant   virtue i.e. virtuous talk and rebukes

For in the fatness of these pursy times
Virtue itself of vice must pardon beg,
160   Yea, curb and woo for leave to do him good.
GERTRUDE O Hamlet, thou hast cleft my heart in twain.
HAMLET O, throw away the worser part of it,
And live the purer with the other half.
Goodnight. But go not to mine uncle's bed:
165   Assume a virtue, if you have it not.
Refrain tonight,
And that shall lend a kind of easiness
To the next abstinence. Once more, goodnight:
And when you are desirous to be blessed,
170   I'll blessing beg of you. For this same lord,   *Points to the body*
I do repent, but heaven hath pleased it so
To punish me with this, and this with me,
That I must be their scourge and minister.
I will bestow him, and will answer well
175   The death I gave him. So, again, goodnight.
I must be cruel, only to be kind:
Thus bad begins and worse remains behind.
GERTRUDE What shall I do?
HAMLET Not this by no means that I bid you do:
180   Let the bloat king tempt you again to bed,
Pinch wanton on your cheek, call you his mouse,
And let him, for a pair of reechy kisses,
Or paddling in your neck with his damned fingers,
Make you to ravel all this matter out,
185   That I essentially am not in madness,
But mad in craft. 'Twere good you let him know,
For who that's but a queen, fair, sober, wise,
Would from a paddock, from a bat, a gib,
Such dear concernings hide? Who would do so?
190   No, in despite of sense and secrecy,
Unpeg the basket on the house's top,
Let the birds fly, and like the famous ape,

---

158 pursy short-winded/fat   **160 curb and woo** bow and entreat   **173 That** so that   **scourge and minister** agent of retribution   **174 bestow** dispose of/stow away   **answer well** justify/pay for **177 behind** yet to come   **180 bloat** bloated/flabby/swollen with self-indulgence   **181 Pinch wanton** in pinching your cheeks leave marks that proclaim you a wanton (lewd woman)   **mouse** common term of endearment   **182 reechy** filthy, squalid (literally 'smoky')   **184 ravel ... out** unravel (i.e. reveal) all this business   **186 in craft** through cunning, by design   **188 paddock ... gib** toad, bat, tom-cat (creatures popularly supposed to be the familiars of witches)   **189 dear concernings** important matters   **191 Unpeg** unfasten (thus letting the birds out)   **192 famous ... down** a reference to a lost story; presumably the ape attempted to imitate the birds who had been released from the basket by climbing in, then leaping out in the hope of flying, only to succeed in breaking his neck

To try conclusions, in the basket creep,
And break your own neck down.

195 GERTRUDE Be thou assured, if words be made of breath
And breath of life, I have no life to breathe
What thou hast said to me.

HAMLET I must to England: you know that?

GERTRUDE Alack,
200 I had forgot: 'tis so concluded on.

HAMLET This man shall set me packing:
I'll lug the guts into the neighbour room.
Mother, goodnight. Indeed this counsellor
Is now most still, most secret and most grave,
205 Who was in life a foolish prating knave.—
Come, sir, to draw toward an end with you.—
Goodnight, mother.   *Exit Hamlet tugging in Polonius*
Enter King

KING There's matter in these sighs, these profound
      heaves,
You must translate: 'tis fit we understand them.
210 Where is your son?

GERTRUDE Ah, my good lord, what have I seen tonight!

KING What, Gertrude? How does Hamlet?

GERTRUDE Mad as the seas and wind when both
         contend
Which is the mightier: in his lawless fit,
215 Behind the arras hearing something stir,
He whips his rapier out and cries, 'A rat, a rat!'
And in his brainish apprehension kills
The unseen good old man.

KING O, heavy deed!
220 It had been so with us, had we been there.
His liberty is full of threats to all:
To you yourself, to us, to everyone.
Alas, how shall this bloody deed be answered?
It will be laid to us, whose providence
225 Should have kept short, restrained and out of haunt
This mad young man: but so much was our love,
We would not understand what was most fit,
But, like the owner of a foul disease,

---

193 try conclusions experiment   **201 set me packing** cause me to be sent away at once/make me begin plotting   **204 still…grave** quiet, trustworthy and dignified/dead   **205 prating** prattling, chattering
206 draw…you finish my dealings with you/haul you to your grave   **208 matter** significance
217 brainish apprehension headstrong conviction/deluded understanding   **219 heavy** sorrowful
223 answered accounted for   **224 providence** foresight/arrangements   **225 short** on a tight leash
haunt company

To keep it from divulging, lets it feed
230   Even on the pith of life. Where is he gone?
     GERTRUDE To draw apart the body he hath killed,
         O'er whom his very madness, like some ore
         Among a mineral of metals base,
         Shows itself pure: he weeps for what is done.
235 KING O Gertrude, come away!
         The sun no sooner shall the mountains touch,
         But we will ship him hence, and this vile deed
         We must with all our majesty and skill,
         Both countenance and excuse.—
     Enter Rosencrantz and Guildenstern
                                        Ho, Guildenstern!
240   Friends both, go join you with some further aid.
         Hamlet in madness hath Polonius slain,
         And from his mother's closet hath he dragged him:
         Go seek him out, speak fair, and bring the body
         Into the chapel. I pray you haste in this.
                         Exeunt Gentlemen [Ros. and Guild.]
245   Come, Gertrude, we'll call up our wisest friends
         To let them know, both what we mean to do
         And what's untimely done. O, come away!
         My soul is full of discord and dismay.   *Exeunt*

[Act 4 Scene 1]   *running scene 11*

Enter Hamlet

     HAMLET Safely stowed.
     GENTLEMEN Hamlet, Lord Hamlet!   *Within*
     HAMLET What noise? Who calls on Hamlet? O, here they
         come.
     Enter Rosencrantz and Guildenstern   *With Attendants?*
5   ROSENCRANTZ What have you done, my lord, with the
         dead body?
     HAMLET Compounded it with dust, whereto 'tis kin.
     ROSENCRANTZ Tell us where 'tis, that we may take it
         thence and bear it to the chapel.
10   HAMLET Do not believe it.
     ROSENCRANTZ Believe what?

---

229 divulging becoming apparent **231 apart** away **232 ore** precious metal **233 mineral** mine or its products **239 countenance** confront/bear out **247 what's untimely done** i.e. Polonius' premature death **4.1 1 Stowed** lodged (refers to Polonius' body); plays on slang sense of 'kept quiet', 'shut up' **2 GENTLEMEN** i.e. Rosencrantz and Guildenstern **7 Compounded** united, mingled

HAMLET That I can keep your counsel and not mine
own. Besides, to be demanded of a sponge, what
replication should be made by the son of a king?

15 ROSENCRANTZ Take you me for a sponge, my lord?

HAMLET Ay, sir, that soaks up the king's countenance,
his rewards, his authorities. But such officers do the
king best service in the end: he keeps them, like an
ape an apple, in the corner of his jaw, first mouthed

20 to be last swallowed: when he needs what you have
gleaned, it is but squeezing you, and, sponge, you
shall be dry again.

ROSENCRANTZ I understand you not, my lord.

HAMLET I am glad of it: a knavish speech sleeps in a

25 foolish ear.

ROSENCRANTZ My lord, you must tell us where the body
is, and go with us to the king.

HAMLET The body is with the king, but the king is not
with the body. The king is a thing—

30 GUILDENSTERN A thing, my lord?

HAMLET Of nothing. Bring me to him. Hide fox, and all
after.   *Exeunt*   *Running*

[Act 4 Scene 2]   *running scene 11 continues*

Enter King

KING I have sent to seek him and to find the body.
How dangerous is it that this man goes loose!
Yet must not we put the strong law on him:
He's loved of the distracted multitude,

5 Who like not in their judgement, but their eyes,
And where 'tis so, th'offender's scourge is weighed,
But ne'er the offence. To bear all smooth and even,
This sudden sending him away must seem
Deliberate pause. Diseases desperate grown

12 **keep . . . own** keep your secrets and not my own/follow your advice (and tell you where the body is) and
yet keep my own secret   13 **demanded of** questioned by   14 **replication** response   16 **countenance**
favour   17 **authorities** power, influence   19 **mouthed** taken into the mouth   24 **sleeps in** i.e. is wasted
on   28 **The . . . body** Claudius has a physical body, but he does not possess true kingship/the body is here in
the castle, like Claudius; however he, not being dead, is not with Polonius/Polonius is with the true king,
dead Hamlet senior, not with the usurping Claudius/Polonius is with God, rather than Claudius
31 **Hide . . . after** refers to a children's game in which one person (the **fox**) hides and the others pursue him
4.2   4 **of** by   **distracted** deranged/confused/foolish   6 **scourge** punishment   **weighed** considered
7 **bear . . . even** manage matters smoothly and evenly   9 **Deliberate pause** i.e. the result of careful
consideration

10   By desperate appliance are relieved,
      Or not at all.
      Enter Rosencrantz
                        How now? What hath befall'n?
      ROSENCRANTZ Where the dead body is bestowed, my lord,
          We cannot get from him.
      KING But where is he?
15   **ROSENCRANTZ** Without, my lord, guarded, to know
              your pleasure.
      KING Bring him before us.
      ROSENCRANTZ Ho, Guildenstern! Bring in my lord.   *Calls*
      Enter Hamlet and Guildenstern   *With Attendants?*
      KING Now, Hamlet, where's Polonius?
      HAMLET At supper.
20   **KING** At supper? Where?
      HAMLET Not where he eats, but where he is eaten: a
          certain convocation of worms are e'en at him. Your
          worm is your only emperor for diet: we fat all creatures
          else to fat us, and we fat ourselves for maggots: your
25   fat king and your lean beggar is but variable service,
          two dishes, but to one table. That's the end.
      KING Alas, alas!
      HAMLET A man may fish with the worm that hath eat of a
          king, and eat of the fish that hath fed of that worm.
30   **KING** What dost thou mean by this?
      HAMLET Nothing but to show you how a king may go a
          progress through the guts of a beggar.
      KING Where is Polonius?
      HAMLET In heaven, send thither to see. If your
35   messenger find him not there, seek him i'th'other
          place yourself. But indeed, if you find him not this
          month, you shall nose him as you go up the stairs
          into the lobby.
      KING Go seek him there.   *To Rosencrantz or Attendants*
40   **HAMLET** He will stay till ye come.
                        [*Exit Rosencrantz or Attendants*]
      KING Hamlet, this deed of thine, for thine especial safety —
          Which we do tender, as we dearly grieve
          For that which thou hast done — must send thee
              hence

---

10 appliance remedy   **15 Without** outside   **22 convocation**...**diet** a punning allusion to the Diet (i.e. assembly) of the German city of Worms   **convocation** political assembly   **e'en** even now   **25 variable service** different dishes in the same meal   **28 eat** eaten   **32 progress** official journey of state undertaken by the monarch   **42 tender** hold dear

With fiery quickness: therefore prepare thyself.
45   The bark is ready and the wind at help,
Th'associates tend and everything at bent
For England.

HAMLET For England?

KING Ay, Hamlet.

50   **HAMLET** Good.

KING So is it, if thou knew'st our purposes.

HAMLET I see a cherub that sees them. But come, for
England! Farewell, dear mother.

KING Thy loving father, Hamlet.

55   **HAMLET** My mother. Father and mother is man and wife:
man and wife is one flesh, and so, my mother. Come,
for England!   *Exit*

KING Follow him at foot, tempt him with speed aboard:
Delay it not, I'll have him hence tonight.
60   Away! For everything is sealed and done
That else leans on th'affair: pray you make haste.
        [Exit Guildenstern and perhaps Rosencrantz]
And, England, if my love thou hold'st at aught —
As my great power thereof may give thee sense,
Since yet thy cicatrice looks raw and red
65   After the Danish sword, and thy free awe
Pays homage to us — thou mayst not coldly set
Our sovereign process, which imports at full,
By letters conjuring to that effect,
The present death of Hamlet. Do it, England,
70   For like the hectic in my blood he rages,
And thou must cure me. Till I know 'tis done,
Howe'er my haps, my joys were ne'er begun.   *Exit*

[Act 4 Scene 3]   *running scene 12*

Enter Fortinbras with an army

FORTINBRAS Go, captain, from me greet the Danish king:
Tell him that by his licence Fortinbras

---

45 **bark** ship 46 **tend** await **at bent** ready 52 **cherub** angel possessed of insight and knowledge 58 **at foot** closely 61 **leans on** appertains to 62 **aught** any worth 63 **thereof . . . sense** may give you an awareness of the value of my love 64 **cicatrice** scar 65 **free awe** voluntary submission, uncompelled deference 66 **coldly set** disregard/regard coolly 67 **process** command **imports at full** is fully concerned with/conveys detailed instructions for 68 **conjuring** solemnly charging/conspiring 69 **present** immediate 70 **hectic** fever 72 **Howe'er my haps** whatever my fortunes **4.3** *Location: the Danish border* (see 'Second Quarto Passages that do not appear in the Folio', lines 81–139 (pp. 147–8), for a longer version of this scene, in which Hamlet witnesses the army's march and speaks his soliloquy 'How all occasions do inform against me / And spur my dull revenge') 2 **licence** permission

Claims the conveyance of a promised march
Over his kingdom. You know the rendezvous.
5   If that his majesty would aught with us,
We shall express our duty in his eye,
And let him know so.
CAPTAIN I will do't, my lord.
FORTINBRAS Go softly on.   *Exeunt*

[Act 4 Scene 4]   *running scene 13*

Enter Queen and Horatio

GERTRUDE I will not speak with her.
HORATIO She is importunate, indeed distract:
Her mood will needs be pitied.
GERTRUDE What would she have?
5   **HORATIO** She speaks much of her father; says she hears
There's tricks i'th'world, and hems, and beats her
heart,
Spurns enviously at straws, speaks things in doubt
That carry but half sense: her speech is nothing,
Yet the unshapèd use of it doth move
10 The hearers to collection; they aim at it,
And botch the words up fit to their own thoughts,
Which, as her winks and nods and gestures yield
them,
Indeed would make one think there might be
thought,
Though nothing sure, yet much unhappily.
15 **GERTRUDE** 'Twere good she were spoken with, for she
may strew
Dangerous conjectures in ill-breeding minds.
Let her come in.   *Horatio goes to the door or may exit*
To my sick soul — as sin's true nature is —   *Aside*
Each toy seems prologue to some great amiss:
20 So full of artless jealousy is guilt,
It spills itself in fearing to be spilt.

3 **conveyance of** granting of/Danish escort for   6 **duty** respect   **eye** presence   9 **softly** slowly,
carefully   **4.4** *Location: within the royal castle at Elsinore*   2 **importunate** insistent, pressing
distract agitated/deranged   6 **hems** makes 'hmm' noises   7 **Spurns . . . straws** strikes out spitefully at
trifles   **in doubt** of unclear meaning   9 **use** manner/utterance   10 **collection** a gathering of meaning
aim guess   11 **botch** patch, stitch clumsily together   12 **Which** which words   **yield** convey, deliver
13 **thought** intended   14 **unhappily** ominously near the truth/maliciously   16 **ill-breeding** mischief-
making   19 **toy** trifle   **amiss** wrong, calamity   20 **artless jealousy** unskilled suspicion   21 **It . . . spilt** its
excessive fear of being revealed ends up betraying it ('to spill' means both to destroy and to reveal)

Enter Ophelia, distracted   *With Horatio?*

OPHELIA Where is the beauteous majesty of Denmark?

GERTRUDE How now, Ophelia!

OPHELIA How should I your true love know   *Sings*

25   From another one?

            By his cockle hat and staff,

            And his sandal shoon.

GERTRUDE Alas, sweet lady, what imports this song?

OPHELIA Say you? Nay, pray you, mark.

30   He is dead and gone, lady,   *Sings*

            He is dead and gone.

            At his head a grass-green turf,

            At his heels a stone.

Enter King

GERTRUDE Nay, but, Ophelia—

35 **OPHELIA** Pray you, mark.

            White his shroud as the mountain snow—   *Sings*

GERTRUDE Alas, look here, my lord.

OPHELIA Larded with sweet flowers   *Sings*

            Which bewept to the grave did not go

40   With true-love showers.

KING How do ye, pretty lady?

OPHELIA Well, God yield you! They say the owl was a

            baker's daughter. Lord, we know what we are, but

            know not what we may be. God be at your table!

45 **KING** Conceit upon her father.

OPHELIA Pray you let's have no words of this, but when

            they ask you what it means, say you this:

            'Tomorrow is Saint Valentine's day,   *Sings*

            All in the morning betime,

50   And I a maid at your window,

            To be your Valentine.'

            Then up he rose, and donned his clothes,

            And dupped the chamber door:

            Let in the maid, that out a maid

55   Never departed more.

---

26 cockle hat hat with a cockleshell on it, showing that the wearer had visited the Spanish shrine of Santiago (Saint James) of Compostela; a **staff** and sandals were also typical of such a pilgrim   **27 shoon** shoes   **38 Larded** strewn, covered   **40 showers** i.e. of tears   **42 yield** reward; a common way to express thanks   **owl...daughter** refers to the tale of a baker's daughter who was turned into an owl after she had been ungenerous to Jesus when he begged for bread   **45 Conceit upon** fanciful thinking about/brooding on   **49 betime** early   **51 Valentine** sweetheart, supposedly the first person of the opposite sex one saw on Valentine's Day   **52 rose** the sexual innuendo of Ophelia's language suggests possible erectile connotations   **53 dupped** opened (perhaps punning on 'tupped', i.e. 'had sex with')   **chamber door** playing on vaginal connotations   **54 maid** virgin

KING Pretty Ophelia.

OPHELIA Indeed, la, without an oath, I'll make an end
      on't:

      By Gis and by Saint Charity,   *Sings*
      Alack, and fie for shame!
60   Young men will do't, if they come to't,
      By cock, they are to blame.
      Quoth she, 'Before you tumbled me,
      You promised me to wed.'
      'So would I ha' done, by yonder sun,
65   An thou hadst not come to my bed.'

KING How long hath she been thus?

OPHELIA I hope all will be well. We must be patient, but I
      cannot choose but weep to think they should lay him
      i'th'cold ground. My brother shall know of it: and so I
70   thank you for your good counsel. Come, my coach!
      Goodnight,   ladies,   goodnight,   sweet   ladies,
      goodnight, goodnight.   *Exit*

KING Follow her close: give her good watch, I pray you.   *To Horatio*
                                  [Exit Horatio]

      O, this is the poison of deep grief: it springs
75   All from her father's death. O Gertrude, Gertrude,
      When sorrows come, they come not single spies
      But in battalions. First, her father slain:
      Next, your son gone, and he most violent author
      Of his own just remove: the people muddied,
80   Thick and unwholesome in their thoughts and
         whispers
      For good Polonius' death, and we have done but
         greenly
      In hugger-mugger to inter him: poor Ophelia
      Divided from herself and her fair judgement,
      Without the which we are pictures or mere beasts:
85   Last, and as much containing as all these,
      Her brother is in secret come from France,
      Feeds on his wonder, keeps himself in clouds,
      And wants not buzzers to infect his ear
      With pestilent speeches of his father's death,

---

58 Gis Jesus   **60 do't** have sex   **61 cock** euphemism for God, plays on sense of 'penis'   **62 tumbled** had sex with   **65 An** if   **76 spies** scouts sent ahead of the main army   **79 remove** removal   **muddied** stirred up   **81 greenly** foolishly   **82 hugger-mugger** secrecy   **85 as much containing** of as much significance   **87 wonder** bewilderment/doubt (about his father's death)   **in clouds** in a state of confusion (or suspicion)/ aloof and inscrutable   **88 wants** lacks   **buzzers** gossips, rumour-mongers

90   Wherein necessity, of matter beggared,
        Will nothing stick our persons to arraign
        In ear and ear. O, my dear Gertrude, this,
        Like to a murdering-piece, in many places
        Gives me superfluous death.

A noise within

Enter a Messenger

95 **GERTRUDE** Alack, what noise is this?

    KING Where are my Switzers? Let them guard the
            door.—
        What is the matter?

    MESSENGER Save yourself, my lord.
        The ocean, overpeering of his list,
100   Eats not the flats with more impiteous haste
        Than young Laertes, in a riotous head,
        O'erbears your officers. The rabble call him lord,
        And, as the world were now but to begin,
        Antiquity forgot, custom not known,
105   The ratifiers and props of every word,
        They cry 'Choose we! Laertes shall be king.'
        Caps, hands and tongues, applaud it to the clouds:
        'Laertes shall be king, Laertes king!'

    GERTRUDE How cheerfully on the false trail they cry!
110   O, this is counter, you false Danish dogs!

Noise within

Enter Laertes   *His followers remain at the door*

    KING The doors are broke.

    LAERTES Where is the king?— Sirs, stand you all
            without.

    ALL FOLLOWERS No, let's come in.   *At the door*

    LAERTES I pray you give me leave.

115 **ALL** We will, we will.

    LAERTES I thank you: keep the door.— O thou vile king,
        Give me my father!

    GERTRUDE Calmly, good Laertes.   *Restrains him or blocks his way*

    LAERTES That drop of blood that's calm proclaims me
            bastard,

---

90 **of matter beggared** deprived of facts and solid evidence   91 **nothing . . . ear** not hesitate to accuse me to one listener after another   93 **murdering-piece** small cannon which scattered its shot and so could kill more people   94 **Gives . . . death** kills me over and over   96 **Switzers** Swiss guards (mercenaries commonly employed in royal households)   99 **overpeering . . . list** rising over its boundary   100 **flats** flat or low-lying land near the shore   101 **head** insurrection   103 **as** as if   104 **Antiquity** ancient tradition   105 **The . . . word** (antiquity and custom are) the things that confirm and support every utterance
107 **Caps** thrown into the air in support   110 **counter** following the scent in the wrong direction (hunting term)   **false** disloyal/erring   112 **without** outside   116 **keep** guard

120 Cries cuckold to my father, brands the harlot
Even here, between the chaste unsmirchèd brow
Of my true mother.

KING What is the cause, Laertes,
That thy rebellion looks so giant-like?—

125 Let him go, Gertrude: do not fear our person:
There's such divinity doth hedge a king
That treason can but peep to what it would,
Acts little of his will.— Tell me, Laertes,
Why thou art thus incensed.— Let him go,
Gertrude.—

130 Speak, man.

LAERTES Where's my father?

KING Dead.

GERTRUDE But not by him.

KING Let him demand his fill.

135 LAERTES How came he dead? I'll not be juggled with:
To hell, allegiance! Vows, to the blackest devil!
Conscience and grace, to the profoundest pit!
I dare damnation. To this point I stand,
That both the worlds I give to negligence,

140 Let come what comes, only I'll be revenged
Most throughly for my father.

KING Who shall stay you?

LAERTES My will, not all the world:
And for my means, I'll husband them so well,

145 They shall go far with little.

KING Good Laertes,
If you desire to know the certainty
Of your dear father's death, is't writ in your revenge,
That, sweepstake, you will draw both friend and foe,

150 Winner and loser?

LAERTES None but his enemies.

KING Will you know them then?

LAERTES To his good friends thus wide I'll ope my arms,
And like the kind life-rend'ring pelican,

155 Repast them with my blood.

---

120 **cuckold** man with an unfaithful wife   121 **between** in the middle of   **unsmirchèd** unstained
122 **true** faithful   125 **fear** fear for   126 **hedge** protect   127 **but...will** only peep through at what it
desires, and carry out little of its intention   135 **juggled with** tricked, deceived   138 **To...stand** I am
fixed in this resolve   139 **both...negligence** I disregard both this world and the next   141 **throughly**
thoroughly, completely   142 **stay** prevent   143 **My...world** by my will, not all the world shall stop
me   144 **husband** manage   149 **sweepstake** indiscriminately (from gambling, where one person sweeps
up all the stakes on the table)   **draw** gather   154 **pelican** supposedly this bird fed its young with its own
blood   155 **Repast** feed

KING Why, now you speak
　　　　Like a good child and a true gentleman.
　　　　That I am guiltless of your father's death,
　　　　And am most sensible in grief for it,
160　　It shall as level to your judgement pierce
　　　　As day does to your eye.
A noise within
ALL FOLLOWERS Let her come in!
Enter Ophelia
LAERTES How now? What noise is that?
　　　　O, heat dry up my brains, tears seven times salt　　　*Sees Ophelia*
165　　Burn out the sense and virtue of mine eye!
　　　　By heaven, thy madness shall be paid by weight,
　　　　Till our scale turns the beam. O rose of May,
　　　　Dear maid, kind sister, sweet Ophelia!
　　　　O heavens, is't possible a young maid's wits
170　　Should be as mortal as an old man's life?
　　　　Nature is fine in love, and where 'tis fine,
　　　　It sends some precious instance of itself
　　　　After the thing it loves.
OPHELIA They bore him barefaced on the bier,　　　　　*Sings*
175　　　Hey non nonny, nonny, hey nonny,
　　　　　And on his grave rains many a tear—
　　　　Fare you well, my dove.
LAERTES Hadst thou thy wits and didst persuade
　　　　　revenge,
　　　　It could not move thus.
180　OPHELIA You must sing 'a-down a-down', and you call
　　　　him 'a-down-a'. O, how the wheel becomes it! It is
　　　　the false steward that stole his master's daughter.
LAERTES This nothing's more than matter.
OPHELIA There's rosemary, that's for remembrance:
185　　pray, love, remember: and there is pansies, that's
　　　　for thoughts.　　　　　　　*Gives real or imaginary flowers*

---

159 **sensible** feeling   160 **level** directly   165 **virtue** power, efficacy   167 **turns the beam** tilts the
crossbar of the scales (i.e. tips in our favour)   171 **Nature** human nature   **fine in** refined by   172 **instance**
sign, token   173 **After ... loves** i.e. after Polonius, to the grave   174 **bier** movable stand on which a corpse
is carried to the grave   175 **Hey ... nonny** a refrain more usually associated with merry love songs
179 **move** affect (me)/**persuade**   180 **You** Ophelia assigns parts to the individuals in the room
'a-down ... well-known refrains   181 **wheel** refrain   182 **false ... daughter** refers to a story or ballad
that remains unidentified   183 **This ... matter** this nonsense is actually more meaningful than sane talk/
this nonsense contains significance that is beyond the reach of sense   184 **rosemary** herb symbolizing
remembrance   185 **pansies** flowers symbolic of love, named from French *pensées* (**thoughts**)

LAERTES A document in madness, thoughts and
remembrance fitted.
OPHELIA There's fennel for you, and columbines: there's
190   rue for you, and here's some for me: we may call it
herb-grace o'Sundays: O, you must wear your rue
with a difference. There's a daisy: I would give you
some violets, but they withered all when my father
died: they say he made a good end—
195   For bonny sweet Robin is all my joy.   *Sings*
LAERTES Thought and affliction, passion, hell itself,
She turns to favour and to prettiness.
OPHELIA And will he not come again?   *Sings*
And will he not come again?
200   No, no, he is dead:
Go to thy death-bed,
He never will come again.
His beard as white as snow,
All flaxen was his poll:
205   He is gone, he is gone,
And we cast away moan.
Gramercy on his soul!
And of all Christian souls, I pray God. God buy ye.
                    Exeunt Ophelia [and Gertrude?]
LAERTES Do you see this, you gods?
210   KING Laertes, I must commune with your grief,
Or you deny me right. Go but apart,
Make choice of whom your wisest friends you will,
And they shall hear and judge 'twixt you and me:
If by direct or by collateral hand
215   They find us touched, we will our kingdom give,
Our crown, our life, and all that we call ours
To you in satisfaction. But if not,
Be you content to lend your patience to us,
And we shall jointly labour with your soul
220   To give it due content.

---

187 **document** lesson   188 **fitted** put together   189 **fennel** herb said to symbolize flattery   **columbines**
flowers symbolic of infidelity   190 **rue** herb symbolizing repentance   191 **o'Sundays** on Sundays
192 **difference** variation on a coat of arms to distinguish different members or branches of a family (or
Ophelia may simply mean 'differently')   **daisy** possibly symbolic of deception; alternatively, a springtime
flower associated with love   193 **violets** flowers symbolic of faithfulness and of chastity   195 **For . . . joy** a
line from a well-known song   196 **Thought** melancholy   **passion** extreme grief   197 **favour** charm,
attractiveness   204 **flaxen** white   **poll** head, i.e. hair   206 **cast away moan** waste our laments
207 **Gramercy** great mercy   208 **God buy ye** goodbye (literally, 'God be with you')   212 **whom**
whichever of   213 **'twixt** between   214 **collateral** indirect   215 **touched** implicated

LAERTES Let this be so:
  His means of death, his obscure burial —
  No trophy, sword, nor hatchment o'er his bones,
  No noble rite nor formal ostentation —
225 Cry to be heard, as 'twere from heaven to earth,
  That I must call in question.
KING So you shall,
  And where th'offence is, let the great axe fall.
  I pray you go with me.   *Exeunt*

[Act 4 Scene 5]   *running scene 14*

Enter Horatio with an Attendant

HORATIO What are they that would speak with me?
SERVANT Sailors, sir: they say they have letters for you.
HORATIO Let them come in.   [*Exit Servant*]
  I do not know from what part of the world
5 I should be greeted, if not from Lord Hamlet.
Enter Sailor
SAILOR God bless you, sir.
HORATIO Let him bless thee too.
SAILOR He shall, sir, an't please him. There's a letter for   *Gives a letter*
  you, sir: it comes from th'ambassador that was
10 bound for England, if your name be Horatio, as I am
  let to know it is.
HORATIO *Reads the letter* 'Horatio, when thou shalt
  have overlooked this, give these fellows some means
  to the king: they have letters for him. Ere we were
15 two days old at sea, a pirate of very warlike
  appointment gave us chase. Finding ourselves too
  slow of sail, we put on a compelled valour, in the
  grapple I boarded them: on the instant they got clear
  of our ship, so I alone became their prisoner. They
20 have dealt with me like thieves of mercy, but they
  knew what they did: I am to do a good turn for them.
  Let the king have the letters I have sent, and repair
  thou to me with as much haste as thou wouldst fly
  death. I have words to speak in your ear will make

223 **trophy** memorial **hatchment** tablet bearing the coat of arms of the dead person, placed over the tomb 224 **ostentation** ceremony 226 **That** so that **call in question** demand an explanation
4.5 8 **an't** if it 13 **overlooked** looked over, read **means** means of access 16 **appointment** equipment 17 **compelled** necessary **grapple** forcible seizing of a ship for the purpose of boarding 20 **thieves of mercy** merciful thieves 22 **repair** come

25 thee dumb, yet are they much too light for the bore of
the matter. These good fellows will bring thee where
I am. Rosencrantz and Guildenstern hold their course
for England: of them I have much to tell thee.
Farewell. He that thou knowest thine, Hamlet.'—
30 Come, I will give you way for these your letters,
And do't the speedier that you may direct me
To him from whom you brought them.   *Exeunt*

[Act 4 Scene 6]   *running scene 15*

Enter King and Laertes

KING Now must your conscience my acquittance seal,
And you must put me in your heart for friend,
Sith you have heard, and with a knowing ear,
That he which hath your noble father slain
5 Pursued my life.
LAERTES It well appears. But tell me
Why you proceeded not against these feats
So crimeful and so capital in nature,
As by your safety, wisdom, all things else,
10 You mainly were stirred up.
KING O, for two special reasons,
Which may to you, perhaps, seem much unsinewed,
And yet to me they are strong. The queen his mother
Lives almost by his looks, and for myself —
15 My virtue or my plague, be it either which —
She's so conjunctive to my life and soul,
That, as the star moves not but in his sphere,
I could not but by her. The other motive,
Why to a public count I might not go,
20 Is the great love the general gender bear him,
Who, dipping all his faults in their affection,
Would like the spring that turneth wood to stone,
Convert his gyves to graces, so that my arrows,

25 **too ... matter** i.e. inadequate to convey the importance of the issue   **bore** calibre of a gun (Hamlet's words are bullets that are too small to fit)   **30 way** access   **4.6 1 my acquittance seal** confirm my innocence   **3 Sith** since   **knowing** understanding/knowledgeable   **7 proceeded not** did not take legal proceedings   **feats** deeds/crimes   **8 capital** punishable by death   **9 As ... up** i.e. given that it was greatly in the interests of safety and prudence to do so   **12 unsinewed** weak   **16 conjunctive** closely united (an astronomical term referring to proximity between planets)   **17 sphere** orbit; individual stars and planets were thought to be contained within concentric hollow spheres that revolved around the earth   **18 but** except, unless I were   **19 count** account, reckoning, indictment   **20 general gender** common people **gender** kind, sort   **22 spring ... stone** a spring with high levels of lime in its water would petrify a piece of wood placed in it   **23 gyves** fetters

        Too slightly timbered for so loud a wind,
25   Would have reverted to my bow again
        And not where I had aimed them.
        LAERTES And so have I a noble father lost,
        A sister driven into desperate terms,
        Who has — if praises may go back again —
30   Stood challenger on mount of all the age
        For her perfections: but my revenge will come.
        KING Break not your sleeps for that: you must not think
        That we are made of stuff so flat and dull
        That we can let our beard be shook with danger
35   And think it pastime. You shortly shall hear more:
        I loved your father, and we love ourself,
        And that, I hope, will teach you to imagine—
        Enter a Messenger
        How now? What news?
        MESSENGER Letters, my lord, from Hamlet:
40   This to your majesty, this to the queen.   *Gives letters*
        KING From Hamlet? Who brought them?
        MESSENGER Sailors, my lord, they say: I saw them not.
        They were given me by Claudio: he received them.
        KING Laertes, you shall hear them.— Leave us.
                              Exit Messenger
45   'High and mighty, you shall know I am set naked on
        your kingdom. Tomorrow shall I beg leave to see your
        kingly eyes, when I shall, first asking your pardon
        thereunto, recount th'occasions of my sudden and
        more strange return. Hamlet.'
50   What should this mean? Are all the rest come back?
        Or is it some abuse? Or no such thing?
        LAERTES Know you the hand?
        KING 'Tis Hamlet's character. 'Naked' —
        And in a postscript here, he says 'alone'.
55   Can you advise me?
        LAERTES I'm lost in it, my lord. But let him come:
        It warms the very sickness in my heart
        That I shall live and tell him to his teeth,
        'Thus diest thou.'

---

24 Too slightly timbered i.e. too light   **28 terms** circumstances   **29 go back again** i.e. recall her as she was   **30 on mount** on high   **34 shook with** tugged (contemptuously) by   **43 Claudio** a bluff, an intermediary, or Shakespeare's slip when he meant 'Horatio'   **45 naked** destitute   **47 pardon** permission   **51 abuse** deceit   **no such thing** not what it seems, a trick   **53 character** handwriting

60   **KING** If it be so, Laertes —
     As how should it be so? How otherwise? —
     Will you be ruled by me?
  LAERTES If so you'll not o'errule me to a peace.
  KING To thine own peace. If he be now returned,
65   As checking at his voyage, and that he means
     No more to undertake it, I will work him
     To an exploit, now ripe in my device,
     Under the which he shall not choose but fall;
     And for his death no wind of blame shall breathe,
70   But even his mother shall uncharge the practice
     And call it accident. Some two months since,
     Here was a gentleman of Normandy.
     I've seen myself, and served against, the French,
     And they can well on horseback; but this gallant
75   Had witchcraft in't; he grew into his seat,
     And to such wondrous doing brought his horse
     As had he been incorpsed and demi-natured
     With the brave beast: so far he passed my thought,
     That I in forgery of shapes and tricks
80   Come short of what he did.
  LAERTES A Norman was't?
  KING A Norman.
  LAERTES Upon my life, Lamond.
  KING The very same.
85   **LAERTES** I know him well: he is the brooch indeed
     And gem of all our nation.
  KING He made confession of you,
     And gave you such a masterly report
     For art and exercise in your defence,
90   And for your rapier most especially,
     That he cried out, 'twould be a sight indeed
     If one could match you. Sir, this report of his
     Did Hamlet so envenom with his envy
     That he could nothing do but wish and beg
95   Your sudden coming o'er, to play with him.
     Now, out of this—

---

63 If so so long as   **65 As checking at** as a result of deviating from or aborting (a falconry term referring to the hawk turning away from its pursuit in mid-flight)   **67 device** devising   **70 uncharge the practice** acquit the plot from blame   **74 can well** are skilled   **gallant** fine young man   **77 As** as if   **incorpsed** of one body   **demi-natured** half of the same nature   **78 brave** splendid   **passed my thought** surpassed anything I could have imagined   **79 forgery ... tricks** imagining feats of horsemanship   **83 Lamond** some editors prefer Quarto's *Lamord*, with its hint of death (*la mort*, French for 'death')   **85 brooch** jewel/ornament   **87 made ... you** testified to your skill   **89 For ... defence** with regard to your skill and performance in self-defence   **93 envenom** embitter/poison   **95 sudden** immediate   **play** compete

LAERTES What out of this, my lord?

KING Laertes, was your father dear to you?
Or are you like the painting of a sorrow,
100   A face without a heart?

LAERTES Why ask you this?

KING Not that I think you did not love your father,
But that I know love is begun by time,
And that I see, in passages of proof,
105 Time qualifies the spark and fire of it.
Hamlet comes back: what would you undertake
To show yourself your father's son in deed
More than in words?

LAERTES To cut his throat i'th'church.

110 KING No place, indeed, should murder sanctuarize;
Revenge should have no bounds. But, good Laertes,
Will you do this, keep close within your chamber.
Hamlet returned shall know you are come home:
We'll put on those shall praise your excellence
115 And set a double varnish on the fame
The Frenchman gave you, bring you in fine together
And wager on your heads: he, being remiss,
Most generous and free from all contriving,
Will not peruse the foils, so that with ease,
120 Or with a little shuffling, you may choose
A sword unbated, and in a pass of practice
Requite him for your father.

LAERTES I will do't,
And for that purpose I'll anoint my sword.
125 I bought an unction of a mountebank
So mortal I but dipped a knife in it,
Where it draws blood no cataplasm so rare,
Collected from all simples that have virtue
Under the moon, can save the thing from death
130 That is but scratched withal: I'll touch my point

103 **begun by time** generated by particular circumstances   104 **passages of proof** events that have proved it   105 **qualifies** weakens, diminishes   110 **sanctuarize** give sanctuary to, protect   112 **Will you** if you are to   **close** secluded   114 **put on** encourage/organize   116 **in fine** in conclusion, finally   117 **remiss** negligent, not vigilant   118 **generous** noble-minded   119 **peruse** examine carefully   **foils** light swords, blunted for use in fencing   121 **unbated** not blunted   **pass of practice** treacherous thrust/ deliberately planned thrust   122 **Requite** repay, have revenge on   125 **unction** ointment   **mountebank** quack doctor who travelled around selling various remedies   126 **I…it** Laertes leaves unfinished the account of what happened when he did this; or perhaps he means 'one need but dip a knife in it'; some editors prefer Quarto's 'so mortal that, but dip'   127 **cataplasm** medicated plaster, poultice   **rare** excellent   128 **simples** medicinal herbs   129 **Under the moon** i.e. anywhere, though gathering herbs by moonlight was thought to lend them extra potency   130 **withal** with it

With this contagion, that if I gall him slightly,
It may be death.

KING Let's further think of this,
Weigh what convenience both of time and means
135 May fit us to our shape: if this should fail,
And that our drift look through our bad performance,
'Twere better not assayed: therefore this project
Should have a back or second, that might hold,
If this should blast in proof. Soft, let me see:
140 We'll make a solemn wager on your cunnings.
I ha't:
When in your motion you are hot and dry —
As make your bouts more violent to the end —
And that he calls for drink, I'll have prepared him
145 A chalice for the nonce, whereon but sipping,
If he by chance escape your venomed stuck,
Our purpose may hold there.—

Enter Queen

How now, sweet queen?

GERTRUDE One woe doth tread upon another's heel,
So fast they'll follow: your sister's drowned, Laertes.

150 LAERTES Drowned? O, where?

GERTRUDE There is a willow grows aslant a brook,
That shows his hoar leaves in the glassy stream:
There with fantastic garlands did she come
Of crow-flowers, nettles, daisies and long purples
155 That liberal shepherds give a grosser name,
But our cold maids do dead men's fingers call them:
There on the pendent boughs her coronet weeds
Clamb'ring to hang, an envious sliver broke,
When down the weedy trophies and herself
160 Fell in the weeping brook. Her clothes spread wide,
And mermaid-like awhile they bore her up,
Which time she chanted snatches of old tunes,
As one incapable of her own distress,

---

131 contagion poison   **gall** graze   **135 fit ... shape** suit our plan/fit us for the roles we are going to play   **136 drift** scheme, intention   **look** becomes visible   **139 blast in proof** explode when put to the test   **140 cunnings** skills (i.e. Laertes' and Hamlet's)   **141 ha't** have it   **143 As** i.e. you should   **bouts** rounds in a fight   **145 nonce** purpose   **146 stuck** thrust   **151 willow** a tree associated with sadness and forsaken love   **152 hoar** greyish-white   **153 fantastic** elaborate/fanciful   **154 crow-flowers** buttercups/ragged robins (both types of wild flower)   **long purples** a type of purple orchid; the roots resemble testicles, hence the **grosser name**   **155 liberal** freely spoken/licentious   **grosser** coarser/more vulgar   **156 cold** chaste   **157 pendent** drooping, overhanging   **158 envious sliver** malicious part of a branch   **159 weedy** made of wild flowers   **163 incapable** uncomprehending/insensible   **distress** affliction, calamity

Or like a creature native and indued
165 Unto that element: but long it could not be
Till that her garments, heavy with their drink,
Pulled the poor wretch from her melodious lay
To muddy death.

LAERTES Alas, then, is she drowned?
170 **GERTRUDE** Drowned, drowned.
LAERTES Too much of water hast thou, poor Ophelia,
And therefore I forbid my tears. But yet
It is our trick: nature her custom holds,
Let shame say what it will: when these are gone,   *Weeps*
175 The woman will be out.— Adieu, my lord:
I have a speech of fire that fain would blaze,
But that this folly douts it.   *Exit*
KING Let's follow, Gertrude:
How much I had to do to calm his rage!
180 Now fear I this will give it start again;
Therefore let's follow.   *Exeunt*

[Act 5 Scene 1]   *running scene 16*

Enter two Clowns   *With a spade and a pickaxe*

FIRST CLOWN Is she to be buried in Christian burial that
wilfully seeks her own salvation?
SECOND CLOWN I tell thee she is: and therefore make her
grave straight: the crowner hath sat on her, and finds
5 it Christian burial.
FIRST CLOWN How can that be, unless she drowned
herself in her own defence?
SECOND CLOWN Why, 'tis found so.
FIRST CLOWN It must be *se offendendo,* it cannot be else.
10 For here lies the point: if I drown myself wittingly, it
argues an act, and an act hath three branches: it is to
act, to do and to perform: argal, she drowned herself
wittingly.
SECOND CLOWN Nay, but hear you, goodman delver—

164 **indued** adapted   167 **lay** song   173 **trick** way, habit   174 **these** i.e. his tears   175 **woman...out**
the woman in me will be finished   177 **folly** i.e. his weeping   **douts** extinguishes   5.1 *Location: a
graveyard near the royal castle at Elsinore*   *Clowns* rustics   1 **Christian burial** suicides were not allowed
Christian burial rites   2 **salvation** probably a malapropism for 'damnation', though perhaps the Clown
suggests Ophelia was trying to get to heaven early   4 **straight** straight away (plays on the sense of 'not
crooked')   **crowner** coroner   **sat** held an inquest (with a play on the literal sense)   9 *se offendendo*
perversion of *se defendendo* (Latin for 'in self-defence', a legal term); literally 'in self-offence'   12 **argal**
perversion of *ergo* (Latin for 'therefore')   14 **goodman** title for a person below the rank of gentleman and
often followed by the individual's occupation (here a **delver** or digger)

15 **FIRST CLOWN** Give me leave: here lies the water; good: here stands the man; good: if the man go to this water, and drown himself, it is, will he, nill he, he goes — mark you that. But if the water come to him and drown him, he drowns not himself: argal, he that
20 is not guilty of his own death shortens not his own life.

SECOND CLOWN But is this law?

FIRST CLOWN Ay, marry, is't: crowner's quest law.

SECOND CLOWN Will you ha' the truth on't? If this had
25 not been a gentlewoman, she should have been buried out of Christian burial.

FIRST CLOWN Why, there thou say'st: and the more pity that great folk should have countenance in this world to drown or hang themselves, more than their
30 even Christian. Come, my spade. There is no ancient gentlemen but gardeners, ditchers and grave-makers: they hold up Adam's profession.

SECOND CLOWN Was he a gentleman?

FIRST CLOWN He was the first that ever bore arms.

35 **SECOND CLOWN** Why, he had none.

FIRST CLOWN What, art a heathen? How dost thou understand the Scripture? The Scripture says 'Adam digged'. Could he dig without arms? I'll put another question to thee: if thou answerest me not to the
40 purpose, confess thyself—

SECOND CLOWN Go to.

FIRST CLOWN What is he that builds stronger than either the mason, the shipwright, or the carpenter?

SECOND CLOWN The gallows-maker, for that frame
45 outlives a thousand tenants.

FIRST CLOWN I like thy wit well, in good faith: the gallows does well; but how does it well? It does well to those that do ill: now thou dost ill to say the gallows is built stronger than the church: argal, the
50 gallows may do well to thee. To't again, come.

SECOND CLOWN Who builds stronger than a mason, a shipwright, or a carpenter?

17 **will . . . he** whether he will or no   23 **quest** inquest   27 **there thou say'st** i.e. how right you are
28 **countenance** authority, permission   30 **even Christian** fellow Christians   31 **ditchers** ditch-makers
32 **Adam's profession** in the Bible, Adam's job was to look after the Garden of Eden   34 **bore arms** had a coat of arms (the sign of a gentleman): with obvious play on sense of 'limbs'   40 **confess thyself** the saying continues 'and be hanged'   47 **does well** i.e. as an answer (the sense then shifts to 'serves well')

FIRST CLOWN Ay, tell me that, and unyoke.

SECOND CLOWN Marry, now I can tell.

55 **FIRST CLOWN** To't.

SECOND CLOWN Mass, I cannot tell.

Enter Hamlet and Horatio afar off   *Hamlet cloaked?*

FIRST CLOWN Cudgel thy brains no more about it, for
your dull ass will not mend his pace with beating;
and when you are asked this question next, say 'A
60 grave-maker: the houses that he makes lasts till
doomsday.' Go, get thee to Yaughan: fetch me a
stoup of liquor.   [*Exit Second Clown*]
    In youth, when I did love, did love,   *Sings*
    Methought it was very sweet,
65   To contract-O-the time, for-a-my behove,
    O, methought there was nothing meet.

HAMLET Has this fellow no feeling of his business that he
sings at grave-making?

HORATIO Custom hath made it in him a property of
70 easiness.

HAMLET 'Tis e'en so: the hand of little employment hath
the daintier sense.

FIRST CLOWN But age with his stealing steps   *Sings*
    Hath caught me in his clutch,
75   And hath shipped me intil the land,
    As if I had never been such.   *Throws up a skull*

HAMLET That skull had a tongue in it and could sing
once: how the knave jowls it to th'ground, as if it
were Cain's jaw-bone, that did the first murder. It
80 might be the pate of a politician, which this ass o'er-
offices, one that could circumvent God, might it not?

HORATIO It might, my lord.

HAMLET Or of a courtier, which could say 'Good morrow,
sweet lord! How dost thou, good lord?' This might be
85 my lord Such-a-one, that praised my lord Such-a-
one's horse when he meant to beg it, might it not?

---

53 **unyoke** give up, stop labouring (literally, unyoke the oxen)   58 **mend** improve   61 **Yaughan** variant
spelling of Vaughan, presumably the name of the local innkeeper, perhaps based on one near the Globe
62 **stoup** tankard   63 **In . . . love** this and the following stanza are loose versions of parts of Thomas Vaux's
poem 'The Aged Lover Renounceth Love', printed in 1557; **O** and **a** may be the gravedigger's grunts as he
goes about his work   65 **contract . . . behove** pass away the time to my own advantage   66 **meet** (more)
fitting   69 **property of easiness** something he can undertake with indifference   71 **hath . . . sense** is
more sensitive/fastidious   75 **shipped . . . land** dispatched me into the earth (i.e. my grave/dust)   **intil**
into   76 **been such** been a young man in love   78 **jowls** strikes, dashes (puns on 'jowl' – i.e. jawbone)
79 **Cain** in the Bible, the first murderer; he killed his brother Abel   80 **politician** crafty schemer   **o'er-
offices** lords it over (on account of his office as gravedigger)   81 **circumvent** cheat, outwit

HORATIO Ay, my lord.

HAMLET Why, e'en so, and now my lady Worm's,
chapless, and knocked about the mazzard with a
90   sexton's spade: here's fine revolution, if we had the
trick to see't. Did these bones cost no more the
breeding, but to play at loggats with 'em? Mine ache
to think on't.

FIRST CLOWN A pickaxe and a spade, a spade,   *Sings*
95   For and a shrouding sheet:
O, a pit of clay for to be made
For such a guest is meet.   *Throws up another skull*

HAMLET There's another: why may not that be the skull
of a lawyer? Where be his quiddities now, his quillets,
100   his cases, his tenures, and his tricks? Why does he
suffer this rude knave now to knock him about the
sconce with a dirty shovel, and will not tell him of his
action of battery? Hum. This fellow might be in's
time a great buyer of land, with his statutes, his
105   recognizances, his fines, his double vouchers, his
recoveries: is this the fine of his fines and the recovery
of his recoveries, to have his fine pate full of fine dirt?
Will his vouchers vouch him no more of his
purchases, and double ones too, than the length
110   and breadth of a pair of indentures? The very
conveyances of his lands will hardly lie in this box;
and must the inheritor himself have no more, ha?

HORATIO Not a jot more, my lord.

HAMLET Is not parchment made of sheepskins?

115   **HORATIO** Ay, my lord, and of calf-skins too.

---

89 chapless jaw-less   **mazzard** head (from the term for a drinking bowl)   **90 revolution** change/turn of
the wheel of fortune   **91 trick** knack   **Did . . . 'em?** Did these people cost so little to bring up that we may
play games with their bones?   **92 loggats** a game where pieces of wood shaped like bowling pins were
thrown at a stake fixed in the ground   **95 For and** and furthermore   **shrouding sheet** sheet in which the
corpse was wrapped   **99 quiddities . . . quillets** subtleties, verbal distinctions, quibbling arguments
100 tenures (documents or cases relating to) conditions on which property is held   **101 rude** ignorant/
rough   **102 sconce** head   **103 action of battery** litigation concerning physical assault   **104 statutes**
legal documents that secured a debt on land and property (similar to a mortgage)   **105 recognizances**
legal documents that formally acknowledged a debt   **fines . . . recoveries** legal processes concerned with
securing the outright ownership of land; **double vouchers** refers to the practice of having two people vouch
for a claimant's ownership of the land   **106 fine . . . fines** end of his fines (the sense of **fine** then shifts to
'elegant, handsome' and then to 'finely powdered')   **108 vouch** guarantee   **109 the . . . indentures** land
(i.e. his grave) only as long and wide as a legal document   **110 pair of indentures** two copies of an
agreement drawn up on the same sheet of paper, which was then halved along a zigzag line to form
documents that, when placed together, were a unique match   **111 conveyances** deeds relating to the
transfer of land and property (plays on the sense of 'light-fingered theft/sleight of hand')   **box** deed-box/
coffin   **112 inheritor** i.e. owner

HAMLET They are sheep and calves that seek out
assurance in that. I will speak to this fellow.—
Whose grave's this, sirrah?

FIRST CLOWN Mine, sir.

120   O, a pit of clay for to be made   *Sings*
For such a guest is meet.

HAMLET I think it be thine, indeed, for thou liest in't.

FIRST CLOWN You lie out on't, sir, and therefore it is not
yours. For my part, I do not lie in't, and yet it is mine.

125 **HAMLET** Thou dost lie in't, to be in't and say 'tis thine:
'tis for the dead, not for the quick: therefore thou liest.

FIRST CLOWN 'Tis a quick lie, sir: 'twill away again, from
me to you.

HAMLET What man dost thou dig it for?

130 **FIRST CLOWN** For no man, sir.

HAMLET What woman, then?

FIRST CLOWN For none, neither.

HAMLET Who is to be buried in't?

FIRST CLOWN One that was a woman, sir; but, rest her

135   soul, she's dead.

HAMLET How absolute the knave is! We must speak by
the card, or equivocation will undo us. By the Lord,
Horatio, these three years I have taken note of it: the
age is grown so picked that the toe of the peasant

140   comes so near the heels of our courtier, he galls his
kibe.— How long hast thou been a grave-maker?

FIRST CLOWN Of all the days i'th'year, I came to't that
day that our last king Hamlet o'ercame Fortinbras.

HAMLET How long is that since?

145 **FIRST CLOWN** Cannot you tell that? Every fool can tell
that: it was the very day that young Hamlet was
born — he that was mad and sent into England.

HAMLET Ay, marry, why was he sent into England?

FIRST CLOWN Why, because he was mad: he shall

150   recover his wits there, or if he do not, it's no great
matter there.

HAMLET Why?

---

117 **assurance in that** security in legal documents   118 **sirrah** sir (used to a social inferior)   **124 not lie**
the First Clown begins a series of puns on the senses of 'dwell/fib'   **126 quick** living (in his reply, the First
Clown plays on the senses of 'quick-witted/speedy')   **136 absolute** strictly accurate   **by the card** precisely
(literally, according to either the sailor's map or compass)   **137 equivocation** verbal ambiguity
139 picked over-refined/fastidious   **140 galls his kibe** chafes his chilblain

FIRST CLOWN 'Twill not be seen in him: there the men
are as mad as he.

155 **HAMLET** How came he mad?

FIRST CLOWN Very strangely, they say.

HAMLET How strangely?

FIRST CLOWN Faith, e'en with losing his wits.

HAMLET Upon what ground?

160 **FIRST CLOWN** Why, here in Denmark: I have been sexton
here, man and boy, thirty years.

HAMLET How long will a man lie i'th'earth ere he rot?

FIRST CLOWN I'faith, if he be not rotten before he die —
as we have many pocky corpses now-a-days, that

165 will scarce hold the laying in — he will last you some
eight year or nine year: a tanner will last you nine
year.

HAMLET Why he more than another?

FIRST CLOWN Why, sir, his hide is so tanned with his

170 trade that he will keep out water a great while, and
your water is a sore decayer of your whoreson dead
body. Here's a skull now: this skull has lain in the
earth three-and-twenty years.

HAMLET Whose was it?

175 **FIRST CLOWN** A whoreson mad fellow's it was: whose do
you think it was?

HAMLET Nay, I know not.

FIRST CLOWN A pestilence on him for a mad rogue! A
poured a flagon of Rhenish on my head once. This

180 same skull, sir, this same skull, sir, was Yorick's skull,
the king's jester.

HAMLET This?

FIRST CLOWN E'en that.

HAMLET Let me see.— Alas, poor Yorick! I knew him,   *Takes the skull*

185 Horatio: a fellow of infinite jest, of most excellent
fancy. He hath borne me on his back a thousand
times — and how abhorred my imagination is! My
gorge rises at it. Here hung those lips that I have
kissed I know not how oft.— Where be your gibes

---

159 ground cause (but the First Clown responds to the literal sense of the word)   **164 pocky** diseased,
especially with the pox (i.e. syphilis)   **165 hold . . . in** hold together long enough to be buried   **166 tanner**
one who converts animal hides into leather by tanning (infusing with an astringent liquid)   **171 whoreson**
wretched (an abusive intensifier used in a jocular manner)   **172 Here's a skull** presumably one of the two
thrown up earlier, but conceivably a third if he is still digging   **178 A** he   **179 Rhenish** German wine from
the area around the River Rhine   **186 fancy** imagination   **187 abhorred** filled with horror   **My gorge
rises** i.e. I feel like vomiting   **gorge** stomach contents

190 now, your gambols, your songs, your flashes of
merriment that were wont to set the table on a roar?
No one now to mock your own jeering? Quite chop-
fallen? Now get you to my lady's chamber and tell
her, let her paint an inch thick, to this favour she
195 must come. Make her laugh at that.— Prithee,
Horatio, tell me one thing.

HORATIO What's that, my lord?

HAMLET Dost thou think Alexander looked o'this fashion
i'th'earth?

200 **HORATIO** E'en so.

HAMLET And smelt so? Puh!   *Places the skull on the ground*

HORATIO E'en so, my lord.   *or throws it down*

HAMLET To what base uses we may return, Horatio!
Why may not imagination trace the noble dust of
205 Alexander till he find it stopping a bung-hole?

HORATIO 'Twere to consider too curiously to consider so.

HAMLET No, faith, not a jot, but to follow him thither
with modesty enough, and likelihood to lead it, as
thus: Alexander died, Alexander was buried,
210 Alexander returneth into dust; the dust is earth; of
earth we make loam, and why of that loam whereto
he was converted might they not stop a beer-barrel?
Imperial Caesar, dead and turned to clay,
Might stop a hole to keep the wind away.
215 O, that that earth, which kept the world in awe,
Should patch a wall t'expel the winter's flaw!
But soft, but soft, aside: here comes the king.

*Enter King, Queen, Laertes, [a Priest] and a coffin with Lords
Attendant*

The queen, the courtiers — who is that they follow?
And with such maimèd rites? This doth betoken
220 The corpse they follow did with desperate hand
Fordo it own life: 'twas of some estate.
Couch we awhile and mark.   *They hide*

LAERTES What ceremony else?

HAMLET That is Laertes, a very noble youth. Mark.   *Aside to Horatio*

225 **LAERTES** What ceremony else?

---

192 No . . . jeering? There's no one left to laugh at the way you mocked and made fun of people?
chop-fallen downcast/lacking the lower jaw **194 favour** facial appearance **198 Alexander** Alexander
the Great, fourth-century King of Macedonia and one of the world's most successful military leaders
205 bung-hole hole in a barrel stoppered with a bung **206 too curiously** too closely/overly ingeniously
208 modesty moderation **211 loam** mortar made of clay, sand and straw **216 flaw** squall, violent gust
of wind **219 maimèd** truncated, insufficient **220 desperate** filled with spiritual despair, suicidal
221 Fordo it destroy its **estate** status **222 Couch** hide

PRIEST Her obsequies have been as far enlarged
　　　As we have warrantise: her death was doubtful,
　　　And but that great command o'ersways the order
　　　She should in ground unsanctified have lodged
230　Till the last trumpet. For charitable prayer,
　　　Shards, flints and pebbles should be thrown on her.
　　　Yet here she is allowed her virgin rites,
　　　Her maiden strewments and the bringing home
　　　Of bell and burial.
235　LAERTES Must there no more be done?
　　　PRIEST No more be done:
　　　We should profane the service of the dead
　　　To sing sage requiem and such rest to her
　　　As to peace-parted souls.
240　LAERTES Lay her i'th'earth:
　　　And from her fair and unpolluted flesh
　　　May violets spring! I tell thee, churlish priest,
　　　A minist'ring angel shall my sister be
　　　When thou liest howling.
245　HAMLET What, the fair Ophelia!　　　　　　　*Aside to Horatio*
　　　GERTRUDE Sweets to the sweet. Farewell!　　*Scatters flowers*
　　　I hoped thou shouldst have been my Hamlet's wife:
　　　I thought thy bride-bed to have decked, sweet maid,
　　　And not t'have strewed thy grave.
250　LAERTES O, treble woe
　　　Fall ten times treble on that cursèd head
　　　Whose wicked deed thy most ingenious sense
　　　Deprived thee of!— Hold off the earth awhile,
　　　Till I have caught her once more in mine arms:
　　　Leaps in the grave
255　Now pile your dust upon the quick and dead,
　　　Till of this flat a mountain you have made,
　　　To o'ertop old Pelion or the skyish head
　　　Of blue Olympus.

226 **obsequies** commemorative rites for the dead　227 **warrantise** authorization　**doubtful** suspicious
228 **o'ersways** overrules　229 **unsanctified** not consecrated by the Church　230 **last trumpet** i.e.
Doomsday, which would, according to the Bible, be heralded by the sound of a trumpet　**For** instead of
231 **Shards** fragments of broken pottery　233 **strewments** flowers strewn on the coffin or grave
bringing . . . burial bringing her to her final resting place accompanied by the funeral bell and burial rites
238 **sage requiem** a solemn funeral chant　**such rest** pray for the same rest　239 **peace-parted**
peacefully departed　242 **violets** the flower was associated with chastity　244 **howling** i.e. in
hell　252 **ingenious sense** quick, intelligent mind　255 **quick** living (i.e. Laertes)　257 **Pelion** the
mountain in Thessaly that, in Greek mythology, the warring giants piled on top of Mount Ossa in their
attempt to scale **Olympus**, the mountain home of the gods

HAMLET What is he whose grief   *Comes forward*
260   Bears such an emphasis? Whose phrase of sorrow
         Conjures the wand'ring stars, and makes them stand
         Like wonder-wounded hearers? This is I,   *Removes cloak?*
         Hamlet the Dane.   *Leaps into the grave*
    LAERTES The devil take thy soul!   *They fight*
265 HAMLET Thou pray'st not well.
         I prithee take thy fingers from my throat,
         Sir: though I am not splenitive and rash,
         Yet have I something in me dangerous,
         Which let thy wiseness fear: away thy hand!
270 KING Pluck them asunder.
    GERTRUDE Hamlet, Hamlet!
    HORATIO Good my lord, be quiet.   *Attendants part them, and they come*
    HAMLET Why I will fight with him upon this theme   *out of the grave*
         Until my eyelids will no longer wag.
275 GERTRUDE O my son, what theme?
    HAMLET I loved Ophelia: forty thousand brothers
         Could not — with all their quantity of love —
         Make up my sum. What wilt thou do for her?
    KING O, he is mad, Laertes.
280 GERTRUDE For love of God, forbear him.
    HAMLET Come, show me what thou'lt do:
         Woo't weep? Woo't fight? Woo't fast? Woo't tear
              thyself?
         Woo't drink up eisel? Eat a crocodile?
         I'll do't. Dost thou come here to whine?
285   To outface me with leaping in her grave?
         Be buried quick with her, and so will I:
         And if thou prate of mountains, let them throw
         Millions of acres on us, till our ground,
         Singeing his pate against the burning zone,
290   Make Ossa like a wart! Nay, an thou'lt mouth,
         I'll rant as well as thou.
    KING This is mere madness,
         And thus awhile the fit will work on him:
         Anon, as patient as the female dove

260 **emphasis** strength of expression (a rhetorical term)   261 **Conjures ... stars** casts a spell on the planets   267 **splenitive** hot-tempered (the spleen was thought to be the seat of the passions)   272 **quiet** calm   274 **wag** open and shut   280 **forbear him** leave him alone   282 **Woo't** wilt thou   **tear** tear violently at (hair, clothing)/injure/destroy   283 **eisel** vinegar   **crocodile** i.e. something tough and dangerous, the creature that was supposed to shed copious hypocritical tears   285 **outface** defy/defeat   288 **our ground** the piled-up earth above us   289 **burning zone** sun's orbit between the tropics   290 **Ossa** in Greek mythology, the mountain on which the giants piled Pelion in their attempt to reach Olympus   **an** if   **mouth** grimace/rant   292 **mere** complete

295   When that her golden couplets are disclosed,
      His silence will sit drooping.
      HAMLET Hear you, sir: *To Laertes*
      What is the reason that you use me thus?
      I loved you ever: but it is no matter.
300   Let Hercules himself do what he may,
      The cat will mew and dog will have his day.   *Exit*
      KING I pray you, good Horatio, wait upon him.—
                                            [*Exit Horatio*]
      Strengthen your patience in our last night's speech: *To Laertes*
      We'll put the matter to the present push.—
305   Good Gertrude, set some watch over your son.—
      This grave shall have a living monument:
      An hour of quiet shortly shall we see;
      Till then, in patience our proceeding be.   *Exeunt*

[Act 5 Scene 2]   *running scene 17*

Enter Hamlet and Horatio

      HAMLET So much for this, sir; now let me see the other:
      You do remember all the circumstance?
      HORATIO Remember it, my lord?
      HAMLET Sir, in my heart there was a kind of fighting
5   That would not let me sleep: methought I lay
      Worse than the mutines in the bilboes. Rashly —
      And praise be rashness for it — let us know
      Our indiscretion sometimes serves us well,
      When our dear plots do pall, and that should teach
          us
10   There's a divinity that shapes our ends,
      Rough-hew them how we will—
      HORATIO That is most certain.
      HAMLET Up from my cabin,
      My sea-gown scarfed about me, in the dark

295 **golden couplets** baby birds covered in golden down   **disclosed** hatched   **298 use** treat
300 **Let…day** i.e. even Hercules could not stop Laertes from his tiresome rant/my turn will come and even
Hercules (or the ranting Laertes) cannot stop me   **303 in** i.e. by remembering   **304 present push**
immediate test (**push** may also be suggestive of the thrust of a weapon)   **306 living** lasting (but also implies
that murdering Hamlet will serve as a memorial)   **5.2** *Location: within the royal castle at Elsinore*
1 **this** the pair enter mid-conversation; **this** refers to what Hamlet has just been telling Horatio   **see the
other** hear the other news   2 **circumstance** details   6 **mutines…bilboes** mutineers in shackles
Rashly on impulse (Hamlet then digresses before returning to his tale in line 13)   7 **know** acknowledge
8 **indiscretion** lack of forethought and prudence   9 **dear** important   **pall** weaken/become flat and stale
11 **Rough-hew** carve roughly   14 **sea-gown** short-sleeved, calf-length sailor's gown made of coarse
material   **scarfed** wrapped loosely

15   Groped I to find out them, had my desire,
        Fingered their packet, and in fine withdrew
        To mine own room again, making so bold —
        My fears forgetting manners — to unseal
        Their grand commission, where I found, Horatio —
20   O, royal knavery! — an exact command,
        Larded with many several sorts of reason
        Importing Denmark's health and England's too,
        With, ho, such bugs and goblins in my life,
        That on the supervise, no leisure bated,
25   No, not to stay the grinding of the axe,
        My head should be struck off.

HORATIO Is't possible?

HAMLET Here's the commission: read it at more leisure.   *Gives a paper*
        But wilt thou hear me how I did proceed?

30 **HORATIO** I beseech you.

HAMLET Being thus benetted round with villainies —
        Ere I could make a prologue to my brains,
        They had begun the play — I sat me down,
        Devised a new commission, wrote it fair:
35   I once did hold it, as our statists do,
        A baseness to write fair and laboured much
        How to forget that learning, but, sir, now
        It did me yeoman's service. Wilt thou know
        The effect of what I wrote?

40 **HORATIO** Ay, good my lord.

HAMLET An earnest conjuration from the king,
        As England was his faithful tributary,
        As love between them as the palm should flourish,
        As peace should still her wheaten garland wear
45   And stand a comma 'tween their amities,
        And many such-like 'As'es of great charge,
        That on the view and know of these contents,
        Without debatement further, more or less,

---

15 them i.e. Rosencrantz and Guildenstern   **16 Fingered** stole   **in fine** finally, in conclusion   **21 Larded** garnished, interspersed   **several** various   **22 Importing** concerning   **23 bugs . . . life** terrors to be feared were I to be allowed to continue living   **bug** hobgoblin, bogeyman   **24 supervise** reading (of the commission)   **leisure bated** time wasted   **25 stay** await   **31 benetted round** snared, surrounded as if in a net   **32 Ere . . . play** i.e. before my brain could begin to consider the issue, I had already taken action   **34 fair** in elegant handwriting   **35 statists** statesmen   **38 yeoman's** i.e. efficient, loyal (a yeoman was an attendant in a royal household)   **39 effect** nature   **41 conjuration** entreaty   **42 tributary** country owing him a tribute (a regular payment after defeat in war)   **44 still** always (i.e. continue)   **wheaten garland** symbolic of peace   **45 comma** the mark of punctuation that indicated only a slight break between words, thus a symbol of closeness and connection between the two countries   **amities** friendship   **46 'As'es** phrases beginning with 'as' (puns on 'asses')   **charge** importance/burden (continuing the play on 'asses')

He should the bearers put to sudden death,
50   Not shriving-time allowed.
HORATIO How was this sealed?
HAMLET Why, even in that was heaven ordinant.
     I had my father's signet in my purse,
     Which was the model of that Danish seal:
55   Folded the writ up in form of the other,
     Subscribed it, gave't th'impression, placed it safely,
     The changeling never known. Now, the next day
     Was our sea-fight, and what to this was sequent
     Thou know'st already.
60 **HORATIO** So Guildenstern and Rosencrantz go to't.
HAMLET Why, man, they did make love to this
          employment:
     They are not near my conscience; their defeat
     Doth by their own insinuation grow.
     'Tis dangerous when the baser nature comes
65   Between the pass and fell incensèd points
     Of mighty opposites.
HORATIO Why, what a king is this!
HAMLET Does it not, think'st thee, stand me now
          upon —
     He that hath killed my king and whored my mother,
70   Popped in between th'election and my hopes,
     Thrown out his angle for my proper life,
     And with such cozenage — is't not perfect
          conscience
     To quit him with this arm? And is't not to be
          damned,
     To let this canker of our nature come
75   In further evil?
HORATIO It must be shortly known to him from England
     What is the issue of the business there.
HAMLET It will be short: the interim is mine,
     And a man's life's no more than to say 'one'.

---

50 shriving-time time for confession and absolution from sin   **52 ordinant** in control   **53 signet** signet ring which acted as a seal   **54 model ... seal** exactly the same as the seal used to secure the commission   **55 writ** letter/written command   **56 Subscribed** signed (in Claudius' name)   **th'impression** the seal   **57 changeling** substitution, i.e. false letter (literally a fairy child substituted for a human one)   **58 to ... sequent** followed this   **61 make love to** court, entreat   **62 defeat** destruction   **63 insinuation** ingratiating behaviour/intrusive involvement   **64 baser** of lower social status/inferior   **65 pass** sword thrust   **fell** fierce   **points** swords   **66 opposites** opponents, enemies   **68 Does ... upon** do you not think that it is now incumbent upon me   **70 th'election** i.e. the designation as king   **71 angle** fishing-hook and line   **proper** own   **72 cozenage** deception (puns on 'cousinage' – i.e. kinship)   **73 quit** requite, repay   **74 canker** spreading ulcer   **come In** spread to, generate   **77 issue** outcome   **79 no ... 'one'** is only as brief as the time it takes to say 'one'

80　　But I am very sorry, good Horatio,
　　　That to Laertes I forgot myself;
　　　For by the image of my cause I see
　　　The portraiture of his. I'll count his favours.
　　　But, sure, the bravery of his grief did put me
85　　Into a tow'ring passion.
　　HORATIO Peace, who comes here?
　　Enter young Osric　　　　　　　　　　　　*Takes off his hat*
　　OSRIC Your lordship is right welcome back to Denmark.
　　HAMLET I humbly thank you, sir.— Dost know this
　　　water-fly?
90　　**HORATIO** No, my good lord.
　　HAMLET Thy state is the more gracious, for 'tis a vice to
　　　know him. He hath much land, and fertile: let a beast
　　　be lord of beasts, and his crib shall stand at the king's
　　　mess; 'tis a chough, but, as I say, spacious in the
95　　possession of dirt.
　　OSRIC Sweet lord, if your friendship were at leisure, I
　　　should impart a thing to you from his majesty.
　　HAMLET I will receive it with all diligence of spirit. Put
　　　your bonnet to his right use: 'tis for the head.
100　**OSRIC** I thank your lordship, 'tis very hot.
　　HAMLET No, believe me, 'tis very cold: the wind is
　　　northerly.
　　OSRIC It is indifferent cold, my lord, indeed.
　　HAMLET Methinks it is very sultry and hot for my
105　　complexion.
　　OSRIC Exceedingly, my lord: it is very sultry, as 'twere, I
　　　cannot tell how. But, my lord, his majesty bade me
　　　signify to you that he has laid a great wager on your
　　　head: sir, this is the matter—
110　**HAMLET** I beseech you remember—　　　*Gestures towards hat*
　　OSRIC Nay, in good faith, for mine ease, in good faith.
　　　Sir, you are not ignorant of what excellence Laertes is
　　　at his weapon.
　　HAMLET What's his weapon?

82 by . . . his i.e. in my situation (having a murdered father) I recognize his also　84 **bravery** extravagance, ostentatious display　88 **water-fly** i.e. buzzing insect　91 **gracious** blessed, fortunate　92 **let . . . mess** even if you are an animal yourself, provided that you own a lot of livestock you shall eat at the king's table (**mess**)　**crib** animal's food receptacle　94 **chough** jackdaw (i.e. chatterer)/chuff (i.e. rustic, churl)　96 **if . . . leisure** i.e. if the two of you have finished talking　99 **bonnet** hat (usually worn indoors when in company)　103 **indifferent** moderately　105 **complexion** constitution　110 **remember** probably 'remember your courtesy', a way of asking someone to put on their hat　111 **for mine ease** a polite way of resisting Hamlet's request

115   OSRIC Rapier and dagger.

       HAMLET That's two of his weapons; but, well.

       OSRIC The king, sir, has waged with him six Barbary
           horses, against the which he imponed, as I take it, six
           French rapiers and poniards, with their assigns, as
120   girdle, hangers or so. Three of the carriages, in faith,
           are very dear to fancy, very responsive to the hilts,
           most delicate carriages, and of very liberal conceit.

       HAMLET What call you the carriages?

       OSRIC The carriages, sir, are the hangers.

125   HAMLET The phrase would be more germane to the
           matter, if we could carry cannon by our sides: I
           would it might be hangers till then. But, on: six
           Barbary horses against six French swords, their
           assigns, and three liberal-conceited carriages: that's
130   the French bet against the Danish. Why is this
           'imponed' as you call it?

       OSRIC The king, sir, hath laid, that in a dozen passes
           between you and him, he shall not exceed you three
           hits: he hath laid on twelve for nine, and that would
135   come to immediate trial, if your lordship would
           vouchsafe the answer.

       HAMLET How if I answer 'no'?

       OSRIC I mean, my lord, the opposition of your person in
           trial.

140   HAMLET Sir, I will walk here in the hall: if it please his
           majesty, 'tis the breathing time of day with me; let
           the foils be brought, the gentleman willing, and the
           king hold his purpose, I will win for him if I can: if
           not, I'll gain nothing but my shame and the odd hits.

145   OSRIC Shall I re-deliver you e'en so?

115 Rapier long, pointed, double-edged sword (the flexible épée of modern fencing had not yet been invented)   116 well very well, never mind   117 Barbary horses valued North African horses, noted for their speed   118 imponed wagered (impawned; or an affected coinage from the Latin *imponere*, meaning 'to pile or lay on')   119 poniards daggers   assigns accessories   as such as   120 girdle sword belt hangers loops on sword belts, from which the sword was hung; often richly ornamented   carriages an affected word for hangers   121 dear to fancy pleasing to the fancy/delightfully tasteful   responsive ... hilts well-matched to the sword handle   122 delicate finely made   liberal conceit elaborate design 123 call you do you mean by   125 germane relevant   126 cannon ... sides 'carriage' is the word for the wheeled support on which a cannon is mounted   132 laid wagered   in ... nine famously incomprehensible and much-debated wager; Claudius bets that, in a series of twelve rounds, Laertes' total number of hits will not exceed Hamlet's by three or more, but it is unclear what is meant by 'twelve for nine', where 'he' may be Claudius or Laertes   passes rounds   133 him i.e. Laertes   136 vouchsafe the answer be pleased to accept the challenge (Hamlet interprets answer more literally as 'reply')   138 opposition ... trial presenting of yourself as an opponent in a contest   141 breathing time time for exercise   144 odd occasional/extra three   145 re-deliver you report back what you say

HAMLET To this effect, sir, after what flourish your nature will.

OSRIC I commend my duty to your lordship.

HAMLET Yours, yours.— [*Exit Osric*]
150 He does well to commend it himself, there are no tongues else for's turn.

HORATIO This lapwing runs away with the shell on his head.

HAMLET He did comply with his dug, before he sucked
155 it. Thus has he — and many more of the same bevy that I know the drossy age dotes on — only got the tune of the time and outward habit of encounter, a kind of yeasty collection, which carries them through and through the most fond and winnowed opinions;
160 and do but blow them to their trials, the bubbles are out.

HORATIO You will lose this wager, my lord.

HAMLET I do not think so: since he went into France, I have been in continual practice; I shall win at the
165 odds. But thou wouldst not think how ill all's here about my heart, but it is no matter.

HORATIO Nay, good my lord—

HAMLET It is but foolery; but it is such a kind of gain-giving as would perhaps trouble a woman.

170 **HORATIO** If your mind dislike anything, obey it: I will forestall their repair hither, and say you are not fit.

HAMLET Not a whit, we defy augury: there's a special providence in the fall of a sparrow. If it be now, 'tis not to come: if it be not to come, it will be now: if it be
175 not now, yet it will come: the readiness is all. Since no man has aught of what he leaves, what is't to leave betimes?

---

146 after what flourish according to whatever lavish gesture or manner of speaking you choose
148 commend entrust (part of a standard phrase, but Hamlet responds to the sense of 'recommend, praise') **151 for's turn** to do it for him **152 lapwing** bird proverbial for youthful precocity as it left the nest soon after being hatched; **shell . . . head** may suggest that Osric has just put his hat on **154 comply . . . dug** pay courteous compliments to his mother's (or nurse's) nipple **155 bevy** company/group of birds **156 drossy** worthless, impure **157 tune** i.e. fashionable speech/general style **habit of encounter** custom of social interaction/fashionable dress **158 yeasty** frothy **collection** i.e. of fashionable words and manners **carries them through** enables them to successfully pass off/enables them to hold their own amongst **159 fond** foolish **winnowed** selective (literally refers to the blowing away of chaff from grain) **160 and . . . out** yet test them by blowing on them and the bubbles will burst/test their opinions and they are lost for words **164 at the odds** given the odds that have been laid **168 gain-giving** misgiving, foreboding **171 repair** coming **172 augury** prophecy (literally, making predictions based on an interpretation of the behaviour of birds) **there's . . . sparrow** i.e. God's hand is in every slightest thing – alluding to Matthew 10:29 **173 it** i.e. his own death **175 readiness** i.e. to meet death **176 has aught of** really owns, can take with him **177 betimes** early

Enter King, Queen, Laertes and Lords, with [Osric and] other
Attendants with foils and gauntlets, a table and flagons of
wine on it

KING Come, Hamlet, come and take this hand from me.   *Puts Laertes'*
HAMLET Give me your pardon, sir: I've done you wrong,   *hand into*
180   But pardon't, as you are a gentleman.   *Hamlet's*
        This presence knows,
        And you must needs have heard, how I am punished
        With sore distraction. What I have done
        That might your nature, honour and exception
185   Roughly awake, I here proclaim was madness.
        Was't Hamlet wronged Laertes? Never Hamlet:
        If Hamlet from himself be ta'en away,
        And when he's not himself does wrong Laertes,
        Then Hamlet does it not, Hamlet denies it.
190   Who does it, then? His madness. If't be so,
        Hamlet is of the faction that is wronged,
        His madness is poor Hamlet's enemy.
        Sir, in this audience,
        Let my disclaiming from a purposed evil
195   Free me so far in your most generous thoughts
        That I have shot mine arrow o'er the house,
        And hurt my brother.
LAERTES   I am satisfied in nature,
        Whose motive in this case should stir me most
200   To my revenge: but in my terms of honour
        I stand aloof, and will no reconcilement
        Till by some elder masters, of known honour
        I have a voice and precedent of peace,
        To keep my name ungored. But till that time,
205   I do receive your offered love like love,
        And will not wrong it.
HAMLET   I do embrace it freely,
        And will this brother's wager frankly play.—
        Give us the foils. Come on.
210 **LAERTES** Come, one for me.

---

gauntlets protective gloves used for fencing **181 presence** assembly/royal company **184 nature** natural feeling/filial loyalty **exception** disapproval, objection **191 faction** party **194 disclaiming from** disavowal, denial of **purposed** intentional **195 generous** noble-minded/magnanimous **196 That I have** as to think that I have **200 my ... honour** where my honour is concerned **201 will** want, will have **203 voice** (authoritative) endorsement **peace** reconciliation **204 name ungored** reputation uninjured **208 frankly** freely, with no ill will

HAMLET I'll be your foil, Laertes: in mine ignorance
    Your skill shall, like a star i'th'darkest night,
    Stick fiery off indeed.

LAERTES You mock me, sir.

215 HAMLET No, by this hand.

KING Give them the foils, young Osric. Cousin Hamlet,
    You know the wager?

HAMLET Very well, my lord:
    Your grace hath laid the odds o'th'weaker side.

220 KING I do not fear it: I have seen you both:
    But since he is bettered, we have therefore odds.

LAERTES This is too heavy, let me see another.   *Looks over the foils*

HAMLET This likes me well. These foils have all a length?

Prepare to play

OSRIC Ay, my good lord.

225 KING Set me the stoups of wine upon that table:
    If Hamlet give the first or second hit,
    Or quit in answer of the third exchange,
    Let all the battlements their ordnance fire:
    The king shall drink to Hamlet's better breath,
230   And in the cup an union shall he throw
    Richer than that which four successive kings
    In Denmark's crown have worn. Give me the cups,
    And let the kettle to the trumpets speak,
    The trumpet to the cannoneer without,
235   The cannons to the heavens, the heaven to earth,
    'Now the king drinks to Hamlet.' Come, begin:
    And you, the judges, bear a wary eye.

HAMLET Come on, sir.

LAERTES Come on, sir.   *They play*

240 HAMLET One.

LAERTES No.

HAMLET Judgement.

OSRIC A hit, a very palpable hit.

LAERTES Well, again.

245 KING Stay, give me drink.— Hamlet, this pearl is thine: *Drinks, then puts*
    Here's to thy health.— Give him the cup.   *the pearl in the cup?*

Trumpets sound and shot goes off

---

211 **foil** background material used to set off the lustre of a jewel (shifting the sense away from 'sword')
213 **Stick fiery off** stand out and sparkle brilliantly   219 **laid the odds** backed   221 **he is bettered**
Laertes is considered to be better   **odds** the advantage (Laertes is handicapped by having to score three hits
over Hamlet)   223 **likes** pleases   **have...length** are all of the same length   225 **stoups** cups
227 **quit...exchange** repays Laertes (for winning the first two bouts) by scoring a hit in the third bout
228 **ordnance** cannon   229 **better breath** increased energy and vigour   230 **union** valuable pearl
233 **kettle** kettle-drum

HAMLET I'll play this bout first: set by awhile.— Come.   *They play*
Another hit; what say you?
LAERTES A touch, a touch, I do confess.
250 **KING** Our son shall win.
GERTRUDE He's fat, and scant of breath.—
Here's a napkin, rub thy brows: *To Hamlet*
The queen carouses to thy fortune, Hamlet.
HAMLET Good madam.
255 **KING** Gertrude, do not drink!
GERTRUDE I will, my lord; I pray you, pardon me.   *Drinks*
KING It is the poisoned cup: it is too late.   *Aside*
HAMLET I dare not drink yet, madam: by and by.
GERTRUDE Come, let me wipe thy face.
260 **LAERTES** My lord, I'll hit him now.   *To the King*
KING I do not think't.
LAERTES And yet 'tis almost gainst my conscience.   *Aside*
HAMLET Come, for the third: Laertes, you but dally.
I pray you pass with your best violence:
265 I am afeard you make a wanton of me.
LAERTES Say you so? Come on.   *Play*
OSRIC Nothing, neither way.
LAERTES Have at you now!   *In scuffling they
change rapiers*

KING Part them: they are incensed.
270 **HAMLET** Nay, come, again.   *Gertrude falls?*
OSRIC Look to the queen there, ho!
HORATIO They bleed on both sides.— How is it, my lord?   *To Hamlet*
OSRIC How is't, Laertes?
LAERTES Why, as a woodcock to mine own springe,
Osric:
275 I am justly killed with mine own treachery.
HAMLET How does the queen?
KING She swoons to see them bleed.
GERTRUDE No, no, the drink, the drink — O my dear
Hamlet —
The drink, the drink! I am poisoned.   *Dies*
280 **HAMLET** O, villainy! Ho! Let the door be locked:
Treachery! Seek it out.
LAERTES It is here, Hamlet. Hamlet, thou art slain:
No medicine in the world can do thee good,

---

251 **fat** may suggest greasy/sweaty, but primary sense is corpulent, overweight   252 **napkin** handkerchief
253 **carouses to** toasts   264 **pass** thrust   265 **make . . . me** toy with me/indulge me   **wanton** spoilt
child   *scuffling* fighting at close quarters   *change* exchange, probably via the manoeuvre known as
'left-hand seizure' (see Introduction, pp. 9–10)   274 **woodcock** proverbially stupid, easily caught birds
springe snare

In thee there is not half an hour of life;
285   The treacherous instrument is in thy hand,
Unbated and envenomed. The foul practice
Hath turned itself on me: lo, here I lie,
Never to rise again. Thy mother's poisoned.
I can no more. The king, the king's to blame.
290 **HAMLET** The point envenomed too!
  Then, venom, to thy work.   *Hurts the King*
ALL Treason! Treason!
KING O, yet defend me, friends, I am but hurt.
HAMLET Here, thou incestuous, murd'rous, damnèd
  Dane,
295   Drink off this potion. Is thy union here?
Follow my mother.   *King dies*
LAERTES He is justly served:
It is a poison tempered by himself.
Exchange forgiveness with me, noble Hamlet:
300   Mine and my father's death come not upon thee,
Nor thine on me.   *Dies*
HAMLET Heaven make thee free of it! I follow thee.—
I am dead, Horatio.— Wretched queen, adieu!—
You that look pale and tremble at this chance,
305   That are but mutes or audience to this act,
Had I but time — as this fell sergeant, death,
Is strict in his arrest — O, I could tell you.
But let it be.— Horatio, I am dead:
Thou liv'st: report me and my causes right
310   To the unsatisfied.
HORATIO Never believe it.
I am more an antique Roman than a Dane:
Here's yet some liquor left.
HAMLET As thou'rt a man,
315   Give me the cup: let go, by heaven, I'll have't.
O, good Horatio, what a wounded name —
Things standing thus unknown — shall live behind
  me!
If thou didst ever hold me in thy heart,
Absent thee from felicity awhile,

---

286 practice plot   **295 Drink off** drink up, drain   **union** pearl (plays on the sense of 'marriage')
298 tempered mixed   **304 chance** mischance/event   **305 mutes** silent onlookers/actors without
speaking parts   **act** event/theatrical performance   **306 fell** cruel   **307 strict** rigorously just/unrelenting,
stern   **arrest** taking into custody/halting (of my words)   **309 causes** grievances, grounds for revenge
310 unsatisfied uninformed/those who wish to know   **312 antique Roman** one of the ancient Romans,
who viewed suicide as a noble alternative to an unworthy life   **319 felicity** happiness, bliss

320   And in this harsh world draw thy breath in pain,
        To tell my story.
     March afar off and shot within
                       What warlike noise is this?

     Enter Osric
     OSRIC Young Fortinbras, with conquest come from
          Poland,
        To th'ambassadors of England gives
        This warlike volley.
325   **HAMLET** O, I die, Horatio:
        The potent poison quite o'er-crows my spirit.
        I cannot live to hear the news from England,
        But I do prophesy th'election lights
        On Fortinbras: he has my dying voice,
330   So tell him, with the occurrents more and less
        Which have solicited. The rest is silence. O, o, o, o!
                                        Dies

     HORATIO Now cracks a noble heart. Goodnight, sweet
          prince,
        And flights of angels sing thee to thy rest!—
        Why does the drum come hither?
     Enter Fortinbras and English Ambassador, with Drum,
     Colours and Attendants
335   **FORTINBRAS** Where is this sight?
     HORATIO What is it ye would see?
        If aught of woe or wonder, cease your search.
     FORTINBRAS This quarry cries on havoc. O proud death,
        What feast is toward in thine eternal cell,
340   That thou so many princes at a shot
        So bloodily hast struck?
     AMBASSADOR The sight is dismal,
        And our affairs from England come too late:
        The ears are senseless that should give us hearing,
345   To tell him his commandment is fulfilled,
        That Rosencrantz and Guildenstern are dead.
        Where should we have our thanks?
     HORATIO Not from his mouth,
        Had it th'ability of life to thank you:

---

326 o'er-crows triumphs over (an image from cockfighting)   **328 th'election** i.e. the selection of the next King of Denmark   **329 voice** vote/support   **330 occurrents** events   **331 solicited** prompted this **O … o!** a dying groan is represented thus in several plays of the period   *Colours* battle flags   **336 would** wish to   **338 quarry … havoc** mound of bodies proclaims total slaughter and destruction   **quarry** pile of dead game after a hunt   **339 toward** imminent/being prepared   **cell** small dwelling   **342 dismal** ominous/calamitous/depressing   **344 The ears** i.e. Claudius' ears

350 He never gave commandment for their death.
But since, so jump upon this bloody question,
You from the Polack wars, and you from England,
Are here arrived, give order that these bodies
High on a stage be placèd to the view,
355 And let me speak to th'yet unknowing world
How these things came about: so shall you hear
Of carnal, bloody and unnatural acts,
Of accidental judgements, casual slaughters,
Of deaths put on by cunning and forced cause,
360 And, in this upshot, purposes mistook
Fall'n on the inventors' heads: all this can I
Truly deliver.

FORTINBRAS Let us haste to hear it,
And call the noblest to the audience.
365 For me, with sorrow I embrace my fortune:
I have some rights of memory in this kingdom,
Which now to claim my vantage doth invite me.

HORATIO Of that I shall have also cause to speak,
And from his mouth whose voice will draw on more:
370 But let this same be presently performed,
Even while men's minds are wild, lest more
mischance
On plots and errors happen.

FORTINBRAS Let four captains
Bear Hamlet, like a soldier, to the stage,
375 For he was likely, had he been put on,
To have proved most royally: and for his passage,
The soldiers' music and the rites of war
Speak loudly for him.
Take up the body: such a sight as this
380 Becomes the field, but here shows much amiss.
Go, bid the soldiers shoot.

Exeunt marching. After the which
a peal of ordnance are shot off

---

351 **jump** precisely **question** dispute/affair 354 **stage** platform **view** general view 358 **accidental judgements** punishments happening by chance **casual** occurring by chance 359 **put on** instigated/arranged **forced cause** deliberate contrivance/false grounds 360 **upshot** conclusion, outcome 362 **deliver** report 366 **of memory** old/traditional/unforgotten 367 **vantage** advantage, favourable opportunity 369 **voice** speaking voice/vote **draw on** encourage, rally the support of 370 **this same** i.e. the displaying of the bodies and explanation of events **presently** immediately 371 **wild** bewildered/agitated 372 **On** on top of/as a result of 375 **put on** put to the test (as king) 376 **passage** journey into death 378 **Speak** i.e. let them speak 380 **Becomes the field** suits the battlefield **shows much amiss** is very out of place

TEXTUAL NOTES

Q1 = First Quarto text of 1603 (of uncertain authority)
Q2 = Second Quarto text of 1604–05
Q1/Q2 = a reading in which the First Quarto and Second Quarto texts
    agree
F = First Folio text of 1623
F2 = a correction introduced in the Second Folio text of 1632
Ed = a correction introduced by a later editor
SD = stage direction
SH = speech heading (i.e. speaker's name)

List of parts = Ed

1.1.70 he = Q1/Q2. *Not in* F **72 steelèd** = Ed. Q1/Q2 = sleaded. F = sledded **pole-axe** = F *(Pollax). Sometimes emended to* Polacks **104 designed** = F2. F = designe **126 haply** *spelled* happily *in* F **151 say** = Q1/Q2. F = sayes **167 Let's** = Q1/Q2. F = Let
1.2.8 sometime = Q2. F = sometimes **67 SH GERTRUDE** = Ed. F = *Queen.* **129 solid** = F. Q2 = sallied, *sometimes emended to* sullied **134 Seem** = Q2. F = Seemes **141 beteem** = Q2. F = beteene **208 distilled** = Q1/Q2. F = bestil'd **213 Where, as** = Ed. F = Whereas **222 its** = Q4. F = it **233 SH MARCELLUS** *and* **BARNARDO** = Ed. F = *Both.* **250 SH MARCELLUS** *and* **BARNARDO** = Ed. F = *All.* **255 walk** = Q1/Q2. F = wake **261 tenable** = Q1/Q2. F = treble
1.3.18 will = Q2. F = feare **23 sanctity** = F. Q2 = safety. Ed = sanity **whole** = Q2. F = weole **48 watchman** Q2. F = watchmen **68 new-hatched** = Q2. F = vnhatch't **77 chief** *spelled* cheff *in* F **113 Running** = Ed. F = Roaming **121 Lends** = Q1/Q2. F = Giues **132 dye** = Q2. F = eye **134 bawds** = Ed. F = bonds
1.4.10 wassail = Q1/Q2. F = wassels **23 intents** = Q1/Q2. F = euents **37 the** = Q1/Q2. F = thee; **54 summit** = Ed. F = Sonnet **64 artery** = Ed. F = Artire
1.5.23 on *spelled* an *in* F **33 I** = Q2. *Not in* F **38 roots** = Q1/Q2. F = rots **48 wit** = Ed. F = wits **with** = Q1/Q2. F = hath **50 to his** = Q1/Q2. F = to to this **74 eager** *spelled* Aygre *in* F **76 barked** = Q1/Q2. F = bak'd **112–13 My tables, My tables** = F *(in one line).* Q1/Q2 *does not repeat* **122 SH HAMLET** = Q2. F = *Mar.* **123 Hillo** *spelled* Ilio *in* F **146 whirling** *spelled* hurling *in* F **150 Horatio** = Q2. F = my Lord **174 our** = Q1/Q2. F = for **194 they** = Q1/Q2. F = there
2.1.1 this = Q1/Q2. F = his **3 marvellous** *spelled* maruels *in* F **15 As** = Q2. F = And **67 carp** = Q2. F = Cape **120 feared** = Q2. F = feare
2.2.0 SD *with others* F *has the Latin 'Cum alijs'* **17 Whether** . . . **thus** = Q2. *Not in* F *(compositor's eyeskip?)* **46 lord? I** = Q2. F = lord? **48 and** = Q1/Q2. F = one **55 fruit** = Q2. F = Newes **129 solicitings** = Q2. F = soliciting **169 does** = Q2. F = ha's **205 that you read** = Q2. F = you meane **209 lack** = Q2. F = locke **229 SD** *Enter* . . . *Guildenstern placed one line later in* F **243 favours** = Q2. F = fauour **279 of** = Q1/Q2. *Not in* F **306 discovery, and** = Q2. F = discouery of **309 heavily** = Q2. F = heauenly **313 firmament** = Q2. *Not in* F **354 berattle** = F2. F = be-ratled **361 most like** = Ed. F = like most **403 Roscius, an** = F *(Rossius* an). Q1/Q2 = *Rossius* was an **407 came** = Q2. F = can **411 individable** = Q2. F = indiuible **431 pious** = Q2. F = *Pons*

435 valanced = Q2. F = valiant 448 caviar *spelled Caviarie in* F 456 as . . . fine = Q2. *Not in* F 457 One = Q2. F = One cheefe 469 total = Q1/Q2. F = to take 477 So, proceed you. = Q2. *Not in* F 483 matched = Q2. F = match 487 this = Q2. F = his 507 fellies *spelled* Fallies *in* F 515 mobled = Q1/Q2. F = inobled *(throughout)* 565 wanned = Q2. F = warm'd 592 bawdy = Q2. F = a Bawdy 595 Why = Q2. F = Who

3.1.33 here = Q2. F = there 48 please you = Q2. F = please ye 53 sugar = Q2. F = surge 77 proud = Q2. F = poore 82 would these = F. Q2 = would 93 away = F. Q2 = awry 104 I know = F. Q2 = you know 106 their perfume lost = Q2. F = then perfume left 117 with = Q1/Q2. F = your 141 nowhere = Q2. F = no way 151 paintings = Q1/Q2. F = pratlings 152 face = Q1/Q2. F = pace 153 jig *spelled* gidge *in* F 164 And = Q2. F = Haue 186 this = F. Q2 = his

3.2.5 with = Q2. *Not in* F 20 o'erstep = Q2. F = ore-stop 33 nor no man = Ed. F = or Norman 63 lick = Q2. F = like 65 fawning = Q2. F = faining 66 her = Q2. F = my 82 thy = Q2. F = my 87 stithy *spelled* Stythe *in* F heedful = Q2. F = needfull 101 mine now. = Ed. F = mine. Now 153 SH PROLOGUE = Ed. *Not in* F 159 SH PLAYER KING = Ed. F = *King.* 168 former = Q2. F = forme 188 you think = Q2. F = you. Think 198 either = Q2. F = other 199 enactures = Q2. F = ennactors 243 wince *spelled* winch *in* F 253 mis-take = Ed. F = mistake your = Q1/Q2. *Not in* F 295 SD *Enter . . . Guildenstern occurs four lines earlier in* F 324 as you = Q2. F = you 372 speak = Q2. *Not in* F 380 mass = Q2. F = Misse

3.3.15 weal = Q2. F = spirit 19 summit = Ed. F = Somnet

3.4.4 silence = F. *Sometimes emended to* sconce = conceal 13 a wicked = Q2. F = an idle *(probably picked up by compositor from previous line)* 37 better = Q2. F = Betters 50 sets = Q2. F = makes 72 brother = Q2. F = breath 86 And = Q2. F = As 120 do = Q2. *Not in* F 121 th'incorporal = Q2. F = their corporall 125 on = Ed. F = an 150 a = F. Q2 = that 157 ranker = Q2. F = ranke 158 these = Q2. F = this 180 bloat = Ed. F = blunt. Q2 = blowt 242 mother's closet = Q2. F = Mother Clossets

4.1.19 ape an apple = Ed. F = Ape. Q = an apple

4.2.7 ne'er *spelled* neerer *in* F 24 ourselves = Q2. F = our selfe 27 SH KING Alas . . . worm = Q2. *Not in* F *(probably due to printer's error)* 52 them = Q2. F = him

4.4.13 might = Q2. F = would 42 yield *spelled* dil'd *in* F 76 sorrows come = Q2. F = sorrows comes 77 battalions = Q2. F = Battaliaes 87 Feeds = Q2. F = Keepes 113 SH ALL FOLLOWERS = Ed. F = *All.* 119 that's calm = Q2. F = that calmes 148 is't = Q2. F = if 149 sweepstake *spelled* Soop-stake *in* F 154 pelican = Q2. F = Politician 162 SH ALL FOLLOWERS = Ed. *Not in* F 180 sing a-down = Q2. F = sing downe 185 pansies = Q2. F = Paconcies 210 commune = Q2. F = common

4.5.9 ambassador = Q2. F = Ambassadours 12 SH HORATIO = Ed. *Not in* F

4.6.26 aimed = Q2. F = arm'd 29 has = Ed. F = was 59 diest = Ed. F = diddest 71 since = Q2. F = hence 74 can = Q2. F = ran 97 What = Q2. F = Why 140 cunnings = Q2. F = commings 147 How now = F2. F = how 166 their = Q1/Q2. F = her 167 lay = Q2. F = buy

5.1.1 SH FIRST CLOWN = Ed. F = *Clown* 3 SH SECOND CLOWN = Ed. F = *Other* 11 to = Q2. F = an 99 of = Q2. F = of of quiddities = Q2. F = Quiddits 118 sirrah = Q2. F = Sir 160 sexton = Q2. F = sixteene 221 of = Q2. *Not in* F 250 treble woe = Q2. F = terrible woer 259 grief = Q2. F = griefes 261 Conjures = Q2. F = Coniure 272 SH HORATIO = Q2. F = *Gen.* 282 Woo't fast? = Q2. *Not in* F 295 couplets = Q2. F = Cuplet 303 your = Q2. F = you

5.2.31 villainies = Ed. F = Villaines 39 effect = Q2. F = effects 52 ordinant = Q2. F = ordinate 58 sequent = Q2. F = sement 62 defeat = Q2. F = debate 78 interim is = Q2. F = *interim's* 94 say = Q2. F = saw 117 king, sir = Q2. F = sir King 130 bet = Q2. F = but 134 laid on = Q2. F = one nine = Q2. F = mine 151 turn = Q2. F = tongue 155 has = Q2. F = had many = Q2. F = mine 165 ill all's = Q2. F = all 170 it = Q2. *Not in* F

197 brother = Q2. F = Mother   **204 ungored** = Q2. F = vngorg'd **274 own** = Q2. *Not in* F **277 swoons** *spelled* sounds *in* F **280 Ho!** *spelled* How! *in* F **321 SD** *shot* = Ed. F = *shout* **332 cracks** = Q2. F = cracke **338 This** = Q2. F = His **340 shot** = Q2. F = shoote **367 now** = Q1/Q2. F = are **368 also** = Q2. F = alwayes **371 while** = Q2. F = whiles

SECOND QUARTO PASSAGES THAT DO NOT APPEAR IN THE FOLIO

Lines are numbered continuously, for ease of reference.

Following 1.1.117:

BARNARDO I think it be no other but e'en so:
Well may it sort that this portentous figure
Comes armèd through our watch, so like the king
That was and is the question of these wars.

5   **HORATIO** A mote it is to trouble the mind's eye.
In the most high and palmy state of Rome,
A little ere the mightiest Julius fell,
The graves stood tenantless and the sheeted dead
Did squeak and gibber in the Roman streets:
10   As stars with trains of fire and dews of blood,
Disasters in the sun, and the moist star
Upon whose influence Neptune's empire stands
Was sick almost to doomsday with eclipse:
And even the like precurse of feared events,
15   As harbingers preceding still the fates
And prologue to the omen coming on,
Have heaven and earth together demonstrated
Unto our climatures and countrymen.—

Following 1.2.59:

      wrung from me my slow leave
20   By laboursome petition, and at last
Upon his will I sealed my hard consent.

---

1 e'en even, i.e. exactly   **2 sort** fit   **4 question** cause (of dispute)   **5 mote** speck, irritating particle   **6 palmy** triumphant, flourishing   **7 ere** before   **Julius** Julius Caesar, murdered by conspirators in 44 BC   **8 sheeted** shrouded   **9 squeak** ghosts were traditionally supposed to have thin high-pitched voices   **10 As** editors have speculated that a preceding line is missing **stars . . . fire** i.e. comets, signs of ill omen   **11 Disasters** unfavourable aspects (astrological term)   **moist star** i.e. the moon, which controls the tides   **12 Neptune** Roman god of the sea   **stands** depends   **13 to doomsday** as if it were Judgement Day (when, according to the Bible, the moon would grow dark)   **14 even . . . precurse** exactly the same foreshadowing **15 As harbingers** like forerunners   **still** always   **16 omen** calamity   **18 climatures** regions   **20 petition** entreaty **21 will** plays on the sense of 'legal document' (which Polonius fixed his seal on)   **hard** reluctant

Following 1.4.18:

This heavy-headed revel east and west
Makes us traduced and taxed of other nations:
They clepe us drunkards, and with swinish phrase
25 Soil our addition: and indeed it takes
From our achievements, though performed at height,
The pith and marrow of our attribute.
So, oft it chances in particular men
That for some vicious mole of nature in them,
30 As in their birth — wherein they are not guilty,
Since nature cannot choose his origin —
By their o'ergrowth of some complexion,
Oft breaking down the pales and forts of reason,
Or by some habit that too much o'erleavens
35 The form of plausive manners, that these men,
Carrying, I say, the stamp of one defect,
Being nature's livery, or fortune's star,
His virtues else — be they as pure as grace,
As infinite as man may undergo —
40 Shall in the general censure take corruption
From that particular fault: the dram of eale
Doth all the noble substance often douse,
To his own scandal.

Following 1.4.58:

The very place puts toys of desperation,
45 Without more motive, into every brain
That looks so many fathoms to the sea
And hears it roar beneath.

Following 3.2.174:

Where love is great, the littlest doubts are fear:
Where little fears grow great, great love grows there.

Following 3.2.219:

50 To desperation turn my trust and hope!
An anchor's cheer in prison be my scope,

---

22 east and west i.e. everywhere   **23 traduced . . . of** dishonoured and censured by   **24 clepe** call   **with swinish phrase** by calling us pigs   **25 addition** name, reputation   **takes** removes   **26 though . . . height** even though they are outstanding   **27 pith . . . attribute** very essence of our distinguished reputation   **29 for** because of   **mole** blemish   **30 As** for example   **32 o'ergrowth . . . complexion** excessive growth of some natural trait   **33 pales** fences, safeguards   **34 too much o'erleavens** spoils (as too much leaven ruins dough)   **35 plausive** pleasing, praiseworthy   **37 nature's livery** uniform designating one's servitude to nature   **38 virtues else** other virtues   **39 undergo** sustain   **40 general censure** public opinion/view of the man as a whole   **41 the . . . scandal** unclear; the general sense is 'even a tiny portion (**dram**) of polluting matter can bring a **noble substance** into disrepute' (or perhaps ' . . . corrupt a noble substance to its own shameful nature')   **eale** ale   **44 toys** wild thoughts   **desperation** the hopelessness or spiritual despair preceding suicide   **46 fathoms** a fathom is approximately six feet   **51 anchor's cheer** the provisions or lifestyle of an anchorite (i.e. hermit)   **scope** limit

Following 3.4.78 (before 'What devil was't'):

Sense sure, you have,
Else could you not have motion: but sure that sense
Is apoplexed, for madness would not err
55   Nor sense to ecstasy was ne'er so thralled
But it reserved some quantity of choice,
To serve in such a difference.

Following 3.4.79:

Eyes without feeling, feeling without sight,
Ears without hands or eyes, smelling *sans* all,
60   Or but a sickly part of one true sense
Could not so mope.

Following 3.4.165:

That monster, custom, who all sense doth eat
Of habits devil, is angel yet in this,
That to the use of actions fair and good
65   He likewise gives a frock or livery,
That aptly is put on.

Following 3.4.168 (before 'Once more, goodnight'):

the next more easy,
For use almost can change the stamp of nature,
And either [ ] the devil, or throw him out
70   With wondrous potency.

Following 3.4.177:

One word more, good lady.

Following 3.4.200:

HAMLET There's letters sealed: and my two schoolfellows,
Whom I will trust as I will adders fanged,
They bear the mandate, they must sweep my way,
75   And marshal me to knavery. Let it work:
For 'tis the sport to have the enginer
Hoist with his own petard: and't shall go hard
But I will delve one yard below their mines
And blow them at the moon. O, 'tis most sweet
80   When in one line two crafts directly meet.

---

52 Sense senses, feeling (in the following line the sense shifts to 'reason')   **53 motion** the power of movement/emotions and impulses **54 apoplexed** paralysed **err** err in this manner/err to this degree **55 ecstasy** madness **thralled** enslaved **56 quantity** small amount **57 serve ... difference** enable it to distinguish between the two men **59 *sans*** without **61 mope** be stupefied/wander aimlessly **62 sense ... devil** destroys all sensitivity to devilish practices **64 use** habit/ undertaking **65 frock** monk's clothing/man's coat/dress **livery** uniform **66 aptly** readily **68 use** habit **69 [ ]** a verb is missing here; editors often insert 'master' or, more recently, 'shame' **70 wondrous potency** extraordinary power **74 sweep my way** clear my path **75 marshal** guide **76 enginer** constructor of military engines (weaponry)/plotter **77 Hoist ... petard** blown up by his own bomb **and't ... But** and unless luck is against me **78 delve ... mines** i.e. countermine by digging deeper than and intercepting the enemy mines **80 crafts** cunning plots

Following 4.3.9:

Exeunt all [but the Captain]

Enter Hamlet, Rosencrantz and others

HAMLET Good sir, whose powers are these?

CAPTAIN They are of Norway, sir.

HAMLET How purposed, sir, I pray you?

CAPTAIN Against some part of Poland.

85   **HAMLET** Who commands them, sir?

CAPTAIN The nephew to old Norway, Fortinbras.

HAMLET Goes it against the main of Poland, sir,
    Or for some frontier?

CAPTAIN Truly to speak, and with no addition,
90   We go to gain a little patch of ground
    That hath in it no profit but the name.
    To pay five ducats, five, I would not farm it:
    Nor will it yield to Norway or the Pole
    A ranker rate, should it be sold in fee.

95   **HAMLET** Why, then the Polack never will defend it.

CAPTAIN Yes, it is already garrisoned.

HAMLET Two thousand souls and twenty thousand ducats
    Will not debate the question of this straw!
    This is th'imposthume of much wealth and peace,
100   That inward breaks, and shows no cause without
    Why the man dies. I humbly thank you, sir.

CAPTAIN God buy you, sir.   *[Exit]*

ROSENCRANTZ Will't please you go, my lord?

HAMLET I'll be with you straight: go a little

[Exeunt all but Hamlet]

105   How all occasions do inform against me,
    And spur my dull revenge. What is a man,
    If his chief good and market of his time
    Be but to sleep and feed? A beast, no more.
    Sure he that made us with such large discourse,
110   Looking before and after, gave us not
    That capability and godlike reason
    To fust in us unused. Now, whether it be
    Bestial oblivion, or some craven scruple
    Of thinking too precisely on th'event —
115   A thought which, quartered, hath but one part wisdom
    And ever three parts coward — I do not know
    Why yet I live to say this thing's to do,
    Sith I have cause and will and strength and means
    To do't. Examples gross as earth exhort me:

81 **powers** troops   87 **main** main part   89 **addition** exaggeration   92 **farm** rent   94 **ranker** higher   **fee** fee simple, i.e. sold outright, with no conditions   98 **Will...straw** are not enough to fight out this trifling issue   99 **th'imposthume** the abscess   102 **buy** i.e. be with   104 **straight** straight away   105 **inform against** betray/bring a charge against 107 **market** profit   109 **discourse** powers of reasoning   110 **Looking...after** able to look ahead and to assess what is past   112 **fust** moulder   113 **oblivion** forgetfulness   **craven** cowardly   114 **Of** resulting from   **precisely** scrupulously th'**event** the outcome   117 **to do** i.e. yet to be done   118 **Sith** since   119 **gross** obvious/large/material, earthly

120   Witness this army of such mass and charge
         Led by a delicate and tender prince,
         Whose spirit with divine ambition puffed
         Makes mouths at the invisible event,
         Exposing what is mortal and unsure
125   To all that fortune, death and danger dare,
         Even for an eggshell. Rightly to be great
         Is not to stir without great argument,
         But greatly to find quarrel in a straw
         When honour's at the stake. How stand I then,
130   That have a father killed, a mother stained,
         Excitements of my reason and my blood,
         And let all sleep, while to my shame I see
         The imminent death of twenty thousand men
         That, for a fantasy and trick of fame,
135   Go to their graves like beds, fight for a plot
         Whereon the numbers cannot try the cause,
         Which is not tomb enough and continent
         To hide the slain? O, from this time forth,
         My thoughts be bloody, or be nothing worth!   *Exit*

Following 4.6.43:

140   Of him that brought them.

Following 4.6.71 (before 'Some two months since'):

LAERTES My lord, I will be ruled,
         The rather, if you could devise it so
         That I might be the organ.

KING It falls right.
145   You have been talked of since your travel much,
         And that in Hamlet's hearing, for a quality
         Wherein they say you shine: your sum of parts
         Did not together pluck such envy from him
         As did that one, and that, in my regard,
150   Of the unworthiest siege.

LAERTES What part is that, my lord?

KING A very ribbon in the cap of youth,
         Yet needful too, for youth no less becomes
         The light and careless livery that it wears
155   Than settled age his sables and his weeds
         Importing health and graveness.

120 mass and charge size and cost   **121 delicate** fine/skilled/elegant   **tender** youthful   **123 Makes mouths** makes faces, i.e. is scornful   **invisible event** unforseeable outcome   **125 dare** can do/can threaten   **126 Rightly...great** i.e. true greatness   **127 stir** i.e. take up arms   **great argument** a noble cause   **128 greatly...straw** to find great cause for contention over a trifle   **131 Excitements** incitements, provocations   **blood** anger/passion   **134 fantasy and trick** illusory and deceptive whim   **fame** reputation, honour   **135 plot** plot of land   **136 Whereon...cause** which is not big enough to hold the soldiers who are to fight for it   **137 continent** (sufficiently large) container; plays on the sense of 'land'   **143 organ** instrument, agent (of Hamlet's death)   **144 falls right** fits well   **147 your...parts** all of your other qualitites   **150 unworthiest siege** least importance   **152 ribbon** i.e. mere adornment/crowning accomplishment   **153 becomes** suits   **155 sables** garments trimmed with sable fur   **weeds** clothing/mourning garments   **156 health** well-being/ prosperity

Following 4.6.92 (before 'Sir, this report'):

> The scrimers of their nation,
> He swore had neither motion, guard, nor eye,
> If you opposed them.

Following 4.6.105:

160 There lives within the very flame of love
A kind of wick or snuff that will abate it:
And nothing is at a like goodness still,
For goodness, growing to a pleurisy,
Dies in his own too much. That we would do,
165 We should do when we would, for this 'would' changes
And hath abatements and delays as many
As there are tongues, are hands, are accidents,
And then this 'should' is like a spendthrift sigh
That hurts by easing. But, to the quick of th'ulcer:

Following 5.2.111:

170 Sir, here is newly come to court Laertes — believe me, an absolute
gentleman, full of most excellent differences, of very soft society and great
showing: indeed, to speak feelingly of him, he is the card or calendar of
gentry, for you shall find in him the continent of what part a gentleman
would see.

175 **HAMLET** Sir, his definement suffers no perdition in you, though I know, to
divide him inventorially would dizzy th'arithmetic of memory, and yet but
yaw neither, in respect of his quick sail. But, in the verity of extolment, I
take him to be a soul of great article and his infusion of such dearth and
rareness as, to make true diction of him, his semblable is his mirror and
180 who else would trace him his umbrage, nothing more.

OSRIC Your lordship speaks most infallibly of him.

HAMLET The concernancy, sir? Why do we wrap the gentleman in our more
rawer breath?

OSRIC Sir?

185 **HORATIO** Is't not possible to understand in another tongue? You will do't, sir,
really.

---

157 scrimers fencers (from the French *escrimeur*)   **158 motion** skilled and trained movements   **eye** quick perception
162 is … still remains always at the same degree of goodness   **163 pleurisy** excess/chest inflammation   **164 too much**
excess   **That** that which   **would** wish to   **167 tongues … accidents** i.e. tongues to dissuade one, hands to prevent one and
chance events to get in the way   **168 spendthrift** i.e. wasteful; each **sigh** was thought to drain a drop of blood from the
heart   **169 hurts by easing** harms the heart at the same time as it eases the immediate emotional pain of the sufferer   **quick**
tender central part   **170 absolute** perfect, accomplished   **171 differences** fine qualities   **soft society** pleasant company/
sociable manners   **great showing** fine appearance   **172 feelingly** to the purpose, with just perception   **card or calendar**
map or guide   **173 the … see** one who contains any quality a gentleman would wish to see   **175 definement** definition
(Hamlet begins to mock Osric's affected language)   **perdition** loss   **you** i.e. your account of him   **to … inventorially** to list his
qualities, to itemize him   **176 but … sail** merely swing unsteadily off course in comparison to his speedy sailing (i.e. Laertes
outstrips attempts to define his virtues)   **177 in … extolment** to praise him truthfully   **178 of great article** highly
accomplished, with many qualities to list in an inventory   **infusion** essence (literally, what has been infused into him)   **dearth**
rarity/costliness   **179 make … diction** speak truly   **his … mirror** the only person truly like him is his reflection in a
mirror   **who** whoever   **180 trace** follow/imitate   **his umbrage** is his shadow   **181 infallibly** absolutely truly   **182 The
concernancy, sir?** Why is all this relevant?   **183 rawer breath** crude words that cannot do him justice   **185 in another
tongue** i.e. when someone speaks your own elaborate language   **do't** get there in the end

HAMLET What imports the nomination of this gentleman?

OSRIC Of Laertes?

HORATIO His purse is empty already: all's golden words are spent.

190 HAMLET Of him, sir.

OSRIC I know you are not ignorant—

HAMLET I would you did, sir. Yet in faith if you did, it would not much approve me. Well, sir?

OSRIC You are not ignorant of what excellence Laertes is—

195 HAMLET I dare not confess that, lest I should compare with him in excellence: but to know a man well were to know himself.

OSRIC I mean, sir, for his weapon: but in the imputation laid on him, by them in his meed, he's unfellowed.

Following 5.2.122:

HORATIO I knew you must be edified by the margent ere you had done.

Following 5.2.161:

Enter a Lord

200 LORD My lord, his majesty commended him to you by young Osric, who brings back to him that you attend him in the hall: he sends to know if your pleasure hold to play with Laertes or that you will take longer time.

HAMLET I am constant to my purposes, they follow the king's pleasure: if his fitness speaks, mine is ready. Now or whensoever, provided I be so able as

205 now.

LORD The king and queen and all are coming down.

HAMLET In happy time.

LORD The queen desires you to use some gentle entertainment to Laertes before you fall to play.

210 HAMLET She well instructs me.

[*Exit Lord*]

---

187 nomination naming **193 approve me** commend me, be to my credit **195 I ... himself** I do not dare to admit that I know just how excellent a man Laertes is lest I should seem to be comparing myself favourably with him: to know a man well one must first know oneself **197 for** i.e. with **in ... unfellowed** in the estimation of those in his pay (i.e. servants/fencing masters), he is unparalleled/in the estimation of others, he's unmatched by any man of comparable worth and honour **199 edified ... margent** instructed by the explanatory notes in the margin **201 that** if **203 if ... ready** my readiness waits on his convenience **207 In happy time** at an opportune moment **208 use ... entertainment** give a courteous reception

TEXTUAL NOTES

Q2 = Second Quarto text of 1604/05
Q3 = a correction introduced in the Third Quarto text of 1611
Ed = a correction introduced by a later editor

5 mote *spelled* moth *in* Q2 **14 feared** = Ed. Q2 = feare **24 clepe** *spelled* clip *in* Q2 **42 often douse** = Ed. Q2 = of a doubt **51 An anchor's** = Ed. Q2 = And Anchors **168 spendthrift** = Ed. Q2 = spend thirfts **172 feelingly** = Q3. Q2 = fellingly *(in some copies)* sellingly *(in other copies)* **176 dizzy** = Q3. Q2 = dosie *(in some copies)* dazzie *(in other copies)* **181 SH OSRIC** = F. Q2 = *Cour. (for courtier)*

SCENE-BY-SCENE ANALYSIS

ACT 1 SCENE 1

Lines 1–14: The play begins with a question, as the guards Barnardo and Francisco swap shifts and Barnardo asks 'Who's there?', evoking the themes of identity, uncertainty and existence which indicate that this is a reflective play, often with more emphasis on thought and speech than on action. The information that it is midnight reinforces setting, with ideas of night and darkness and the associated themes of secrecy/deception. It also introduces the concept of 'balance' between two opposites: the play begins at the point between one day and another, a literal representation of this 'balance' between key themes and motifs such as day/night, words/actions, physical/spiritual and appearance/reality.

Lines 15–117: Marcellus brings Horatio to witness an 'apparition' that he and the sentinels have previously seen, as Horatio thinks they have imagined the whole thing. Barnardo begins to describe a previous encounter when the Ghost appears. Commenting on its resemblance to the late king, they urge it to speak, but the Ghost leaves in silence. Shaken, Horatio says that he would not believe it 'Without the sensible and true avouch' of his 'own eyes', a statement that raises the theme of sight/perception. He adds that the appearance of the Ghost 'bodes some strange eruption to our state', establishing that the play functions on a national/public level, often in tension with the individual/personal. Marcellus asks why Denmark appears to be preparing for war. Horatio explains that the late king conquered lands belonging to Norway and that the young Norwegian prince, Fortinbras, is preparing to take them back.

Lines 118–168: The Ghost reappears and, as Horatio attempts to make it speak, a cock crows. Horatio instructs Marcellus to 'Stop it' and Marcellus strikes at the Ghost, which leaves again. Horatio suggests that they tell Prince Hamlet what they have seen, as, if it really is the Ghost of his father, it will speak to him.

ACT 1 SCENE 2

Lines 1–128: King Claudius (whose name is never mentioned in the dialogue) makes a speech to court, expressing his grief at the death of his brother and announcing that he has married his brother's widow, Queen Gertrude: 'With mirth in funeral and with dirge in marriage, / In equal scale weighing delight and dole', again suggesting balance between opposites. The speech is formal and ceremonious, as Claudius emphasizes his new role as king, but it seems awkward as well: it is difficult to reconcile his apparent grief with his happiness at his marriage. Claudius also announces that Fortinbras is demanding the 'surrender' of the captured Norwegian lands, and he sends two Ambassadors to inform the King of Norway, Fortinbras' elderly uncle, of his nephew's actions. Laertes asks for permission to return to his studies in France now that he has shown his duty in attending Claudius' coronation. Claudius agrees, provided Laertes has Polonius' permission, which is given. Three sets of father/son relationships have now been established, emphasizing the importance of this particular family dynamic to the play. Claudius turns to Hamlet, addressing him as 'my son', and asks him why 'the clouds still hang' on him, to which Hamlet replies that he is 'too much i'th'sun'. This pun on 'son/sun' establishes the wordplay that is a key feature of this play, particularly in Hamlet's speeches. Language/words are focused on and explored throughout in terms of the complexities of 'meaning', and also as an opposition to action. Gertrude asks Hamlet to stop wearing mourning for his father, but Hamlet responds that his grief goes much deeper than 'the trappings and the suits of woe', reinforcing the theme of appearance and reality and the motif of clothing. He argues that there is a difference between what is 'within' and external appearances, which are something a 'man might play', an expression that raises the theme of performance/theatre. Claudius accuses Hamlet of 'impious stubbornness', and calls his grief 'unmanly', one of several reflections on gender. In a more conciliatory tone, he asks Hamlet to think of him as a father, and says that he would prefer him to remain in court rather than returning to university in Wittenberg. Gertrude adds her 'prayers' that Hamlet will remain, and he agrees.

Lines 129–272: Alone, Hamlet embarks on the first of the many soliloquies that reveal his introspective nature. He wishes that he could die and that his 'too solid flesh would melt', emphasizing the opposing elements of physical and spiritual as he also regrets that suicide is a sin against God. He contemplates the 'stale' nature of the world, comparing it to an 'unweeded garden' filled with 'things rank and gross in nature', establishing the recurring motif of decay/infection. He reveals his disgust at his mother's remarriage and the 'wicked speed' with which she moved between 'incestuous sheets'. He recalls how much she appeared to love his father, blaming her behaviour on the fickle nature of her sex: 'frailty, thy name is woman!' Horatio, Barnardo and Marcellus arrive. Horatio tells Hamlet about seeing his father's Ghost. Hamlet resolves to watch that night and to try to speak to it. After they leave, he contemplates what the appearance of the 'armed' Ghost means, suspecting 'some foul play'.

ACT 1 SCENE 3

Laertes says goodbye to his sister, Ophelia. He warns her against 'Hamlet and the trifling of his favours', saying that, while Hamlet may love her now, their difference of rank is too great for him to marry Ophelia and so she must not open her 'chaste treasure' to him. Ophelia says that she will do as he asks, but reminds him that he must not preach virtue to her and then behave immorally himself. Polonius arrives and urges his son to board the ship, which is ready to sail. He kindly, but pompously, gives Laertes a great deal of advice and bids him farewell. Laertes urges Ophelia to remember what he has said and leaves. Polonius asks Ophelia what Laertes meant and, hearing that it concerns Hamlet, repeats Laertes' advice in harsher, more realistic terms. He forbids Ophelia to 'give words or talk with the Lord Hamlet', and Ophelia obeys with a readiness that demonstrates her father's authority over her.

ACT 1 SCENE 4

Hamlet, Horatio and Marcellus wait for the Ghost as sounds of revelry from the court are heard in the background. The Ghost appears and Hamlet declares his intention to speak to it, whether it is 'a spirit of health or goblin damned', raising the possibility that the Ghost is a malevolent force and reminding us that appearances are subjective. The Ghost beckons and Hamlet follows, despite Horatio and Marcellus' attempts to stop him.

ACT 1 SCENE 5

Lines 1–118: The Ghost tells Hamlet that he is his father's spirit, 'Doomed for a certain time to walk the night', and asks Hamlet to revenge his murder. The ghostly request for revenge is a key element of the 'revenge tragedy', a genre that is acknowledged throughout the play, but also consciously explored and challenged. Hamlet begs to hear more, so that he may 'sweep' to his revenge. The Ghost explains that Hamlet's father was not, as everyone believes, killed by a snake's bite. He tells Hamlet that Claudius first seduced the 'seeming virtuous queen', Gertrude, and then killed him by pouring poison in his ear as he slept (a literal representation of the rumour and plotting in the play). He urges Hamlet to kill Claudius, but says that he must spare Gertrude, who will be punished by her own guilt: 'the thorns that in her bosom lodge'. Morning approaches and the Ghost leaves, urging Hamlet to remember him. Alone, Hamlet swears that he will remember nothing else.

Lines 119–207: Horatio and Marcellus find Hamlet and question him, but he reveals nothing except that 'There's ne'er a villain dwelling in all Denmark / But he's an arrant knave', a statement that is both true and meaningless, showing the ambiguity of language and Hamlet's control over it. Hamlet asks his companions to swear on his sword that they will never reveal what they have seen that night. The voice of the Ghost repeats 'swear', and Horatio and Marcellus do so. Hamlet's disjointed speech reveals his state of mind as he thinks about what he has heard. Establishing the theme of sanity/madness, he hints that he may in the future pretend to be mad: 'put an antic disposition on', and asks them not to reveal what they know, whatever happens.

ACT 2 SCENE 1

Polonius sends Reynaldo to Paris with messages and money for his son, but tells him that first he is to spy on Laertes and spread rumours about him to the effect that he is 'very wild'. Ironically, he explains that the purpose behind these lies is to discover the truth about Laertes' behaviour. He shows Reynaldo how to subtly generate rumours, demonstrating the potential distance between words and truth. The conversation reveals tensions in the characterization of Polonius: his instructions to Reynaldo show cunning, but the reason for them seems nonsensical and foolish. The latter aspect to his character is emphasized by his long-windedness and temporary forgetfulness mid-speech, requiring Reynaldo to 'prompt' him in a moment that becomes almost meta-theatrical. Reynaldo leaves and Ophelia enters, telling Polonius that she has been 'affrighted' by Hamlet, who appeared in her chamber half-dressed and looking 'As if he had been loosèd out of hell'. She reports that Hamlet did not speak, but just held her arm and stared at her face. Polonius decides that Hamlet has gone mad with love for Ophelia and goes to tell Claudius.

ACT 2 SCENE 2

Lines 1–89: Claudius greets Rosencrantz and Guildenstern, former schoolfellows of Hamlet. He explains that he is worried about Hamlet and suggests that they might spend time with him and find out whether there is anything 'unknown' afflicting him. Although Claudius presents this as kindly concern, revealing his capacity as an 'actor', we are reminded of Polonius' attempts to spy on Laertes. Rosencrantz and Guildenstern agree to help, and are taken to find Hamlet. Polonius brings the news that the Ambassadors have arrived back from Norway and adds that he has found the 'very cause of Hamlet's lunacy'. He insists that Claudius sees the Ambassadors first, however, and goes to fetch them. The Ambassadors report that the king of Norway believed Fortinbras was preparing for war on Poland, but found out that it was really against Denmark. He ordered Fortinbras to cease plotting against Denmark and genuinely prepare to fight Poland. The King of Norway sends a request that Claudius will grant him 'quiet pass' through his lands, and Claudius promises to consider it.

Lines 90–232: Despite declaring that he will be brief, Polonius embarks on a lengthy and rambling explanation of Hamlet's madness that demonstrates his obsequious attitude to the king and queen. He reads out a love letter from Hamlet to Ophelia and explains that he instructed Ophelia not to encourage Hamlet because of the difference in their status. He explains that Hamlet's madness stems from being 'repulsèd' by Ophelia. Claudius and Gertrude ask Polonius if he is certain and he offers to prove it, suggesting a plan: he will 'loose' Ophelia to Hamlet, and then hide behind an arras with Claudius to watch the encounter. His choice of vocabulary reduces Ophelia to the level of an animal, demonstrating her powerlessness and her status as one her father's possessions. Claudius agrees to the plan and, as Hamlet enters, he and Gertrude leave. Polonius greets Hamlet, who appears not to recognize him. Hamlet's disjointed and nonsensical speech suggests madness, but many of his remarks contain implicit comments/criticisms on Polonius' character. This uncertainty as to the extent and veracity of Hamlet's madness has been the subject of much debate in the play's critical history, as the audience remains uncertain as to whether he is really mad or merely acting, or, perhaps, there is a genuine disturbance due to his father's death that he is exaggerating for his own purposes. Rosencrantz and Guildenstern arrive and Polonius leaves.

Lines 233–391: Hamlet seems pleased to see Rosencrantz and Guildenstern, but asks them why they have come to the 'prison' of Denmark. They cheerfully claim that they have come solely to see Hamlet, but he tells them that he knows that Claudius and Gertrude sent for them. Our perception of Hamlet's sanity is further confused during this exchange, as his manner towards Rosencrantz and Guildenstern is introspective and melancholy, but shows nothing of the 'madness' he portrayed to Polonius. Rosencrantz tells him that they have engaged a group of 'Players', 'the tragedians of the city', that Hamlet has previously enjoyed watching. The presence of the Players further develops the theme of theatre/performance and the conversation about them establishes a meta-theatrical commentary on the conventions of genre, as Hamlet lists various recognizable 'roles' (the 'adventurous knight', the 'lover' and the 'clown', for example). A flourish announces the arrival of the Players and Hamlet tells Rosencrantz and Guildenstern that they are 'welcome to Elsinore', adding that his 'uncle-father and aunt-mother are deceived' about his madness, a description that emphasizes the 'incestuous' nature of Claudius and Gertrude's relationship, and the uncomfortably close nature of various family dynamics in the play.

Lines 392–559: Polonius returns, and Hamlet switches back to a more disjointed pattern of speech. He breaks off to welcome the Players and asks one man to recite a speech about the fall of Troy, which he begins and which is then taken up by the First Player, emphasizing Hamlet's potential role as an 'actor'. Pleased with the recital, Hamlet asks Polonius to 'see the players well bestowed' and asks for a performance of *The Murder of Gonzago* the next day, adding that he has written 'some dozen or sixteen lines' that he would like them to add.

Lines 560–617: Hamlet's soliloquy reveals his anguish at his own inaction, a factor that conflicts with his potential role of revenge hero and one of the ways in which the play challenges expectations of genre. He comments that the player who gave the speech was able to summon emotion for a character in a play, whereas he himself is a 'dull and muddy-mettled rascal' who remains unmotivated by a genuine 'cue for passion'. The tensions between actions and words are explored again, as Hamlet comments that, despite being 'Prompted to [his] revenge by heaven and hell', all he does is 'unpack' his heart 'with words'. He outlines his plan to establish Claudius' guilt: the Players will act out 'something like' the death of his father, while he watches Claudius' reaction. This will give him proof that Claudius really did commit the murder and allay his concern that the spirit might have been 'the devil', working to damn him, rather than the genuine Ghost of his father.

ACT 3 SCENE 1

Lines 1–61: Claudius questions Rosencrantz and Guildenstern. They report that they cannot find out what is troubling Hamlet, who has evaded their questions 'with a crafty madness'. The king tells them to encourage Hamlet's interest in the players and they leave. Claudius asks Gertrude to leave, so that he and Polonius may secretly observe the arranged meeting between Ophelia and Hamlet. Polonius 'directs' Ophelia in how she is to act, drawing attention once more to theatre/performance and appearance/reality as he comments on how a 'pious action' can 'sugar o'er / The devil himself'. This prompts an aside about his 'conscience' from Claudius, the first implicit acknowledgement of his guilt that he has made. Hearing Hamlet approach, they withdraw, forming a dual audience to the action, further revealing the play's self-conscious theatricality.

Lines 62–170: Hamlet appears to be contemplating suicide as he asks himself: 'To be, or not to be', although the question can be considered in a more abstract way than just Hamlet's choice over whether to live or die, and can potentially transcend the action of the play as a philosophical argument. It returns us to the concept of 'balance', between flesh/spirit and action/inaction, as Hamlet is torn between a passive acceptance of life's events, 'to suffer / The slings and arrows of outrageous fortune', and definitive resistance to them: 'to take arms against a sea of troubles, / And by opposing end them'. Hamlet breaks off as he sees Ophelia, who tries to return some love-tokens that he has previously given her. Hamlet's disjointed responses become a wild verbal attack on Ophelia that further complicates our understanding of his mental state, seeming too extreme to be merely acting. It is also difficult to distinguish whether Hamlet's outburst is personal and related directly to his feelings for Ophelia, or an attack on all women and their sexuality, possibly generated by his disgust at his mother's relationship with his uncle. He repeatedly tells Ophelia to go 'to a nunnery', and then leaves abruptly. Ophelia laments the loss of Hamlet's 'sovereign reason'.

Lines 171–198: Claudius and Polonius discuss what they have overheard. Claudius is not convinced that Hamlet's madness is the result of love, nor, indeed, that Hamlet is actually mad. He says that there is something in Hamlet's soul 'O'er which his melancholy sits on brood' and that he is worried that the 'hatch and the disclose' of this thing will be 'some danger' (although he does not acknowledge aloud the fear that the danger will be to himself). He resolves to send Hamlet to England, claiming that the change might 'expel' the 'something-settled matter' from his heart. Polonius agrees, but still insists that Hamlet's problem is 'neglected love'. He suggests a further test of this: Queen Gertrude will speak 'all alone' to her son, and 'entreat him / To show his griefs', while Polonius will conceal himself again and listen to the exchange.

ACT 3 SCENE 2

The performance of the play-within-the-play makes the theme of theatre/performance explicit and focuses attention on the nature of 'reality'. The presence of a dual audience also emphasizes the theme of sight/perception, as we watch the characters watching a play, and, more specifically, Hamlet secretly observing Claudius (neatly reversing their roles of observed/observer from the previous scene).

Lines 1–139: Hamlet directs the players as to how he wants them to deliver the lines he has written, urging them to 'suit the action to the word, the word to the action' – an ironic instruction given the apparent disparity between words and actions in the wider play. The players go to prepare and Hamlet sends Polonius, Rosencrantz and Guildenstern to 'hasten' them. Horatio arrives and Hamlet excitedly explains his plan and tells him to watch Claudius. Horatio agrees, and the king and queen enter in a formal procession with other members of the court, accompanied by guards and torchbearers. This ceremony emphasizes the public setting for this scene, which contrasts with the concealed secrets, emotions and intentions of the various characters. Hamlet continues to disconcert everyone with his changeable speech, including some bawdy wordplay directed at Ophelia that emphasizes his fixation with women in terms of their sexuality. Music sounds, and the dumb show begins.

Lines 140–271: The dumb show establishes the plot of the play-within-the-play, and the events surrounding the death of Hamlet's father in the wider play. This paralleling of storylines creates meta-theatrical awareness, emphasized by Ophelia's comment, 'Belike this show imports the argument of the play'. The full performance begins, with asides from Hamlet as he comments on and explains the action for the others. Ophelia says that he makes a 'good chorus', emphasizing his capacity as an 'actor' but also highlighting that, despite this, he is often slightly distanced from the action, observing and commenting rather than participating. Hamlet responds to Ophelia with his usual harsh, deliberately sexual, wordplay. As we reach the point in the play-within-the-play where 'Lucianus' kills 'Gonzago' by pouring poison in his ear, Claudius rushes out, calling for light and throwing the court into confusion.

Lines 272–402: Hamlet and Horatio discuss Claudius' behaviour and Horatio's more measured response contrasts with Hamlet's wild exclamations of conviction as to his uncle's guilt. Rosencrantz and Guildenstern come to report that the king is 'marvellous distem-pered' and that they have been sent by Gertrude to fetch Hamlet. Despite their attempts to make Hamlet respond in a more reasoned way and put his 'discourse into some frame', he continues to disconcert them with his unpredictable speech and behaviour. He accuses them of trying to 'play' him as they might play a musical instrument. Polonius interrupts and tells Hamlet to go to his mother. When he is left alone, Hamlet prepares himself to see Gertrude, declaring that he will be 'cruel', but 'not unnatural' and that although he will 'speak daggers' he will 'use none'.

ACT 3 SCENE 3

Claudius tells Rosencrantz and Guildenstern that he is sending Hamlet to England immediately as he does not feel that it is safe 'To let his madness range'. He instructs them that they are to accompany Hamlet, and they go to prepare for the voyage. Polonius brings the news that Hamlet is going to speak to Gertrude and that he intends to conceal himself so as to 'hear the process'. Once alone, Claudius makes his first direct admission of guilt: he has committed an act that has 'the primal eldest curse upon't, / A brother's murder'. Claudius' conscience appears to be troubling him as he tries to pray but cannot and, although he wishes to be forgiven for his sin, he does not wish to give up the 'effects' it has brought him: his 'crown', his 'ambition' and his 'queen'. He wonders whether it is possible to 'be pardoned and retain th'offence'. He kneels and attempts to pray. Hamlet enters and, seeing Claudius, prepares to kill him. Once more, however, the expected progress of the revenge tragedy is frustrated as Hamlet shifts from a definite declaration of action, 'now I'll do't', to further uncertainty. Emphasizing the opposing concepts of the physical/spiritual aspects to humanity, he considers the spiritual consequences of killing Claudius. He argues that, if he kills Claudius while he is at prayer, then Claudius' soul will go to heaven, which would be more of a reward than a punishment. Deciding to wait until Claudius is 'about some act / That has no relish of salvation in't' so that 'his soul may be as damned and black / As hell, whereto it goes', Hamlet puts up his sword and leaves. Claudius, unaware of Hamlet's presence, rises and ironically announces that he could not pray, as 'Words without thoughts never to heaven go'.

ACT 3 SCENE 4

Lines 1–43: Polonius arranges with Gertrude that he will conceal himself behind the arras to overhear her conversation with Hamlet. Hamlet arrives, and Gertrude accuses him of offending his father (meaning Claudius). He responds that it is she who has offended, referring to his actual father. He continues to parry her attempts to question him, demonstrating his characteristic verbal dexterity, and then insists that she sit down so that he may show her 'the inmost part' of herself. Frightened that Hamlet intends to attack her, Gertrude cries out and Polonius responds, calling for help from behind the arras. In an unusual moment of spontaneous action, Hamlet stabs the concealed figure, believing it to be Claudius. When he discovers that he has killed Polonius, he is unmoved, merely saying 'Thou wretched, rash, intruding fool, farewell', before turning once more to his mother.

Lines 44–104: Gertrude asks what she has done to deserve Hamlet's anger. He shows her two pictures, one of his father and one of Claudius, 'The counterfeit presentment of two brothers', a visual symbol of the theme of identity. He urges her to look at the picture of his father, 'Jove himself', and to compare it with a picture of Claudius, who is 'like a mildewed ear' of corn. He asks her how she could 'step' from one to the other, showing his bitterness and disgust. Despite Gertrude's attempts to stop him, he continues to accuse her, focusing particularly on the sexual aspect of her betrayal. Distressed, Gertrude claims that Hamlet has revealed her 'very soul', which has 'such black and grained spots'. As she begs 'No more!' the Ghost appears.

Lines 105–207: Hamlet fears that the Ghost has come to 'chide' him for not taking revenge on Claudius, and the Ghost urges him to act, claiming that he is there 'to whet' Hamlet's 'almost blunted purpose'. As they talk, it becomes clear that Gertrude cannot see the Ghost. Hamlet urges her to 'look' as the Ghost leaves them, but Gertrude takes this as a sign of his insanity. Hamlet insists that he is 'But mad in craft' and urges his mother to repent of her sins and avoid any further relationship with Claudius. He asks her to keep his feigned madness a secret and she agrees. He leaves, dragging Polonius' body with him.

Lines 208–248: Gertrude tells Claudius that Hamlet is 'Mad as the seas and wind' in a storm, although it is uncertain whether she is lying to Claudius or still believes this to be true. She reports how Hamlet killed Polonius, and Claudius uses this as his excuse to send Hamlet to England. Sustaining his performance of grief at his nephew's behaviour, he orders Rosencrantz and Guildenstern to find Hamlet and take Polonius' body to the chapel.

ACT 4 SCENE 1

Hamlet enters, commenting that Polonius is 'safely stowed'. Rosencrantz and Guildenstern come to ask what he has done with the body and Hamlet accuses them of being 'sponges' out of which Claudius may squeeze information. He agrees to see the king, but leaves, running, with Rosencrantz and Guildenstern following.

ACT 4 SCENE 2

Claudius contemplates the danger he is in while Hamlet 'goes loose', but says that he cannot 'put the strong law on him' because Hamlet is loved by Denmark's people. He compares sending Hamlet away to ridding himself of a disease, reinforcing previous references to infection/decay. Rosencrantz arrives and reports that Hamlet will not reveal the whereabouts of the body, but that they have managed to get him to come to Claudius. Guildenstern brings Hamlet in and Claudius demands Polonius' body. Hamlet gives a nonsensical, macabre response, but eventually tells them that they will 'nose him' in the lobby, another image of decay that emphasizes the corporeal, rather than spiritual, aspect of death. Claudius sends someone to find the body and, pretending great sorrow, informs Hamlet that he must go to England immediately as a result of his actions. Hamlet apparently agrees and Claudius sends Rosencrantz and Guildenstern to hurry Hamlet on board the ship. When they have left, Claudius' soliloquy reveals that he is sending letters to the English, instructing them to kill Hamlet.

ACT 4 SCENE 3

Fortinbras, marching across stage with his army, sends a messenger to tell Claudius that he is claiming safe passage across Denmark. In the Quarto version of the play (see 'Second Quarto Passages that do not appear in the Folio'), Hamlet witnesses the march and contrasts Fortinbras' willingness to 'find quarrel in a straw' when his honour is affronted to his own inaction in the face of monstrous provocation.

ACT 4 SCENE 4

Lines 1–110: Horatio persuades Gertrude to see Ophelia, who has been sent mad by the death of her father. Ophelia reveals a genuine, pitiful, madness that contrasts with the potentially more contrived or exaggerated moments of Hamlet's insanity. She speaks mostly in rhyme and, while her ideas are disjointed and largely nonsensical, they focus on death and sex. Ophelia leaves and Claudius sends Horatio to watch over her. He laments recent events, and comments to Gertrude that the people of Denmark are stirred up by Polonius' death and have become 'Thick and unwholesome in their thoughts and whispers'. They are interrupted by a messenger, bringing the news that Laertes has stormed Elsinore.

Lines 111–229: Laertes breaks in, demanding vengeance for his father's death, creating parallels and contrasts with Hamlet, as Laertes also becomes a potential 'revenge hero'. In contrast to Hamlet's hesitant and thoughtful approach, Laertes is intent on action and his assertion that he will 'dare damnation' shows that he has less consideration for the moral/spiritual issues raised by revenge. The king and queen explain that Claudius is not responsible for Polonius' death and Laertes is calmer, until Ophelia returns. He is aghast at the change in his sister, who continues to sing in a distracted way and distributes flowers (possibly imaginary) such as 'rosemary' for 'remembrance' and 'pansies' for 'thoughts'. She sings a lament, and leaves. Laertes calls on the gods as Claudius tries to calm him. He promises to help Laertes get revenge, saying that 'where th'offence is, let the great axe fall'.

ACT 4 SCENE 5

Sailors bring Horatio a letter from Hamlet. Hamlet explains that he was captured by pirates who have returned him to Denmark, while Rosencrantz and Guildenstern are still bound for England. He asks Horatio to see that some enclosed letters are given to Claudius and then to come to him.

ACT 4 SCENE 6

Laertes asks why Claudius did not take public action against Hamlet for Polonius' death. Claudius persuades him that it was because both the queen and the Danish people love Hamlet and he did not wish to upset her or cause trouble. A messenger brings the letter from Hamlet, announcing that he has returned to Denmark and asking to see Claudius the next day. The king is confused, but Laertes is pleased as it means he can confront and kill Hamlet. Claudius sees a way to rid himself of Hamlet and urges Laertes to take his revenge and show that he is his father's son 'in deed / More than in words', again forcing a comparison with Hamlet, who generally seems more concerned with words than deeds. Claudius reminds Laertes that Hamlet has always been jealous of his abilities with a sword, and has long wished to fence with him. Claudius suggests that they tempt Hamlet into fencing with Laertes but that Laertes uses an 'unbated' sword rather than a blunted one. Laertes agrees and announces his intention to anoint the tip of the sword with poison. Claudius further suggests poisoning a cup of wine to give to Hamlet if he should win the duel. Gertrude interrupts with the news that Ophelia has drowned, describing how she went to a 'glassy stream', dressed in a crown of flowers, and fell in. Gertrude seems to suggest that the fall was an accident, but Ophelia sang serenely as the weight of her clothes dragged her down. Laertes leaves, distraught.

ACT 5 SCENE 1

Lines 1–222: Two rustics are digging Ophelia's grave and discussing the fact that she is to have a Christian burial, despite appearing to have committed suicide. Their witty exchange creates dark humour when juxtaposed with their task. Hamlet and Horatio approach, unaware of who the grave is for. Hamlet observes that the gravedigger has no finer feelings as he sings while he digs and unceremoniously throws down any skulls that he unearths. Hamlet muses that status has no meaning once you are dead. He banters with the gravedigger, sustaining the witty wordplay that began the scene and ironically discussing the madness of 'young Hamlet' as the gravedigger does not recognize him. Hamlet's discussion of himself in the third person emphasizes the divisions in his character that have been evident throughout. The banter continues until the rustic identifies one of the skulls as belonging to Yorick, a court jester that Hamlet knew as a child. Hamlet immediately becomes more introspective, philosophizing on the inevitability of death and commenting that no matter how great the man, he will eventually die and decompose: 'Alexander [the Great] died, Alexander was buried, Alexander returneth into dust'. This seems to mark a new turn in Hamlet's thoughts concerning death: until now he has largely been concerned with the spiritual, rather than corporeal, aspects of dying. He sees a funeral procession approach, led by the king, queen and Laertes, and notes that the funeral rites have been shortened, guessing that it is for a suicide. He and Horatio conceal themselves to watch.

Lines 223–308: Hamlet recognizes Laertes, who is asking the priest why the ceremony is so short. The priest explains that because Ophelia's death 'was doubtful', she should really have been buried in 'ground unsanctified' and that he has done as much as he has 'warrantise' to do. Furious, Laertes retorts that his sister will become 'a minist'ring angel' and Hamlet realizes that the funeral is for Ophelia. Gertrude scatters flowers in the grave, emphasizing the repeated association between Ophelia and flowers, which represent the transience and beauty of nature. Overcome, Laertes curses Hamlet for sending Ophelia mad and leaps into her grave, demanding to be buried with her. Hamlet steps forward and reveals his identity, also jumping into the grave. Laertes and Hamlet fight and Hamlet declares that he did love Ophelia. He rushes off, followed by Horatio. Claudius speaks to Laertes, obliquely reassuring him that the subject of their 'last night's speech' will be put 'to the present push.'

ACT 5 SCENE 2

Lines 1–177: Hamlet tells Horatio the circumstances of his return to Denmark. He explains that while on board the ship he crept from his cabin and took the letter entrusted to Rosencrantz and Guildenstern by Claudius, containing the instructions for his execution. He explains how he forged a replacement letter from Claudius, asking that the English put Rosencrantz and Guildenstern 'to sudden death'. The next day he was captured by the pirates, leaving Rosencrantz and Guildenstern to sail to their deaths, a fate he feels that they deserved. He repeats his intention to kill Claudius and expresses regret at his behaviour towards Laertes, acknowledging the similarities in their circumstances. They are interrupted by Osric, whose long-winded and obsequious manner is mocked by Hamlet. Osric explains that he has been sent to tell Hamlet that the king has placed a bet that he will win a fencing match against Laertes and to ask if Hamlet will take up the challenge. Hamlet agrees and Osric goes to report this. Horatio warns Hamlet that he will 'lose this wager', but Hamlet says that he has been in 'continual practice' and, anyway, it does not matter if he is killed as everyone must die: it is not important when, but 'the readiness is all'.

Lines 178–239: Claudius and Gertrude enter with Laertes, other courtiers and attendants, emphasizing the public nature of the duel in contrast to the secret intentions of Claudius and Laertes. The king joins Hamlet and Laertes' hands and Hamlet asks for Laertes' pardon, explaining that his actions were 'Never Hamlet', but the result of 'madness' which caused 'Hamlet from himself [to] be taken away', again reinforcing the fragmented nature of his identity. Laertes will not consider 'reconcilement' until he has consulted 'some elder masters' on the matter of honour, but he accepts Hamlet's 'offered love'. They begin to fence.

Lines 240–334: The fight signifies a shift from 'words' to 'action'. After all the contemplation and conversation, we are presented with fast and confusing activity, added to by the various characters brief comments and asides. There is a switch of rapiers, resulting in both Hamlet and Laertes being stabbed with the poisoned blade. Gertrude, meanwhile, mistakenly drinks the poisoned wine. She dies and Hamlet demands that they seek out the treachery that killed her. Laertes, realizing that he and Hamlet are both dying, explains everything and blames Claudius. Hamlet kills Claudius with the poisoned sword, finally fulfilling his quest for revenge. Laertes begs Hamlet to 'exchange forgiveness' with him and dies. Hamlet forgives Laertes and curses the courtiers who stand around and watch as 'but mutes or audience to this act', sustaining the theatrical awareness to the end. Horatio wishes to drink the poison and die, but Hamlet begs him to remain alive 'in this harsh world', so as to tell Hamlet's story. A 'warlike noise' is heard, and Osric explains that Fortinbras and the English ambassadors have arrived. Hamlet announces that Fortinbras will be the next King of Denmark and dies.

Lines 335–381: Fortinbras asks what has happened, and Horatio promises to tell him. We learn that Rosencrantz and Guildenstern are dead. Fortinbras claims the Danish throne and orders that Hamlet is given a military funeral.

HAMLET IN
PERFORMANCE:
THE RSC AND BEYOND

The best way to understand a Shakespeare play is to see it or ideally to participate in it. By examining a range of productions, we may gain a sense of the extraordinary variety of approaches and interpretations that are possible – a variety that gives Shakespeare his unique capacity to be reinvented and made 'our contemporary' four centuries after his death.

We begin with a brief overview of the play's theatrical and cinematic life, offering historical perspectives on how it has been performed. We then analyse in more detail a series of productions staged over the last half-century by the Royal Shakespeare Company. The sense of dialogue between productions that can only occur when a company is dedicated to the revival and investigation of the Shakespeare canon over a long period, together with the uniquely comprehensive archival resource of promptbooks, programme notes, reviews and interviews held on behalf of the RSC at the Shakespeare Birthplace Trust in Stratford-upon-Avon, allows an 'RSC stage history' to become a crucible in which the chemistry of the play can be explored.

Finally, we go to the horse's mouth. Modern theatre is dominated by the figure of the director. He, or sometimes she (like musical conducting, theatre directing remains a male-dominated profession), must hold together the whole play, whereas the actor must concentrate on his or her part. The director's viewpoint is therefore especially valuable. Shakespeare's plasticity is wonderfully revealed when we hear directors of highly successful productions answering the same questions in very different ways.

FOUR CENTURIES OF *HAMLET*: AN OVERVIEW

Hamlet is the best-known and most discussed of all Shakespeare's plays. It is also one of the most frequently performed. The many early references to it suggest that this has always been the case. There is then a remarkably full stage history which reveals a certain continuity and predictability by way of a perpetual focus on the figure of the prince himself, claims for the 'naturalistic' quality of the actor's performance, a sense of the play's special capacity to catch the contemporary *Zeitgeist*, cutting and rearranging of the text, and the international dimension and appeal of the play. The legendary centrality of the prince – with nearly forty per cent of the lines – has led to the focus on the performance of the leading actor in the main part, particularly in historical productions in which the cutting of the text increased the relative size of the role. Such a focus is problematic but inevitable and does have some value, as the modern critic Anthony Dawson recognizes:

> I am aware of perpetuating the discredited tradition of equating performance history with detailed accounts of how one or another famous actor played a single role. But one explanation is that the available source materials make such an emphasis almost unavoidable; moreover, leading actors express in heightened ways features of cultural style, and when they take on Hamlet they help to reveal an era's understanding of subjectivity.[1]

Thanks to an anonymous elegist writing on the death of Richard Burbage, the leading actor in Shakespeare's company, we know that Burbage played the part in the early seventeenth century:

> He's gone and with him what a world are dead!
> Which he reviv'd, to be revived so,
> No more young Hamlet, old Hieronymo
> Kind Lear, the grieved Moor, and more beside,
> That lived in him; have now forever died,
> Oft have I seen him, leap into the grave
> Smiting the person which he seem'd to have

Of a sad lover with so true an eye
That there I would have sworn, he meant to die;
Oft have I seen him, play this part in jest,
So lively, that spectators, and the rest
Of his sad crew, whilst he but seem'd to bleed,
Amazed, thought even then he died indeed.[2]

Assuming that the lines describe the graveyard scene in Act 5 scene 1 of *Hamlet*, we are also given some idea of how he played the part. In general Burbage is praised for the realism of his performances. It is striking that all the great actors who followed in his footsteps are similarly praised despite very different conceptions of the part and performance styles. There is also a tendency for actors themselves to trace a lineal descent for their performance, as though perhaps this might validate or authenticate their interpretation. This was certainly the case after the Restoration of the monarchy in 1660 when the part was played for Sir William Davenant's company by Thomas Betterton. John Downes, company book-keeper and prompter, reports that

> *Hamlet* being Perform'd by Mr *Betterton*, Sir *William* (having seen Mr *Taylor* of the *Black-Fryars* Company Act it, who being Instructed by the Author Mr *Shaksepeur*) taught Mr *Betterton* in every Particle of it; which by his exact Performance of it, gain'd him Esteem and Reputation, Superlative to all other Plays . . . No more succeeding Tragedy for several Years got more reputation, or Money to the Company than this.[3]

In fact Joseph Taylor, who inherited Burbage's roles, joined the King's Men at the Blackfriars three years after Shakespeare's death so could not have been personally instructed by the author, but he probably performed them in a similar way. Betterton played Hamlet to great acclaim until he was seventy:

> had you been to-night at the play-house, you had seen the force of action in perfection: your admired Mr Betterton behaved himself so well, that though now about seventy, he acted youth; and by the prevalent power of proper manner, gesture, and voice, appeared through the whole drama a young man of great expectation,

vivacity, and enterprise. The soliloquy where he began the celebrated sentence of 'To be or not to be?', the expostulation, where he explains with his mother in the closet, the noble ardour, after seeing his father's ghost; and his generous distress for the death of Ophelia, are each of them circumstances which dwell strongly upon the minds of his audience, and would certainly affect their behaviour on any parallel occasions in their own lives.[4]

The early eighteenth century actor-manager Colley Cibber described Betterton's performance as restrained, 'governed by decency, manly, but not braving; his voice never rising into that seeming outrage, or wild defiance of what he naturally revered'.[5] The actor seems to have attended to Hamlet's advice to the players at the beginning of Act 3 scene 2, although these lines were cut in the so-called 'Players' Quarto' (1676) which was used, as were the Ambassadors, Polonius' talk with Reynaldo, his advice to his son, Laertes' advice to Ophelia, and most of Fortinbras. Many other speeches were thinned, including all the soliloquies apart from 'To be, or not to be', which was presumably too well-known to be cut. *Hamlet*'s complicated textual history and length has led to a stage history characterized by cuts and exclusions designed to create a fast-paced script concentrating on narrative and action.

David Garrick, the outstanding eighteenth-century Hamlet, used a version of the same text for much of his theatrical career until 1772 when he decided to cut most of the fifth act and have Hamlet reappear after Ophelia's final exit, fight and forgive Laertes and kill Claudius. This drastic action had the positive effect of enabling much of the material from the first four acts to be restored, adding depth to the other characters and making Hamlet a more complex, ambiguous figure. Garrick's performance was noted for its liveliness and energy and was based on a conviction of Hamlet's deeply-felt love for his dead father. In an age of feeling, 'The basis of Hamlet's character seems to be an extreme sensibility of mind, apt to be strongly impressed by its situation, and overpowered by the feelings which that situation excites.'[6] Walter Scott characterized Garrick's acting as 'impetuous, sudden, striking, and versatile'.[7] He was also known for carefully thought-out stage business, including a collapsing chair, a wig wired so that the hair stood on end and his famous 'start' on first seeing the Ghost. The German scientist and Anglophile Georg Lichtenberg described how

> His whole demeanour is so expressive of terror that it made my flesh creep even before he began to speak. The almost terror-struck silence of the audience, which preceded this appearance and filled one with a sense of insecurity, probably did much to enhance this effect. At last he speaks, not at the beginning, but at the end of a breath, with a trembling voice: 'Angels and ministers of grace defend us!'[8]

The liveliness of Garrick's interpretation contrasted markedly with the late eighteenth-century actor John Philip Kemble's melancholy prince. The memoirist Mary Russell Mitford thought him 'the only satisfactory Hamlet I ever saw – owing much to personal grace and beauty – something to a natural melancholy, or rather pensiveness of manner – much, of course, to consummate art'.[9] The Regency star Edmund Kean, by contrast, was passionate and impetuous. At the end of Act 3 scene 1, for example, according to the Scottish poet Theodore Martin, after screaming 'get thee to a nunnery' at Ophelia, he was about to leave

> when he stops, turns round, and casting back the saddest, almost tearful look, stands lingering for some time, and then with a slow, almost gliding step, comes back, seizes Ophelia's hand, imprints a lingering kiss upon it with a deep-drawn sigh, and straightway dashes more impetuously than before out of the door, which he slams violently behind him.[10]

William Charles Macready's performance in the mid-nineteenth century was described as a 'composite',[11] combining 'the classical dignity of John Kemble with the intense earnestness and colloquial familiarity of Edmund Kean'.[12] Reviewers praised his naturalism and ability to suggest subtle, complex feelings, but in his diary Macready confesses how difficult he found it to achieve 'the ease and dignified familiarity, the apparent levity of manner, with the deep purpose that lies beneath'.[13] Edwin Booth, the great American actor, was praised for his portrait of a 'reflective, sensitive, gentle, generous nature, tormented, borne down and made miserable by an occasion ... to which it is not equal'.[14] Booth softened and refined the role.

Accounts of Henry Irving's performance at the Lyceum are contradictory, although he was astonishingly successful; some critics faulted him for 'the entire absence of tragic passion'[15] while others talked of his 'real frenzy'.[16] He is credited with introducing a 'psychological Hamlet'.[17] Eden Philpotts later analysed his performance in terms of the psychological connection between his intellectuality, insanity and failure to act.[18] Irving's chosen successor as Hamlet was Johnston Forbes-Robertson, whose performance likewise drew contradictory notices. George Bernard Shaw praised his verse-speaking for the way he 'does not utter half a line; then stop to act; then go on with another half line ... he plays as Shakespeare should be played, on the line and to the line, with the utterance and acting simultaneous, inseparable and in fact identical'.[19] While all reviewers agreed on the delicacy of his performance, some found him 'affable' and 'light-hearted'; Shaw talked of 'celestial gaiety'[20] while others mention his 'gentle melancholy'.[21] This production reintroduced Fortinbras in the last act after the character had been banished from the stage for over two hundred years, an innovation suggested by Shaw but regarded as anticlimactic by many at the time.

The matinee idol John Barrymore was praised by James Agate as 'nearer to Shakespeare's whole creation than any other I have seen'.[22] To John Gielgud he suggested 'tenderness, remoteness, and neurosis',[23] and he also impressed the young Laurence Olivier: 'Everything about him was exciting. He was athletic, he had charisma, and to my young mind, he played the part to perfection.'[24] Olivier was impressed also by the way in which Barrymore emphasized certain words in a line, although critics were less enthusiastic. Olivier drew a telling theatrical line directly back through Barrymore to Booth, from Booth to Kean and hence ultimately to Burbage.[25]

Evolving twentieth-century production styles were influenced by the attempts of the late-Victorian producer William Poel to recreate an authentically Elizabethan bare stage as opposed to a cluttered historical realism with elaborate scenery. There was also a trend towards ensemble-playing which meant that focus was no longer exclusively on the star. Interpretations, meanwhile, veered between exploration of the politics of the play and interest in sexuality in the light of Freud's theory of the family romance. Late twentieth and early twenty-first-century productions were often concerned with self-conscious dramatic devices (overhearings, the play-within-the-play) and references to play-acting, a phenomenon that became known as 'meta-theatricality' (theatre about theatre). Performances of *Hamlet* frequently sought to interrogate their own meaning.

The play's contemporary significance was signalled in the 1925 Birmingham Repertory production which became known as 'Hamlet in plus fours' on account of its modern-day set and dress. Post-war disillusionment infected Colin Keith-Johnston's 'snarling prince'.[26] Not all were convinced, but the *Sunday Times'* reviewer was one of many who responded to its modern treatment: 'A certain matter-of-factness of diction, combined with the absence of gesture and pose, do give a

3. Realistic historical staging, with elaborate sets and large casts of spear-carriers in attendance, characterized the play in the eighteenth, nineteenth and early twentieth centuries: this is the duel scene in the 1913 Forbes-Robertson production on the cavernous stage of London's Drury Lane Theatre.

certain added humanity and life, even if sometimes at the expense of majesty.'[27] Gielgud's judgement on the production was 'UNspeakable',[28] but it influenced his own performance at the Old Vic in 1930; as one critic puts it, 'Like Barrymore with his veiled demonic streak and Keith-Johnston with his open hostility, Gielgud brought out the darker side of Hamlet's nature.'[29] The unabridged text in the Gielgud production (conflated from the Quarto and Folio versions of the play) included Hamlet's bawdy talk to Ophelia and his mother, which hitherto had usually been cut. In the course of his career, Gielgud played the part in six different productions in total and critics are divided in their judgement on each. W. A. Darlington sums up his performances over fifteen years in terms of a progression from 'a sensitive youth, aghast at the wickedness of the world which he had just discovered, to a sophisticated man to whom that wickedness is no surprise'.[30] Gielgud's intellectualism is often contrasted, somewhat crudely, with Olivier's physicality, but as Dawson points out, 'Both were "modern" though in different ways.'[31] Olivier's Hamlet is best known for the film version of 1948; the stage version on which it was based a decade earlier and directed by Tyrone Guthrie is regarded as 'more forceful and energetic and volatile'.[32] Both stage and screen versions were strongly influenced by Freud's 'Oedipal' reading of the part of Hamlet, as well as by the Romantic image of the solitary, anguished intellectual: as the opening voiceover of the film put it, 'This is the tragedy of a man who could not make up his mind.'

In recent years there have been many notable Hamlets: Paul Scofield, Richard Burton, David Warner, Nicol Williamson, Michael Pennington, Daniel Day Lewis, Ian Charleson, Ben Kingsley, Jonathan Pryce, Derek Jacobi, Mark Rylance, Kevin Kline, Kenneth Branagh, Alex Jennings, Ralph Fiennes, Sam West, Simon Russell Beale, Adrian Lester, Toby Stephens: the list goes on. Playgoers and critics no longer look for a definitive *Hamlet* and all these productions have been variously praised and appraised. Several had striking innovations and experiments: Pryce, for instance, conjured up the voice of the Ghost from within Hamlet's own body, while Lester (in Peter Brook's supremely lucid, heavily cut production of 2000 at the Bouffes du Nord in Paris) played the 'solid flesh' soliloquy at the very beginning of the action, giving a rationale for a Hamlet that was more modern everyman, 'intelligent, decisive, extremely hurt',[33] than Renaissance prince. The radical spirit of the 1960s interrogated the play's status as cultural icon by deconstructing and reconstructing the text in Charles Marowitz's *Hamlet Collage* (1965) and Joseph Papp's American *Naked Hamlet* (1968). Tom Stoppard's *Rosencrantz and Guildenstern are Dead* (1966) owes its inspiration to the same questioning spirit.

The historical focus on Hamlet tended to exclude the importance of other characters. There have, however, been notable Ophelias including Susannah Cibber playing opposite Garrick, Harriet Smithson with Kemble, Helena Faucit with Macready, Mrs Charles Kean to her husband's prince and Kate Terry with Charles Albert Fechter. Kate's younger sister, Ellen Terry, playing opposite Irving, was much praised and led to the role enjoying greater prominence. The challenge for an actor has been in the title role, though, and there has been a tradition going back to Sarah Siddons in 1775 for women actors to take it on, including Charlotte Cushman, Sarah Bernhardt in a notable 1899 production in Paris, Asta Nielsen (in the silent film of 1921), Eva LeGallienne and more recently Judith Anderson, Diane Venora and Frances de la Tour. Bernhardt indeed argued that the role was more suitable for a mature woman than an immature man, since 'The woman more readily looks the part, yet has the maturity of mind to grasp it.'[34]

From an early date the play has had extraordinary international connections and appeal. One of the first recorded performances was in 1607 off the coast of Sierra Leone by sailors aboard a ship called the *Dragon* on the way to the East Indies. Troupes of visiting English actors performed throughout northern Europe in the sixteenth and seventeenth centuries: indeed, Shakespeare probably knew about the castle at Elsinore because two of his colleagues (Thomas Pope and Will Kempe) had played there in the 1580s. *Hamlet* was certainly seen in Germany not long after it was written.

In the eighteenth century it was the French Enlightenment sage Voltaire who shaped attitudes to Shakespeare in continental Europe. His view of *Hamlet* was that it was a great play, despite breaking neo-classical rules and patent 'absurdités' such as the introduction of

4. Sarah Bernhardt as Hamlet. Of all Shakespeare's male tragic roles the one that has been played most often and most effectively by female actors: in his book *Women as Hamlet* (2007), the critic Tony Howard notes that Bernhardt was the first Hamlet on film and Eve Donne the first Hamlet on radio.

gravediggers in the last act.[35] German Romantics such as Goethe, Schiller and Schlegel claimed a special affinity with *Hamlet* and Schlegel and Ludwig Tieck (c.1795) produced a fine German translation. Successful French Hamlets have included François Joseph Talma and Charles Albert Fechter. In nineteenth-century Russia 'Hamletism' was the term coined by Turgenev to describe the introspective political malaise of the ruling classes. Plays such as Chekhov's *Ivanov* (1887) and *The Seagull* (1896) provided explicit commentary on the character of Hamlet. In Eastern Europe in the twentieth century, productions of *Hamlet* were staged which obliquely critiqued oppressive and corrupt governments, notably Moscow's Taganka Theatre *Hamlet* directed by Yuri Lyubimov, which used a translation by Boris Pasternak and ran from 1971 to 1980, and a Romanian production with Ion Caramitru in the title role – this was recognizably a critique of the tyrannical regime of the Ceausescus, who were evoked by Claudius and Gertrude. When the Ceausescu regime was overthrown in 1989, Caramitru was recognized in the street by a general commanding a tank squadron. The actor was pulled up onto the tank and taken to the television station, where the battle for power was being fought. He was among the men who announced to the world that regime change had taken place. Hamlet had teamed up with Fortinbras to oversee the demise of Claudius and Gertrude.

Hamlet has been no less popular in the cinema than the theatre. The first onscreen Hamlet was Sarah Bernhardt. Johnston Forbes-Robertson starred in a twenty-two-minute silent version in 1913 and the Danish silent film star Asta Nielsen played Hamlet in an astonishing 1921 version in which a female Hamlet has been brought up as male to provide an heir to the Danish throne. Laurence Olivier directed and starred in a brooding black-and-white version (1948), full of vertiginous long shots and use of voiceover for soliloquies. Richard Burton's 1964 stage production directed by Gielgud was filmed, as was Tony Richardson's 1967 Roundhouse production starring Nicol Williamson as a very modern Hamlet. Grigori Kozintsev's rigorous, intellectual 1964 black-and-white Russian version took as its theme 'Denmark's a prison'. This contrasted sharply with Franco Zeffirelli's 1990 version starring Mel

Gibson and Glenn Close set in medieval Denmark which eliminated politics altogether and focused on the play's family dynamics and made Hamlet into a version of the action hero. Kenneth Branagh, like Olivier, directed himself in the lead role: his sumptuous four-hour 1996 version was set in Regency costume and shot at Blenheim Palace with a star-studded cast. Using a conflated Quarto and Folio text, it maintains a balance between the private and the political. Fortinbras' great-coated army arrive in the last act to storm the palace in a scene recalling the storming of the Winter Palace in Sergei Eisenstein's *October* (1926). Michael Almereyda's *Hamlet* (2000) with Ethan Hawke as Hamlet updated the story to modern-day Manhattan where corrupt grey 'suits' run the Denmark Corporation in a spiritual landscape of urban isolation and Hamlet's meditation on his own inadequacy as a man of violence is wittily delivered as he wanders the aisles of a Blockbuster video store, passing the section of movies marked 'Action'.*

AT THE RSC

Young Hamlet: Modernity and Politics

> Hamlet is the best-known play in the history of the world, but no two productions are the same: at the level of text as well as interpretation and stage-business, every director will seek to remint the old familiar words and to make Shakespeare speak in answer to the pressure of new times.
> (Jonathan Bate)[36]

The mutability of *Hamlet* is demonstrated by the wide variety of approaches which the Royal Shakespeare Company have taken in their dozen revivals of the play since the 1960s. Modern concerns regarding politics, psychology, religion, and the meta-theatrical nature of the play have shaped themselves into productions that reflect the time in which they were produced. Whether with the judicious cutting of the lengthy text or with choices in setting, the difficulty in pinning down *Hamlet* is also its director's blessing – an

* See p. 241 for a discography of DVD versions.

opportunity to reflect a uniquely personal vision of the play, with an actor who will bring out the essential elements of that reading:

> Actor and audience alike have an oddly personal relationship with the part and the play. It seems to identify itself with the particular age and body of the time in which it is being played. Productions are often seen as pinpointing the nature and quality of the day's disaffected youth, though this quality can vary from gentle disappointed fatalism to angry violent nihilism without a word being altered.[37]

In 1965, Peter Hall's production had the youth of the day queueing round the block for tickets. Camping out in sleeping bags, they waited determinedly to have the chance of seeing the twenty-four-year-old David Warner speak for their generation. And speak he did: his soliloquies were addressed directly to the audience from the forefront of the stage in a naturalistic language, the text was cut to emphasize his loneliness and isolation,* and the aspect of the individual against officialdom was emphasized.

> Warner found his closest companions to be the theatre audience. . . . Peter Hall . . . began with his reaction to a particular political climate, as [Tony] Church** described it, 'the corrupted end of a long conservative administration . . . sex scandals [Profumo†] and all that going on,' the oppressiveness of which produced disaffection in the youth of Great Britain. On the surface, then, Hall wanted to make a production that was 'relevant' and spoke to the audience of the sixties, a unique and eventful decade.[38]

On the 'How all occasions do inform against me. . .' soliloquy, Warner himself commented that

---

* Seventy-five lines of Horatio's were cut.

** Tony Church played Polonius in this production.

† A political and intelligence scandal in the early 1960s which captured the attention of the British public and helped to discredit and topple the Conservative government of Harold Macmillan. Secretary of State for War John Profumo had an extramarital affair with showgirl Christine Keeler, who was also sleeping with a Russian spy.

5. David Warner as Hamlet, wearing student scarf, japing with Rosencrantz (John Bell, left) and Guildenstern (James Laurenson) in Peter Hall's 1965 production.

There was a lot going on then in the sixties, Vietnam and everything, and although this production was not commenting on that, I . . . was feeling something there about that particular situation, 'The imminent death of twenty thousand men . . . Go to their graves . . .'. I grew to like this speech, and it began to mean more things as one just played with it.[39]

Peter Hall explained in a lecture that

Hamlet is one of mankind's great images. It turns a new face to each century, even to each decade. It is a mirror which gives back the reflections of the age that is contemplating it. And the need to define these reflections produces, on average, a new appreciation of Hamlet every twelve days . . . . For our decade I think the play will be about the disillusionment which produces an apathy of the will so deep that commitment to politics, to religion or to life is impossible. For a man said to do nothing, Hamlet does a great deal. For a man said to refuse experience, he experiences a great deal. He is always on the brink of action, but something inside him, this disease of disillusionment, stops the final, committed action . . . . [Talking of the young intellectuals of his day, Hall felt]: There is a sense of what-the-hell-anyway, over us looms the Mushroom Cloud. And politics are a game and a lie, whether in our own country or in the East/West dialogue which goes on interminably without anything very real being said. This negative response is deep and appalling.[40]

The cold, self-perpetuating nature of the political machine was also prevalent in Steven Pimlott's 2001 production. Whereas in 1965 historical costumes were made with modern fabrics, loosely referencing the twentieth century, Pimlott went for a completely modern interpretation:

Searchlights and swivelling surveillance cameras make spies of everyone in [a] windowless Elsinore . . . . In this contemporary court, the wily new king Claudius (Larry Lamb) is every inch the president. Made over by image consultants as used by Blair and Clinton, he always appears hand-in-hand with his smiling soignée First Lady, Gertrude, a gang of whooping, clapping yes-men, presswomen and suited, armed, security guards in their wake. This is a world we all recognise.[41]

The production started and ended with around twenty anonymous looking sycophantic suited types, clapping Claudius and later his successor, Fortinbras. Despite the momentous events of the play the indifferent world of politics survived. Almost otherworldly and uncanny in their uniformity, they appeared as an unstoppable and timeless crowd, without any sense of loyalty, compassion, or understanding of humanity, homing in on Fortinbras with Hamlet's dead body still warm on stage.

The incapability of an individual and uncorrupted life in this bureaucratic world was emphasized in the setting. The designer Alison Chitty favoured

... minimal furnishing, wide empty spaces, shades of bureau-cratic grey, and you [got] a corresponding sense of watching the play under laboratory conditions. Pimlott is a believer in modern-dress Shakespeare, too, which on this occasion means jeans, leather jackets, name-tags, courtiers dressed like City traders...[42]

David Warner and Sam West, respective Hamlets in 1965 and 2001, wore defining items of clothing which set them apart and marked them as part of contemporary rebellious and disaffected youth. Warner's long, red, student scarf has remained an iconic theatrical image. Sam West first appeared in black jeans and a black 'hoody', a 'hunched and hooded figure squatting with his back to the audience, snooping on the court'.[43] As Rosencrantz and Guildenstern tried to find out his secrets, they plied him with a joint of marijuana.

Pimlott's thoroughly modern production is set upon confounding traditional expectations and sometimes he manages to do so with a vengeance. The guards try to blast the Ghost away with machine-gun fire. A leather-jacketed Hamlet finishes off Polonius with a pistol rather than his knife. On the Prince's orders, Horatio videos the murderous Play scene, so that his close-ups of a twitchy Claudius and Gertrude loom large before us. And Ben Meyjes's splendid Laertes, possessed by the furies, holds up the king with machine-gun fire and what suitably looks like an incipient Palace revolution.[44]

Moving away from politics, Matthew Warchus' quasi-cinematic production of 1997 completely cut out the Fortinbras subplot and focused on the families of the court.

Hamlet is a play absolutely saturated with the words 'father', 'mother,' 'sister', 'brother', 'son', 'daughter', 'uncle' . . . . I cut about 35% of the text of the play in order to focus on the domestic story – on the two families who I imagine in this production live together with their staff in an isolated house.[45]

Warchus conflated the three existing versions of the play, reordering events and including rarely played scenes, such as Horatio's First Quarto reassurance to Gertrude that her banished son is safe. The cuts were justified by the director in an interview with journalist Lyn Gardner in the *Guardian*:

'I know that by cutting the play you could diminish it, but by cutting a couple of courses from a banquet you can also make the flavours sharper and richer' . . . he knows that in excising the political dimension of the play, he risks turning it into a small domestic incident rather than a full-scale tragedy. 'My hope is that when the story is told very vividly, very passionately, audiences will recognise it as a blueprint for what happens more widely. Shakespeare is so good at both macrocosm and microcosm. I feel that what I am doing is taking the play out of the hands of the academics and intellectuals, and bringing [it] back into the arena of relationships. More than any other play I have directed, I am doing this with my heart, not my head.'[46]

Warchus succeeded in creating a Hamlet that was accessible and exciting, 'about a wounded individual rather than the rank corruption within a tyranny'.[47] Its modern setting led to many inventive touches: Hamlet taking Polaroids of Claudius at a wedding party which looked like 'a gaudy purple disco',[48] and later using them to show Gertrude the comparison with her dead husband; the audience unsure if Hamlet, carrying around a revolver in a brown paper bag, was going to use it on himself or others; Ophelia handing out pills instead of flowers.

> There's a clarity and energy here that silences the usual anxieties about updating a classic from Elizabeth I to Elizabeth II. [Alex] Jennings hugs [Derbhla] Crotty, then pushes her away, stubs his cigarette out on the floor and tells her to get to a nunnery. There's a whole new spin to her saying he's blasted with 'ecstasy'.[49]

In 1980 director John Barton picked up on the many references in the play to role-playing and theatricality, making it the central metaphor for his production in collaboration with his cast and designer. Michael Pennington, who played Hamlet, explained how

> the distinction between self-dramatization and real feeling, theatricality and life, runs right through the play, and was beginning to influence my reception of the text; and soon the theatrical world itself – hampers, cloaks and property swords – began to appear in rehearsal.[50]

Reviewing this production, the critic Irving Wardle pointed out that

> Hamlet, everyone agrees, is Shakespeare's most obsessively theatrical work. This production puts that idea to the test of the basic scenic elements, ransacking the text for disguisings and routines, and always allowing the spectator a full view of the concrete instruments that create the sense of illusion. Where is Elsinore? It is a stage. Who is Hamlet? A man who may not be able to take action but who can always put on a show. What happens happens bang centre stage: otherwise characters retreat to the benches and philosophise across wide open space as if they had not part in the events.[51]

Another reviewer noted that

The style of the production is, in a sense, dictated by Ralph Koltai's design: a thrusting wooden platform over which five rehearsal lights hover and behind which are arrayed such necessary props as a thunder-sheet, a table for the swords, a huge dragged suit of armour, for people to hide behind.[52]

Heaven or Hell: Hamlet and the Ghost

'Who's there?' *Hamlet* famously begins. The question, centred on the ambiguous figure of the Ghost, haunts the entire play.

(Stephen Greenblatt)[53]

As the catalyst for the play's action, the staging of the Ghost is key in indicating what type of production and what type of *Hamlet* the audience are about to see. However, one of the difficulties with staging *Hamlet* in the modern era is creating a Ghost that will have the terrifying and awe-inspiring impact that it had on audiences of previous centuries.

Many directors have eschewed any attempt to make the Ghost frightening, especially when the production has a modern setting. In Matthew Warchus' 1997 modern-dress production,

As Hamlet, Alex Jennings appears centre stage, holding his father's ashes in an urn, while on the screen behind we see black and white footage of the father playing in the snow with his son. Over the speakers, we hear the words of the usurping king, Claudius: 'Though yet of Hamlet our dear brother's death the memory be green . . .'. In this strong personal production, which axes the public-political side, Hamlet's memory of his father, the motive for revenge, never loses its freshness. . . . Into [the] wedding celebrations, amid champagne, fireworks, balloons and bridesmaids, walks the ghost of Hamlet's father (Edward Petheridge) . . . [entering] in a smoking jacket, [he] speaks with quick authority, then drifts away.[54]

Steven Pimlott's 2001 production had an extremely animated and fast-moving Ghost. He clutched at the distraught Hamlet and held him in his arms when imparting his story of betrayal. When

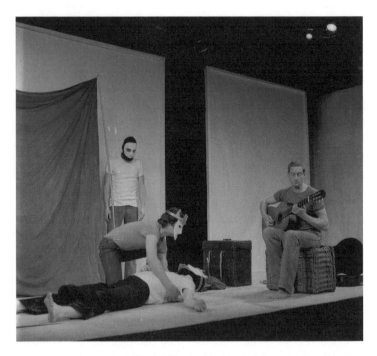

6. *Hamlet* is the most self-consciously theatrical of the tragedies: Hamlet himself is fascinated by actors and the idea of playing a part (does he *act* his madness?) and his deep concern with 'acting' in relation to thinking and feeling introduces a play on the two senses of 'to act'. The presence of the players and the play-within-the-play is crucial to all this, but the highly rhetorical linguistic style of *The Murder of Gonzago* (otherwise known as *The Mousetrap*), together with the dumb show, require a different theatrical style from that of the main play. Masks were used in Buzz Goodbody's intimate 1975 production in the studio theatre The Other Place.

Hamlet went too far in berating his mother the Ghost strode purposefully into the room, rather than just appearing, and almost grabbed Hamlet, as if to say 'That's enough!'

In 1965 David Warner played Hamlet as a man obsessed with his father, not only by the loss of him, but by his inability to match up to him in stature. In order to emphasize this the Ghost appeared as a tremendously tall figure. Roger Howells, the stage manager, explained that the device used to create this effect was like a 'dalek'. When staged in Stratford, two men, one standing on the ground and the other on the platform above him, manoeuvred the Ghost from inside a 'shell'. The voice of Patrick Magee* was sound-recorded and then boomed over the speakers to create an otherworldly effect. Critic Anthony Dawson remarked that

> the sense of being outmanned was the dominant effect. The Ghost entered with raised arms through the doors at the back as the sentries and Prince huddled around the cannon downstage . . . on 'sweep to my revenge', he swept, ironically, to the long arms of his father, to be cradled within them for the remainder of the scene. He seemed to be 'looking for the comforts of the nursery' (*Times*, 20 Aug.), and it was clearly his father rather than his mother, here and throughout, that fired his imagination. But the gap between heroic parent and inadequate child was overtly underlined by the stage image, generated as it were by Hamlet's inner compulsions: the father huge and protective, the son comfortless and unfit. Even after the Ghost's departure under the stage, as he reeled about getting his friends to swear their secrecy, Hamlet kept falling on the ground as if attempting to return to his father's protective embrace. How could such a man effectively take on the polished King or his politic prime minister?[55]

David Warner explained how the powerful image of the Ghost's embrace gave the scene a feeling of 'total love and belief in the father'. Warner 'reacted quite violently to the Ghost's request for revenge even to shouting "WHAT!" (not in text) and then sobbing throughout the Ghost's long speech'.[56]

> For the revenge [Hamlet] really wishes, and achieves, is on himself for not being the great Hamlet his father was . . . . As the hollow voice beneath the stage cries 'Swear!', his son lovingly

---

* Patrick Magee was predominantly a classical stage actor, but his distinctive and impressively eerie voice got him many parts in films playing sinister villains for the horror studios of the 1960s and 1970s, including Hammer, Amacus, and the films of Roger Corman.

measures his length on the ground, as if on a grave; but the voice moves, he cannot cover it. Clutching violently at his mother on her bed he looks up to find the huge presence of his father towering between them.[57]

Obviously, Hamlet's sense of intense grief plays a large part in the way he perceives the world. Grief can often bring with it an exaggeration of the senses, a cruel self-awareness and feelings of isolation. As Stanley Wells points out, Shakespeare's central concern in writing Hamlet was 'Reactions to death'.[58] For Hamlet, actor Michael Pennington believed,

> Grief seems to have sharpened his sense of falsehood in the world around him, but in other ways the immeasurable shock he has received has sent him to sleep. The torpor is deep and disturbing to watch, lifting in utterances – 'My father, methinks I see my father' – which are more hallucinatory than sentimental. Anybody familiar with bereavement can recognise the symptoms. In dramatic terms, until the news of the Ghost's appearance animates him, gives him something to believe in he is a dramatic hero of whom nothing much can be expected.[59]

In the production starring Pennington, the Ghost sat on a bench and quietly told Hamlet what had happened. Director John Barton's highlighting of theatricality also informed his Hamlet's reaction to the Ghost:

> From Hamlet's viewpoint, perhaps even the Ghost is a Satanic actor, until the closet scene when Hamlet gently presses his mother's face round and, in a shared moment of stunned disbelief, she too sees the Ghost.[60]

Hamlet's grief stems from an acute awareness of the importance, the preciousness of human life. Anger at his mother's inability to see, to be aware, of the truth of her situation, prompts one of the most potent dramatic scenes ever written. In this production, Gertrude not only saw into her own soul, but in witnessing the Ghost became fully aware of what Hamlet saw and felt. The effect was so powerful that she fainted.

Michael Boyd's 2004 staging of the supernatural was striking and imaginative. The Ghost appeared with slow progression through the audience to the stage, skeleton-like with his mouth contorted into a silent scream. With its truly frightening visage, this nightmarish apparition was one of the few modern stagings of the Ghost to truly unsettle the audience:

> Instead of the usual stern but fatherly figure, in the 'fair and warlike form' of his living self, old Hamlet here hauls himself into the play as a bowed, deathly-white, half-naked spook, with hollow red sockets for eyes, scraping his broadsword along the ground to nerve-shatteringly ominous effect. He hawks up his speeches in an agonised vomit of vengefulness. That he seems to hail from an alien belief system as well as from another world is entirely deliberate.... Boyd has been inspired by Stephen Greenblatt's recent book *Hamlet in Purgatory*, which highlights the tragedy's unsettling premise: 'A young man from Wittenberg, with a distinctly Protestant temperament, is haunted by a distinctly Catholic ghost.' Or, as the director puts it, 'There has been a political and intellectual revolution, and then Hamlet re-encounters the past in the shape of his father's spirit and has to negotiate with it.'[61]

If we were in any doubt that this Ghost had suffered the terrors of hell, we had none by the end of the scene when a trapdoor opened to reveal intense red light, the fires of Purgatory. The Ghost fell forward, face first, into the awaiting pit.

From the first appearance of the Ghost there is a sense of inevitability in Hamlet's fate. As he progresses through the play, he undergoes an acceptance of his own mortality. Hamlet's acceptance and 'readiness' for death was something which the designer for Boyd's production, Tom Piper, built into the characters' costuming:

> Laertes changes from light, golden boy to black avenger. Hamlet begins as a black avenger and ends up in light grey, a sort of Everyman colour, because on his return in Act 5, Hamlet becomes more accepting, more at peace in a sense. Grey tones also give a

sense of being half in and half out of the world. It's as though, at the end, Hamlet is beginning to accept that he's about to join the world of the ash people – the gravedigger is also in grey.[62]

Greg Hicks, who played the startling Ghost, also played the Player King and the First Gravedigger: 'It's a great treble because there are resonances of Hamlet's father in each one of the roles, especially the gravedigger.'[63]

Michael Boyd's doubling of roles provided a sense of the dead being present among the living and looking after their loved ones in spirit:

When I asked her [Meg Fraser who played Ophelia] to play the second gravedigger too it was because I thought there was something very moving in the fact that, in that benign scene, Hamlet was with people who loved him: his father and Ophelia.[64]

Meg Fraser commented on this comforting but macabre idea: 'I also play the second gravedigger – Ophelia digs her own grave! . . . And now I wear the same make-up for both parts because it's about making connections rather than being naturalistic.'[65]

The references to grief and death were markedly used in the set for the Adrian Noble production in 1992:

The unweeded garden of Elsinore exists downstage in Bob Crowley's design. The right arm of the subterranean ghost pushes through like the arm in John Boorman's *Deliverance*, and Ophelia plucks her flowers here shortly before the gravediggers prepare her tomb. If Denmark is a prison, it is also, finally, a graveyard. The stage is littered with pink garlands and funeral mounds.[66]

As indicated, the Ghost in this production emerged from a garden, which formed the front part of the stage, and was later used for Ophelia's madness scene and the burial.

What you are left with after Hamlet's return from England is a landscape of grief. By the end the whole stage is a huge graveyard, not literally with tombstones, but just dead flowers everywhere.[67]

Love and Madness

> Hamlet evokes the long-distance loneliness and isolation of three lost,
> young things – Hamlet, Laertes and Ophelia – caught up in a political and
> personal revenge that's the death of them.
>
> (Nicholas de Jongh)[68]

The parallel stories of two families and how their children cope with
the death of their fathers is central to the plot of *Hamlet*. Hamlet's
dilemma after seeing the Ghost lies in the fact that he is too aware of
the possible consequences of his actions. The intelligence of his
imagination is such that he knows that the Ghost's request for
revenge has two possible outcomes for him: death or madness. As
hot-blooded avenger he will provoke the punishment of the state,
whereas not to act – to withdraw – would only compound and
multiply his already unbearable grief and frustration to a state of
madness. Both of these options are against his nature and his
sensibility. However, Shakespeare demonstrates their tragic consequences in the reactions of Polonius' children, Laertes and Ophelia.

Most actors, although they may reach a peak of frenzy, do not
play Hamlet as genuinely mad. In Ron Daniels' 1989 production,
however, the disintegrating mind of Hamlet was evidenced in
Elsinore's state of collapse.

> Set in what appears as an exclusive sanatorium with extensive
> views over the North Sea, Ron Daniels's production presents a
> group of cheerfully contented inmates who all fall victim to
> a killer disease.... Antony McDonald's vertiginously angled,
> hydraulically operated set suggests that Elsinore is sliding into
> the sea.
>
> Its opening court scene presents an image of harmony and
> political health, with only Mark Rylance's spiritlessly dejected
> Hamlet signalling the plague that will strike them down.[69]

The large planes of flat, subdued colour and sparse detail have a
two-fold effect. They highlight the characters and, at the same
time, emphasize their littleness against the massive ruins and the
stormy sea.

The heart of Denmark is rotten, and Daniels concentrates on that heart. Questions of legitimacy, kingship and ambition are treated in terms not of the State but of individual fate. Intrigue is social, courtly, politic, not broadly political. The huge windows open on the sea and the rabble is heard only as an electronic noise, as of sirens. Daniels seems to want to lift the court out of history, to a plane on which the psychological and metaphysical themes can be purely explored.[70]

Known as 'the pyjama Hamlet', due to the fact that Mark Rylance wore pyjama bottoms from entering for the 'To be, or not to be' soliloquy to his exile to England, Rylance's performance took Hamlet's loss of sanity to extreme and believable levels. When the production toured and did a special performance at Broadmoor, a hospital for the criminally insane, one inmate wrote to his local paper, explaining that Rylance 'was able to capture every aspect of a person's slip into the world of psychopathic, manipulative paranoia . . . Many of us here in Broadmoor are able to understand Hamlet's disturbed state of mind because we have experienced such traumas.'[71]

In Ron Daniels's RSC production of Hamlet, the hero is . . . a Black Prince of pain and destruction. Antony McDonald's sets are an expressionistic clash between sloping floors and tilted walls, as if the court were in danger of imminent collapse . . . the threat comes from Hamlet. We first see Mark Rylance as a tense, pale, hunched figure tightly buttoned in a long, heavy overcoat. His eyes are glazed over with too much introspection. He is clearly on the brink of a crack-up, and his encounter with the Ghost topples him over. This Hamlet suffers from a combination of obsessional brooding and a retarded emotional maturity. In public, he acts up to his breakdown, until it takes over and he regresses to a difficult, irascible adolescence . . . . Daniels and Rylance show Hamlet to be a moral vessel which is too weak to bear its just cause. When, at the end of a superb, harrowing bedroom scene, he kisses his mother on the mouth, it begins as a kiss of comfort and complicity and ends in a shocked recognition of fear and freedom. Of course, you lose the 'romantic' Hamlet; but you gain in hard emotional authenticity. This is a deeply shocking production in the most crucial sense: it shocks you into the difficult recognition that necessary moral actions can be performed by people who do not carry the usual moral price tag. And so our sympathy and pity for Hamlet is hard-earned and therefore all the more real.[72]

Frances Barber as Ophelia in 1985 was universally praised for her extremely moving performance. She saw Ophelia as an extension of Hamlet's character, presenting

the female counterpart and counterpoint to him. She provides the feminine qualities lacking in his sensibilities. Shakespeare uses her innocence and naiveté to illustrate this imbalance and highlight its consequences; the destruction of a potent feminine force, caught up in a male-dominated power struggle .... I noticed Roger [Rees] as Hamlet became more lucid and reasonable as his obsessions took him over. He also used particular gestures each time he saw his father's ghost, and he was truly in danger of losing his mind. If I was to follow through my theme of Ophelia as a female counterpart to the Prince, it seemed interesting to incorporate some of Hamlet's gestures into the most inappropriate moments of her own madness, high-lighting her then as his female counterpoint. Consequently one of Roger's most striking gestures was that of banging his chest violently after the ghost has appeared to him for the first time, as if his heart truly is breaking .... I decided to bang my chest and beat my heart as violently as I could at the most unexpected moment, during the sweetness of the song ... people are 'certified' if they are likely to do harm to others or to themselves. I wanted to suggest that whilst Hamlet is likely to do harm to others at his most revengeful, Ophelia is capable of doing herself great harm at her most tranquil .... When Laertes enters the scene, I clasped his face, echoing Roger in the nunnery scene, but in this case singing gently and weeping for the loss of everything good in her life – a direct contrast to Hamlet's spitting accusations .... Another gesture that occurred during one rehearsal was coincidentally an echo of the closet scene in which a distraught Gertrude clasps her son to her bosom and strokes his hair. Kenneth Branagh (Laertes) sank into my arms as Ophelia sings, whilst I stroked his hair, unaware at that point of the parallel mother/son image.[73]

Ophelia's loneliness and isolation are equal to, if not greater than, Hamlet's. The loss of Hamlet and the death of her father, the absence of Laertes, leave her no one to turn to in her distraction. Actresses in recent productions have often employed visual associations with Ophelia's loved ones in the madness scenes, indicating a lost mind helplessly turning to those she loves by assimilating their actions, keeping part of them alive and with her even though they are absent. In Meg Fraser's performance in 2005,

Ophelia mimics or echoes her father's gestures when she's mad, for example the authoritative clap. I came by it accidentally in rehearsal but I love the way it gives the audience such a shock! . . . Ophelia's wearing the same colour her dad wears – the Polonius family are in silvers.[74]

This idea was strongly adopted in 1992 when Joanne Pearce's Ophelia wore her dead father's clothes. Her innocence, isolation and vulnerability were highlighted by this effective piece of costuming:

The mad scene began with the shattered young woman shuffling along in her father's clothes, the shirt bloodstained and the shoes, clownlike, much too large.[75]

Many modern productions pick up on the fact that Hamlet and Ophelia are both condemned by paternal domination. Tony Church, who played Polonius twice in 1965 and in 1980, commented:

The appalling news that Hamlet has apparently been driven mad by Ophelia's rejection leads Polonius in the text straight into the problem of reporting this event to the King; here we added the business of the father covering his poor frightened daughter with his robes of state, and leading her protectively from the stage. Later, in the mad scene, Ophelia appeared wearing her dead father's robe, and it was only after the first night that I remembered that Glenda Jackson, the Ophelia in 1965, had used the same business. This led me to reflect on the nature of parental oppression; Glenda's reasoning was based on the suffocation of her spirit by her father – that although he had frightened her, she could not escape him. My Polonius of 1980, it could be said, overpowered his daughter in the end by too much love.[76]

Elsinore, the heart of Denmark, is sterile and corrupt. There is a complete lack of responsibility from the older generation in this play, in caring for the fragility of their young. Despite the larger themes which the play deals with, these productions demonstrated that it is the emotional dependence and twisted parental relationships which gives the play its emotional pull. Everything conspires to kill the young before they have a chance to grow. None survive the cruel parental world in which they live. Although Hamlet returns from England a changed man, he has been condemned from the moment his father utters his dreadful command. 'Remember me': the words in their simplicity echo in the mind with each fresh death of the unprepared or tormented – those that perish before their time.

THE DIRECTOR'S CUT: INTERVIEWS WITH RON DANIELS, JOHN CAIRD AND MICHAEL BOYD

Ron Daniels, who was born in Brazil, was a founding member of the Teatro Oficina in São Paulo. In 1977 he was appointed Artistic Director of the Royal Shakespeare Company's Stratford-upon-Avon studio theatre, The Other Place, and in 1980 he became an Associate Director of the RSC. In 1991 he became Associate Artistic Director of the American Repertory Theatre in Cambridge, Massachusetts. More recently he has worked out of New York as a freelance director. He has directed most of Shakespeare's major tragedies and history plays. He directed two RSC productions of Hamlet: with Roger Rees as the Prince in 1984 and with Mark Rylance in 1989; the interview concentrates principally on the latter, which became known as the 'pyjama Hamlet', with Rylance's performance singled out for particular praise by the critics.

John Caird, born in 1948 in Canada to British parents, staged and directed more than twenty plays, both classic and contemporary, while he was an Associate Director at the Royal Shakespeare Company. He has subsequently directed many musicals, plays and operas, both in London (e.g. for the National Theatre and the Almeida) and internationally. Together with Trevor Nunn, he directed the celebrated production of Charles Dickens' *Nicholas Nickleby* for the RSC in 1980, as well as the internationally successful *Les Misérables* in 1985. His production of *Hamlet* in 2000 for the National Theatre in London on the proscenium-arch Lyttelton stage, featured Simon Russell Beale, one of the outstanding Hamlets of the modern age.

Michael Boyd, born in 1955, trained as a director at the Malaya Bronnaya Theatre in Moscow. He then worked at the Belgrade Theatre in Coventry and the Sheffield Crucible before founding his own company, the Tron in Glasgow. He became an Associate Director of the RSC in 1996, coming to prominence with his millennial staging of the three parts of *Henry VI* and *Richard III* in the company's 'This England' cycle of history plays, which won him an Olivier award for Best Director. In 2003, he took over as Artistic Director, achieving a notable success in 2006–07 with his ambitious Complete Works Festival, whereby all Shakespeare's plays were staged in Stratford-upon-Avon over the course of a year, some by the RSC and others by visiting companies. His 2004 production of *Hamlet* starred Toby Stephens, son of the noted actors Robert Stephens and Dame Maggie Smith, as Hamlet.

Design choices seem crucial in establishing the atmosphere of the first act of *Hamlet*, with its movement between the guards outside on the platform, the formal exchanges at court, where Hamlet's black costume sets him so conspicuously apart, and the private conversations of Polonius and his children: what was the process whereby you arrived at a vision for the look and style of the opening scenes?

RD: Our basic approach was that this was to be a 'domestic' Hamlet. My earlier [1984] production, with Roger Rees in the title role and with designs by Maria Bjornson, had been set somewhere in the vast expanses between heaven and earth – a 'cosmic' and imposing Hamlet set literally among the clouds, some of which were painted on a vast transparent curtain above the stage and others on the huge ramp which finally parted to reveal Ophelia's grave beneath it. Though retaining a few of these elements [the encounter between Hamlet and the Ghost took place literally in the sky, on a platform suspended high above the stage], the 1989 production, designed by Antony McDonald, was to be much more intimate, rooted in personal relationships, a tragedy set in the heart of a family as well as of a state: the action was to take place in a mansion, a home, really, perched on the edge of a cliff high above the turbulent sea.

7. The domestic setting of Ron Daniels' 1989 *Hamlet*: Elsinore as a mansion instead of a castle.

JC: My designer, Tim Hatley, and I didn't think of the opening scenes as a separate issue. We were more concerned with creating a performance space for the whole play. In *Hamlet* one needs a graveyard, a battlement, a fencing ground, a cloister, and so on. I was also keen to give the whole play a suffocatingly religious setting.

In my production the two main design images were graveyard and travel, based on the 'undiscovered country from whose bourn no traveller returns'. There were stone flags on the floor, many of them engraved with the names of the dead, alcoves from which the ghostly characters of the play emerge as if to re-enact an old story, and a large pile of old and dusty luggage out of which all of the settings of the play could be made. The set was part cathedral, part castle, part graveyard, part attic.

MB: We wanted a space which could create tension, allow eavesdropping, open out as Claudius' grip on Hamlet and Denmark weakens, and generally encourage swift and fluid movement of scenes and actors. A rational, cold space for Claudius' 'modern', 'reforming' court. A black circular palisade, with no visible exits or entrances, the only visible way into the world from outside was from the audience, and was used exclusively by the Ghost and Players.

Hamlet's language is famously introspective and self-questioning, while King Claudius is very adept at controlling language for political ends: is this a contrast that you explored in your production?

RD: It seems to me that in Shakespeare, content perfectly defines the form. The words Shakespeare chooses to give Polonius and how he constructs his sentences are a precise indication of who Polonius is as a human being. Claudius' concerns are the affairs of estate – he is a man of action, a consummate political (and sexual) animal who, with the exception of his one moment of soul-searching (which he deals with with a good deal of brusque impatience), demonstrates little if any interest in the workings of his own heart. The language he uses perfectly reflects this 'objective' posture, whereas Hamlet's 'subjective' language reveals his continuing obsession with himself and with the struggles raging deep within him. What other character in Shakespeare agonizes about his own state of mind so relentlessly?

JC: I'm not sure I agree with that statement. Hamlet is incredibly clever with language, both in his political and introspective utterances. He manipulates people every bit as successfully as Claudius does. You could say that he handles Polonius much better than Claudius, who seems at a loss for words in the face of Polonius' loquacity.

It's also not true to say that Claudius isn't introspective. One of the turning points of the plot is a profound introspection from Claudius. The scene in the chapel where he questions his actions and is in despair about the state of his soul is about as introspective as you can imagine anybody ever being. I think almost all characters in Shakespeare manipulate language, because they are Shakespeare's creatures; they do what Shakespeare himself does in creating them.

I think the more interesting question is *why* does Claudius try to manipulate Hamlet when he could quite easily kill him? He has killed Hamlet's father, he has made himself king, he has married Hamlet's mother...if he's such a brutal machiavellian politician, why doesn't he just kill Hamlet? The answer is that he kills his brother so that he can become him. It's an attempted act of transformation. That's why he tries genuinely, desperately, to persuade Hamlet that everything is the same as it used to be. His father may be dead but he has a new father now. It's Hamlet's incapacity to accept this new status quo that throws Claudius into confusion and ultimately forces him into the position of having Hamlet killed. But it takes more than half the play for Claudius to be forced to this point.

MB: We saw the play being driven by the possible actions of a usurped prince in a dangerous court, rather than by a 'given' of Hamlet's state of mind. We chose to celebrate Hamlet's brilliant control of language under extreme pressure rather than relax into a 'state' of introspection. This felt more active, true and exciting. That said, as the production matured, Toby [Stephens, playing Hamlet] was able to give more space to the lyrical wonder in Hamlet's thought, without losing the prevailing sense of danger.

The Ghost appears to come from Roman Catholic Purgatory, whereas young Hamlet is studying at Wittenberg, a university synonymous with Martin Luther and Protestantism: did the religious controversies of the age play any part in your production?

RD: These religious controversies are indeed fascinating but they are perhaps of more interest in the study than in the rehearsal room, where what matters is human behaviour and motivation. What makes Hamlet, who perhaps understands that he is the protagonist of a revenger's tragedy, incapable of carrying out his obligation to revenge his father's death? What other imperative is short-circuiting his will to action? What is forcing him to deviate from the destiny imposed on him?

JC: Religion had a great deal to do with my interpretation but not religious controversies. The main reason I set the play in a discernibly Renaissance period is that I don't think the play works if it's set in a post-Enlightenment world. The central characters are deeply concerned with the mortality of their souls. Without the religious and spiritual context in which Shakespeare was writing it's hard to make sense of the play philosophically and intellectually.

I don't think the difference between Protestantism and Catholicism is so crucial to the meaning of the play and Wittenberg itself is relatively unimportant. Ostensibly the company of players comes from Wittenberg, because one assumes that's where Hamlet and Horatio must have met them. But that would make Wittenberg a town with troupes of child-actors taking over from adult companies and we know that wasn't the case in Wittenberg. As always Shakespeare is using his own experiences and playing fast and loose with geography and chronology. Shakespeare's Wittenberg is more like Oxford than a Lutheran university, and when the Players arrive on the scene it suddenly becomes London.

MB: Shakespeare is clearly writing about the deep damage caused by the English Reformation, the suppression of the old Church, and the resulting schism in the country. Hamlet is of the new 'Protestant' generation, but is forced to learn that 'there are more things in heaven and earth...than are dreamt of' in the reformed thinking of Wittenberg. The fact that 'the time is out of joint' runs through the middle of Hamlet and all of Shakespeare's work.

Greg Hicks was truly supernatural – chalk white, nearly naked, agonized and burdened with a giant broadsword from a bygone heroic age, which he slowly dragged with painful Shinto precision across the metal grating on the floor. It was genuinely frightening and gave Toby Stephens a powerful problem to solve.

8. Greg Hicks: Michael Boyd's terrifying Ghost from Purgatory.

Was your Hamlet's 'antic disposition' always a performance or were there moments when he veered into genuine madness?

RD: I don't think the 'antic disposition' was ever a performance. Certainly, Hamlet out-clowns Polonius in the Fishmonger scene, giving the foolish old man a taste of his own foolishness, and

Hamlet's fury and his pain in the nunnery scene are almost beyond his control. However, these are different responses, one humorous and the other unbearably violent, to specific instances within a larger continuum of despair, a despair that is utterly disabling.

For this production we used the Bad Quarto structure, in which the nunnery scene is placed well before the Fishmonger scene: the first time Hamlet appeared after the battlement sequence was when he came on stage, a forlorn, suicidal figure still dressed in his pyjamas, to agonize over whether he should be or not be – a man in the throes of an unbearable inner crisis, genuinely 'transformed' and very far from the 'understanding of himself'.

JC: I see a lot of *Hamlets* where the actor plays the madness card in order to escape a proper investigation of the part. Of course it's exciting for an actor to walk onto the stage looking or acting completely nuts, but there's nothing in the language of the scenes to suggest madness at all. Hamlet doesn't say anything mad. I came to the view, after rehearsing it and extrapolating all the sense I could from what Hamlet says in each of his scenes, that Hamlet is the only sane person in the play. Almost everyone else is to some extent mad, with the obvious exception of Horatio. Polonius says and does mad things. Ophelia, Gertrude, Claudius, Laertes...they all find themselves in truly mad situations and react madly to them. What's amazing about Hamlet is that in the circumstances in which he finds himself, he doesn't go mad. Instead he gets saner and saner as the play continues. By the time he returns from England he's extraordinarily balanced and wise. He has moments of rashness and anger in the play, one of which results in the death of Polonius, but I can't think of a single thing he does in the play that would suggest for one moment that he's mad.

MB: Hamlet begins the play under great mental stress, but it is the world that is mad. He is in mourning and has been effectively usurped with the collusion of his mother, and yet is being forced to celebrate his mother's wedding to his usurper.

He is probably at his wildest with his dead father, Ophelia, and his mother, i.e. when he is most profoundly emotionally threatened,

9. Mark Rylance as Ron Daniels' pyjama-wearing Hamlet, berating Gertrude (Clare Higgins) in the closet scene: she holds the pictures of the two brothers who became her two husbands.

but he is not mad. As the victim of the mad time and the one born to set it right, he bears the imprint of the madness of the time. The antic disposition is a time honoured camouflage employed by Hieronimo (in *The Spanish Tragedy*) and Arbella Stuart (in her cousin Elizabeth I's court) to make themselves seem harmless to a watchful and oppressive state.

How did you deal with the brutality of Hamlet's behaviour towards Ophelia in the 'nunnery' and 'country matters' exchanges?

RD: In the most brutal way possible. The scene became quite physically as well as verbally explosive. Much as Hamlet believes Gertrude has betrayed the memory of his father by posting 'with such dexterity to incestuous sheets', he also believes Ophelia has betrayed him by obeying her father's orders that she 'lock herself from his resort, admit no messengers, receive no token . . .' – and I've always been fascinated by Hamlet's strange encounter with her when he breaks into her chamber and falls 'to such perusal of my face as he would draw it'. What did Hamlet mean to convey by such a mysterious encounter – and what did Ophelia understand by it that caused her to be so terrified? Did he look into her soul and did he see her guilt at her act of betrayal?

'Frailty, thy name is woman'. All women. Does this then not refer as much to Ophelia as to Gertrude? And what horror does this reveal, of Woman merely as the painted seductress, ambling and lisping and awakening dangerous and uncontrollable desires in all men that can only lead to murder and incest? Tormented and pathological reasoning, certainly, which can only lead to violent and irrational behaviour.

JC: I don't think he is being brutal, or certainly not intentionally. The character of Ophelia has to be seen in thematic terms. She's not a fully drawn character. She represents the possibility of a future life. She is the only nobly born woman in the play of childbearing age and therefore the only available person for Hamlet to marry and have children with. Hamlet's father was called Hamlet, and for all one knows his father was called Hamlet too. The state of Denmark is one in which kings called Hamlet get married and have boys called Hamlet, and so life continues. Claudius aborts this natural order.

The crucial line in the nunnery scene is 'I say we will have no more marriages'. It's a tragic utterance. It says 'I cannot go on pretending with this woman that we're in love and that we're going to get married and have children and everything's going to be happy. It cannot be. The world is diseased, mad and dead. No more children must be born into it.' 'Get thee to a nunnery' means precisely that. It's nothing to do with a whorehouse, as some scholars have suggested. Whorehouses in Shakespeare are bawdy, complicated places, full of life. Look at *Measure for Measure* and the *Henry IV* plays. The Denmark of *Hamlet* is no place for a whorehouse. The nunnery here is the same place as the cold unproductive cloister with which Theseus threatens Hermia in the opening scene of *A Midsummer Night's Dream.*

It is germane that when Ophelia dies, Gertrude brings the news of her death. Gertrude is the other woman in the play; a woman who won't have any more children, and who has forgotten her duty to the child she already has. Ophelia is the woman who should one day have taken over the role of wife and mother from Gertrude as Hamlet should have become his father's successor. Gertrude says this very clearly at Ophelia's obsequies. She had believed that her son would marry Ophelia and life would thereby continue into the future, but by marrying Claudius and forgetting her love for her husband and son she has made a horrible miscalculation, albeit for very human reasons.

If Gertrude was present while Ophelia was drowning, why didn't she help her? If she is reporting what she was told by someone else, who then told her? And why doesn't Shakespeare use that character to report the news to us? Why didn't he use a shepherd or the Gentleman from Ophelia's madness scene? The reason is thematic. If Hamlet is not to marry Ophelia and have children with her, then everything Gertrude has lived for dies with Ophelia. Nothing that she's ever done has any future value. The death of Ophelia contains her own death and ultimately the death of her son. By making her the bearer of these tidings, Shakespeare gives the actress playing Gertrude a pivotal moment in the development of her role.

MB: Hamlet suspects that Ophelia is being abused and reduced to a political chesspiece by her father (and therefore his master the king), but Ophelia is also clearly lying, and Hamlet cannot tell the degree to which she is compliant in an attempt to entrap him. Remember also that Hamlet is under observation in both the nunnery scene and the Players scene, and taking pains to appear mad.

How did you distinguish between the style of the play-within-the-play and that of the main drama?

RD: Clearly a style has to be found for the play-within-a-play which places it outside the boundaries of realistic action. Our solution was to perform it as a shadow play.

JC: Hamlet's advice to the Players is so specific and apt and modern – it's what any director of any age would want to say to his actors. To have the players in the play-within-the-play acting in a different style from the main protagonists you would have to have

10. Toby Stephens and Meg Fraser as Hamlet and Ophelia in Michael Boyd's production.

one or other of the casts ignoring Hamlet's, and therefore also Shakespeare's, instructions!

I used a staging trick. The play-within-the-play was performed at the very edge of the stage with Claudius, Gertrude and Polonius watching from upstage. The two audiences – for *The Mousetrap* at Elsinore and for *Hamlet* at the National Theatre – became reflections of one another. By the device of building false prosceniums on either side of the stage, I created 'wings'. Hamlet stood in the wings reacting as a director or author would in the wings of an actual theatre. The National Theatre audience could thereby watch Hamlet watching the play while he simultaneously observed the reactions of Claudius and Gertrude as they watched from their own auditorium. This solved the problem of Hamlet having to whisper things quietly enough for Claudius and Gertrude not to hear them, but loudly enough for Ophelia and the National Theatre audience to hear.

MB: Our players were brilliant, prone to coarseness, and seemingly harmless cousins of the mechanicals, but they were led by Greg

Hicks, who carried with him the awful authority of the Ghost. Like the inhabitants of Purgatory, they had been driven out of town. Like Shakespeare's own companies at times, they were being used as a political weapon.

Some Hamlets don't kill Claudius while he is trying to pray after the play-scene because they really want to send him to hell rather than heaven, whereas other Hamlets seem to be looking for an excuse not to execute the action. How did you approach this key moment?

JC: I think you have to take Hamlet at face value. In soliloquy Hamlet cannot lie to his audience. If the actor playing Hamlet is to have any moral authority he can't sometimes be telling the truth to the audience and sometimes not. Especially when in other soliloquies he debates the very nature of truth and reality.

I think the sight of Claudius praying sets up a moral perturbation in Hamlet that Shakespeare was fascinated by. Why else would he have created a scene in which Claudius prays? Much easier to have made Claudius an Iago, or a Richard III, a man incapable of remorse. In order to create added layers of moral complexity to the play, Shakespeare puts Claudius at the centre of the drama for the first time. This creates sympathy for him. What would the audience think of their hero if he killed a man while he was praying? The debate in Hamlet's mind is echoed by a debate in the audience's mind.

RD: In performance terms, is it really possible to distinguish between these two approaches? And may not both approaches co-exist at one and the same moment?

It seems to me that one of Hamlet's most astonishing qualities is his rigorous and unwavering honesty. Hamlet never lies to himself or to us – the soliloquies are moments of utter truth-telling. There is absolutely no equivocation as he lays before us his most secret doubts and fears.

So – and though Hamlet is clearly not alone on stage, his speech is another soliloquy, another moment of truth-telling! – does it not follow that we should believe him when he tells us his reason for not cutting Claudius' throat?

What's more, Hamlet is on his way to Gertrude's chamber. His mother stays! Claudius, now guilty beyond doubt, will keep for a more propitious moment.

In both practical and psychological terms, the closet scene presents problems, since Hamlet can see and hear the Ghost, but Gertrude can't. How did you deal with this?

JC: The closet scene gives you the opportunity to see Hamlet and his parents together as a family. Just before the Ghost's final exit I had him and Gertrude move so close to Hamlet that just for a moment he could touch both their faces at the same time. This moment returned him to his childhood. From then on, things become much clearer for him in the play. He has killed Polonius and is therefore no better than Claudius, the man he sought to kill. He starts to understand what his mother has done and the limits of her culpability. He forgives her.

Earlier in the play, other people have seen the Ghost, so you know he isn't a figment of Hamlet's imagination. But he isn't real to Gertrude, or doesn't appear to her. This is psychologically apt. She can't 'see' her husband any longer. If she could still see him she wouldn't have married his brother. It is Hamlet's perception of his father that brings her to her senses. He reminds her of her former happiness and her love for her husband and son. This is the beginning of Gertrude's madness. She never recovers from this scene.

RD: In one sense this presents no problem at all: Hamlet sees the Ghost and Gertrude does not. Those are the givens of the scene. It is a convention that the audience, possibly more trusting than actors and directors, completely and unquestioningly accepts.

Clearly, whatever difficulty we have with the scene, it did not suit Shakespeare's design that Gertrude should see the Ghost – it would probably have taken the scene into a completely different direction were she to have done so.

Perhaps for our benefit, if we cannot accept Shakespeare at face value, we need to ask why is it that Gertrude does not see the now not so monstrous and rather piteous apparition – in night attire? Are only those characters who are guilt-free capable of seeing the Ghost? Is that explanation enough? Sufficient to lay that question to rest?

Did you discuss whether or not Gertrude is having an affair with Claudius *before* the murder of Old Hamlet? Or is that not a useful question for director and actors?

JC: I don't think it's a useful question on its own. Better to link it with another. Does Gertrude know that Claudius has murdered her husband? There's no textual evidence to suggest that she does. At no point does Hamlet accuse her of being complicit. And at no point does she assert her innocence. It's not explored. The question could be rephrased. If Gertrude was having an affair with Claudius before he murdered his brother, is it more likely she was complicit in the murder? One would certainly think the more advanced the affair between Gertrude and Claudius, the more morally blind Gertrude must have been to what Claudius was up to. But Gertrude is to some extent the portrait of a morally blind person, so the question of complicity is an interesting one for the actress to consider. The actor playing Claudius also has a stake in the question. Has an affair with Gertrude propelled him to the murder of his brother?

It is difficult to imagine that Shakespeare intended Gertrude to be complicit in the murder. It would make everything she subsequently says to Hamlet impossibly hypocritical. It would also make Claudius and Gertrude into the Macbeths. Claudius is certainly a sketch for Macbeth, but the crucial difference between Gertrude and Lady Macbeth is complicity. Gertrude is far more interesting a character if her flaw is moral blindness rather than downright amorality.

RD: As useful as asking how many children does Lady Macbeth have? These are questions that fill in the psychological history of the characters and that create performance texture. Questions the actor will answer only for him or herself in whatever way he or she finds most stimulating to the imagination. The answers will inevitably remain a secret since there is no textual evidence for them. They are the actors' private fantasies that the audience can never partake in, but these secrets will inform in subtle but important ways every moment of the characters' lives on stage.

What kind of man was the Old King when he lived? Was he always busy at the office (or off fighting wars) and did he neglect his wife? How unhappy was she and did she turn to Claudius for consolation? Is Gertrude now, on her wedding day, a happy and sexually satisfied woman? How close were Hamlet and his father who, truth be told, seems so forbidding and so aloof, an irascible and bitter old man? And how much time did Hamlet spend as a little boy, playing in his beautiful mother's closet? Do the memories of his innocence, of her motherly love – and of her subsequent betrayal – colour the way he now enters the chamber? The way he speaks to her?

Certainly this is a story about kings and queens and princes and it may feel that questions like these tend to 'suburbanize' the narrative. And it may be that academics feel impatient if not infuriated by such banality. But beyond all the poetry, all the spiritual aspirations and deepest meanings of the plays, the personal relationships between fathers and mothers and their sons and daughters lie at the heart of most if not the entire canon. How many plays centre around the death of a father (or the king, which of course is the same thing)? How many daughters disobey their fathers (or, like Ophelia, pay the price for their obedience)? How many sons struggle with the desire or the need to kill their fathers? Bringing these relationships to life in the most intimate and truest way possible is the task that befalls the director and the actors – and if in doing so the questions asked and strategies adopted (along with a most rigorous analysis of the text, of course) may appear at first to reduce the scope and magnitude of the narratives, these are the very strategies that bring heartfelt immediacy and credibility to the plays and make them leap off the page and pulsate with life.

In many readings, Hamlet seems to have undergone a huge change during the fourth act rest when he is away at sea: was it like that in yours?

RD: Yes, the change is indeed huge. It is as if for Hamlet the agonizing inner struggle is over. His thoughts have indeed become bloody – he may not have actually wielded the knife, but he has sent his old friends Rosencrantz and Guildenstern to their death and they are not near his conscience. There is a curious serenity about him. The landscape of death is now awesomely familiar to him (no accident that at this moment he encounters Yorick once again) and he is not so much resigned as ready to face his own.

JC: Yes, I think it has to be. The temperature of his language is so different from earlier in the play. It's to do with what happens to his mind immediately after he kills Polonius. He's such a deeply moral creature that once he has murdered someone he forfeits the right to his moral superiority over his uncle and his mother. He cannot thereafter decide how his own story should be resolved.

This is a philosophical discovery, and the metaphor for his subsequent mental development is a voyage. As in *Pericles, The Tempest* and *Twelfth Night*, a journey by sea is an escape into a different world, a different way of life, or way of thought. Discovering that Ophelia has died unhinges him for a moment, but it does so only temporarily. In the very next scene he has recovered his equilibrium and seems quite sanguine when Horatio faces him with the possibility of his own death:

> there's a special providence in the fall of a sparrow. If it be now, 'tis not to come: if it be not to come, it will be now: if it be not now, yet it will come: the readiness is all. Since no man has aught of what he leaves, what is't to leave betimes? Let be.

The 'Let be' is not in the Folio, but Simon Russell Beale and I both thought it indispensable. It is the perfect spiritual punctuation for that speech and it must, surely, be by Shakespeare's hand. No other writer could have been at the same time so bold and so succinct.

MB: By the time of his return to Denmark, Hamlet has pondered on the resolute leadership of Fortinbras, killed two men, and arrived at a readiness to die. All of which seems to have stilled his bad dreams, and none of which bodes well for Claudius.

The exchange of rapiers in the duel is sometimes played as a matter of chance, sometimes with Hamlet knowing exactly what he is doing: how did your production handle it?

RD: My sense is that Hamlet perceives very quickly what is happening in the course of the duel. He is no longer an innocent in the face of worldly treachery and he can now give as good as he gets.

JC: Hamlet can't know what's going on when the duel is happening. The text is very clear. As Laertes is dying, he tells Hamlet what he's done and he speaks with what seems like genuine remorse:

LAERTES   The treacherous instrument is in thy hand,
            Unbated and envenomed. The foul practice
            Hath turned itself on me: lo, here I lie,
            Never to rise again. Thy mother's poisoned.
            I can no more. The king, the king's to blame.
HAMLET   The point envenomed too!

Shakespeare wouldn't have had Hamlet speaking that line if he already knew the point was envenomed.

MB: Once Hamlet knows for certain that the duel is a plot to murder him, there is nothing to stop him killing Laertes. Indeed, he'll probably have to if he's going to kill the king.

The play exists in three early texts of greatly differing lengths, suggesting that it evolved in performance in Shakespeare's lifetime and that cuts were applied at various times – in cutting your text to a manageable length, did you have a set of principles or was it more a case of following your directorial instincts?

RD: Common sense, I suppose. A desire to keep the action immediate and exciting, to make sure the text was clear and accessible. And understandable.

JC: A bit of both. There are obvious economies to be made whatever text you use. You don't need the play-with-the-play and the dumb show. One or other suffices. Playing them both means Claudius has to be peculiarly blind or arbitrarily distracted while watching the dumb show. Hamlet asking for his own lines to be inserted in *The Murder of Gonzago* must have been added by Shakespeare for performances where the subsequent soliloquy – 'O, what a rogue and peasant slave am I!' - was to be cut. If you include both, the former lines disable the climax in the latter – where Hamlet says 'About my brain' and goes on to invent the idea of using the play as a means of discerning Claudius' guilt.

But the largest cuts I made were inspired by a clear principle. I took the view that Shakespeare's play is at heart a domestic and philosophical drama, not a history play. In many of the productions of *Hamlet* that I've seen, the scenes that seemed to be more like history play than domestic tragedy were always the dull points in the evening, where you could feel the audience switching off; the plot involving Cornelius, Voltemand, Fortinbras and the Ambassadors; the mention of Norway or Poland seeming to distract the audience from the metaphorical power of the world that is Denmark. I started to feel as I studied the text leading up to rehearsals that there was a case for saying that the more political scenes may have been later additions, though certainly not by another hand. It is not too fanciful to think that Shakespeare may have been warned, or warned himself, that the language with which Hamlet describes the world was apparently so dangerously irreligious, even amoral in its tone, that his audience, and more importantly his noble sponsors, would find it impossible to accept, that it would behove him to set it in a more political framework and especially to give some hope for the future at the end of the play.

In any event it seemed to me that Fortinbras has absolutely no moral right to say what has been written for him. We don't know him, we don't care about him, and yet he's given a moral authority at the end of the play, an authority he hasn't earned and that seems to be written without any irony. He isn't like Malcolm at the end of *Macbeth*, who has lived through the terrible events of the play and, cleansed by his experience, has every right to the crown. So I cut Fortinbras and all that goes with him, ending the play with Horatio's lines:

> Now cracks a noble heart. Goodnight sweet prince,
> And flights of angels sing thee to thy rest!

What more apposite words could there be to end a play about mortality, nobility, philosophy and the meaning of earthly existence?

By the same token, I felt I couldn't do better than begin and end the play on the relationship between Hamlet and Horatio. At the start of the play I had Horatio arriving on the scene as if returning to it after a long absence. The other characters were enshrined in their tombs, all long dead. Horatio's memory of the events of the play brought them back to life. At the end of the play while Hamlet lies dying Horatio threatens to kill himself, but Hamlet stops him. If Horatio dies, who will tell Hamlet's story? Horatio is the only living witness. We may even ask another question: who other than Horatio could have told Shakespeare the story? It is diverting to imagine a silent final scene to *Hamlet* that we, the surviving inhabitants of Elsinore, watch at a distance from the battlements. Horatio is leaving the castle to return to Wittenberg and falls in with the company of Players, starting on their long trip back to London. We see him deep in conversation with the First Player who listens intently. The story is being told for the first time. It has started on its own long circular journey. From Hamlet to Horatio, from Horatio to the Player, from the Player to the page, from the page to the stage. Horatio has survived for the same reason that Kent and Edgar survive at the end of *Lear*, to 'speak what we feel, not what we ought to say'.

MB: We exploited the brevity and directness of the First Quarto, which feels like a cut playing script and propels the action forward, particularly after the death of Polonius; but the suppleness, subtlety and elegance of thought in the Folio reeks of the integrity of original authorship, and so we allowed its style to predominate.

I flirted until late in rehearsal with transposing 'To be' as a 'suicide bomber' speech immediately before 'Lights, lights, lights!', with the whole court frozen as Hamlet advanced slowly on Claudius, surrounded by Switzers. It worked as a thrilling dramatization of the difficulty of direct action, but it pushed the speech's vulnerability out the door, and so we restored it to the moment before Hamlet meets Ophelia.

SHAKESPEARE'S CAREER IN THE THEATRE

BEGINNINGS

William Shakespeare was an extraordinarily intelligent man who was born and died in an ordinary market town in the English Midlands. He lived an uneventful life in an eventful age. Born in April 1564, he was the eldest son of John Shakespeare, a glove-maker who was prominent on the town council until he fell into financial difficulties. Young William was educated at the local grammar in Stratford-upon-Avon, Warwickshire, where he gained a thorough grounding in the Latin language, the art of rhetoric and classical poetry. He married Ann Hathaway and had three children (Susanna, then the twins Hamnet and Judith) before his twenty-first birthday: an exceptionally young age for the period. We do not know how he supported his family in the mid-1580s.

Like many clever country boys, he moved to the city in order to make his way in the world. Like many creative people, he found a career in the entertainment business. Public playhouses and professional full-time acting companies reliant on the market for their income were born in Shakespeare's childhood. When he arrived in London as a man, sometime in the late 1580s, a new phenomenon was in the making: the actor who is so successful that he becomes a 'star'. The word did not exist in its modern sense, but the pattern is recognizable: audiences went to the theatre not so much to see a particular show as to witness the comedian Richard Tarlton or the dramatic actor Edward Alleyn.

Shakespeare was an actor before he was a writer. It appears not to have been long before he realized that he was never going to grow into a great comedian like Tarlton or a great tragedian like Alleyn. Instead, he found a role within his company as the man who patched up old plays, breathing new life, new dramatic twists, into tired repertory pieces. He paid close attention to the work of the university-educated dramatists who were writing history plays and tragedies for the public stage in a style more ambitious, sweeping and poetically grand than anything which had been seen before. But he may also have noted that what his friend and rival Ben Jonson would call 'Marlowe's mighty line' sometimes faltered in the mode of comedy. Going to university, as Christopher Marlowe did, was all well and good for honing the arts of rhetorical elaboration and classical allusion, but it could lead to a loss of the common touch. To stay close to a large segment of the potential audience for public theatre, it was necessary to write for clowns as well as kings and to intersperse the flights of poetry with the humour of the tavern, the privy and the brothel: Shakespeare was the first to establish himself early in his career as an equal master of tragedy, comedy and history. He realized that theatre could be the medium to make the national past available to a wider audience than the elite who could afford to read large history books: his signature early works include not only the classical tragedy *Titus Andronicus* but also the sequence of English historical plays on the Wars of the Roses.

He also invented a new role for himself, that of in-house company dramatist. Where his peers and predecessors had to sell their plays to the theatre managers on a poorly-paid piecework basis, Shakespeare took a percentage of the box-office income. The Lord Chamberlain's Men constituted themselves in 1594 as a joint stock company, with the profits being distributed among the core actors who had invested as sharers. Shakespeare acted himself – he appears in the cast lists of some of Ben Jonson's plays as well as the list of actors' names at the beginning of his own collected works – but his principal duty was to write two or three plays a year for the company. By holding shares, he was effectively earning himself a royalty on his work, something no author had ever done before in England. When the Lord Chamberlain's Men collected their fee for performance at court in the Christmas season of 1594, three of them went along to the Treasurer of the Chamber: not just Richard Burbage the tragedian and Will Kempe the clown, but also Shakespeare the scriptwriter. That was something new.

The next four years were the golden period in Shakespeare's career, though overshadowed by the death of his only son Hamnet, aged eleven, in 1596. In his early thirties and in full command of both his poetic and his theatrical medium, he perfected his art of comedy, while also developing his tragic and historical writing in new ways. In 1598, Francis Meres, a Cambridge University graduate with his finger on the pulse of the London literary world, praised Shakespeare for his excellence across the genres:

> As Plautus and Seneca are accounted the best for comedy and tragedy among the Latins, so Shakespeare among the English is the most excellent in both kinds for the stage; for comedy, witness his *Gentlemen of Verona*, his *Errors*, his *Love Labours Lost*, his *Love Labours Won*, his *Midsummer Night Dream* and his *Merchant of Venice*: for tragedy his *Richard the 2*, *Richard the 3*, *Henry the 4*, *King John*, *Titus Andronicus* and his *Romeo and Juliet*.

For Meres, as for the many writers who praised the 'honey-flowing vein' of *Venus and Adonis* and *Lucrece*, narrative poems written when the theatres were closed due to plague in 1593–94, Shakespeare was marked above all by his linguistic skill, by the gift of turning elegant poetic phrases.

PLAYHOUSES

Elizabethan playhouses were 'thrust' or 'one-room' theatres. To understand Shakespeare's original theatrical life, we have to forget about the indoor theatre of later times, with its proscenium arch and curtain that would be opened at the beginning and closed at the end of each act. In the proscenium arch theatre, stage and auditorium are effectively two separate rooms: the audience looks from one world into another as if through the imaginary 'fourth wall' framed by the proscenium. The picture-frame stage, together with the elaborate scenic effects and backdrops beyond it, created the illusion of a self-contained world – especially once nineteenth-century developments in the control of artificial lighting meant that the auditorium could be darkened and the spectators made to focus on the lighted stage. Shakespeare, by contrast, wrote for a bare platform stage with a standing audience gathered around it in a courtyard in full daylight. The audience were always conscious of themselves and their fellow-spectators, and they shared the same 'room' as the actors. A sense of immediate presence and the creation of rapport with the audience were all-important. The actor could not afford to imagine he was in a closed world, with silent witnesses dutifully observing him from the darkness.

Shakespeare's theatrical career began at the Rose Theatre in Southwark. The stage was wide and shallow, trapezoid in shape, like a lozenge. This design had a great deal of potential for the theatrical equivalent of cinematic split-screen effects, whereby one group of characters would enter at the door at one end of the tiring-house wall at the back of the stage and another group through the door at the other end, thus creating two rival tableaux. Many of the battle-heavy and faction-filled plays that premiered at the Rose have scenes of just this sort.

At the rear of the Rose stage, there were three capacious exits, each over ten feet wide. Unfortunately, the very limited excavation of a fragmentary portion of the original Globe site, also in 1989, revealed nothing about the stage. The first Globe was built in 1599 with similar proportions to those of another theatre, the Fortune, albeit that the former was polygonal and looked circular, whereas the latter was rectangular. The building contract for the Fortune survives and allows us to infer that the stage of the Globe was probably substantially wider than it was deep (perhaps forty-three feet wide and twenty-seven feet deep). It may well have been tapered at the front, like that of the Rose.

The capacity of the Globe was said to have been enormous, perhaps in excess of three thousand. It has been conjectured that about eight hundred people may have stood in the yard, with two thousand or more in the three layers of covered galleries. The other 'public' playhouses were also of large capacity, whereas the indoor Blackfriars theatre that Shakespeare's company began using in 1608 – the former refectory of a monastery – had overall internal dimensions of a mere forty-six by sixty feet. It would have made for a much more intimate theatrical experience and had a much smaller capacity, probably of about six hundred people. Since they paid at least sixpence a head, the Blackfriars attracted a more select or 'private' audience. The atmosphere would have been closer to that of an indoor performance before the court in the Whitehall Palace or at Richmond. That Shakespeare always wrote for indoor production at court as well as outdoor performance in the public theatre should make us cautious about inferring, as some scholars have, that the opportunity provided by the intimacy of the Blackfriars led to a significant change towards a 'chamber' style in his last plays – which, besides, were performed at both the Globe and the Blackfriars. After the occupation of the Blackfriars a five-act structure seems to have become more important to Shakespeare. That was because of artificial lighting: there were musical interludes between the acts, while the candles were trimmed and replaced. Again, though, something similar must have been necessary for indoor court performances throughout his career.

Front of house there were the 'gatherers' who collected the money from audience members: a penny to stand in the open-air yard, another penny for a place in the covered galleries, sixpence for the prominent 'lord's rooms' to the side of the stage. In the indoor 'private' theatres, gallants from the audience who fancied making themselves part of the spectacle sat on stools on the edge of the stage itself. Scholars debate as to how widespread this practice was in the public theatres such as the Globe. Once the audience were in place and the money counted, the gatherers were available to be extras on stage. That is one reason why battles and crowd scenes often come later rather than early in Shakespeare's plays. There was no formal prohibition upon performance by women, and there certainly were women among the gatherers, so it is not beyond the bounds of possibility that female crowd members were played by females.

The play began at two o'clock in the afternoon and the theatre had to be cleared by five. After the main show, there would be a jig – which consisted not only of dancing, but also of knockabout comedy (it is the origin of the farcical 'afterpiece' in the eighteenth-century theatre). So the time available for a Shakespeare play was about two and a half hours, somewhere between the 'two hours' traffic' mentioned in the prologue to *Romeo and Juliet* and the 'three hours' spectacle' referred to in the preface to the 1647 Folio of Beaumont and Fletcher's plays. The prologue to a play by Thomas Middleton refers to a thousand lines as 'one hour's words', so the likelihood is that about two and a half thousand, or a maximum of three thousand lines made up the performed text. This is indeed the length of most of Shakespeare's comedies, whereas many of his tragedies and histories are much longer, raising the possibility that he wrote full scripts, possibly with eventual publication in mind, in the full knowledge that the stage version would be heavily cut. The short Quarto texts published in his lifetime – they used to be called 'Bad' Quartos – provide fascinating evidence as to the kind of cutting that probably took place. So, for instance, the First Quarto of *Hamlet* neatly merges two occasions when Hamlet is overheard, the 'Fishmonger' and the 'nunnery' scenes.

The social composition of the audience was mixed. The poet Sir John Davies wrote of 'A thousand townsmen, gentlemen and whores, / Porters and servingmen' who would 'together throng' at the public playhouses. Though moralists associated female play-going with adultery and the sex trade, many perfectly respectable citizens' wives were regular attendees. Some, no doubt, resembled the modern groupie: a story attested in two different sources has one citizen's wife making a post-show assignation with Richard Burbage and ending up in bed with Shakespeare – supposedly eliciting from the latter the quip that William the Conqueror was before Richard III. Defenders of theatre liked to say that by witnessing the comeuppance of villains on the stage, audience members would repent of their own wrongdoings, but the reality is that most people went to the theatre then, as they do now, for entertainment more than moral edification. Besides, it would be foolish to suppose that audiences behaved in a homogeneous way: a pamphlet of the 1630s tells of how two men went to see *Pericles* and one of them laughed while the other wept. Bishop John Hall complained that people went to church for the same reasons that they went to the theatre: 'for company, for custom, for recreation . . . to feed his eyes or his ears . . . or perhaps for sleep'.

Men-about-town and clever young lawyers went to be seen as much as to see. In the modern popular imagination, shaped not least by *Shakespeare in Love* and the opening sequence of Laurence Olivier's *Henry V* film, the penny-paying groundlings stand in the yard hurling abuse or encouragement and hazelnuts or orange peel at the actors, while the sophisticates in the covered galleries appreciate Shake-speare's soaring poetry. The reality was probably the other way round. A 'groundling' was a kind of fish, so the nickname suggests the penny audience standing below the level of the stage and gazing in silent open-mouthed wonder at the spectacle unfolding above them. The more difficult audience members, who kept up a running commentary of clever remarks on the performance and who occasionally got into quarrels with players, were the gallants. Like Hollywood movies in modern times, Elizabethan and Jacobean plays exercised a powerful influence on the fashion and behaviour of the young. John Marston mocks the lawyers who would open their lips, perhaps to court a girl, and out would 'flow / Naught but pure Juliet and Romeo'.

THE ENSEMBLE AT WORK

In the absence of typewriters and photocopying machines, reading aloud would have been the means by which the company got to know a new play. The tradition of the playwright reading his complete script to the assembled company endured for generations. A copy would then have been taken to the Master of the Revels for licensing. The theatre book-holder or prompter would then have copied the parts for distribution to the actors. A partbook consisted of the character's lines, with each speech preceded by the last three or four words of the speech before, the so-called 'cue'. These would have been taken away and studied or 'conned'. During this period of learning the parts, an actor might have had some one-to-one instruction, perhaps from the dramatist, perhaps from a senior actor who had played the same part before, and, in the case of an apprentice, from his master. A high percentage of Desdemona's lines occur in dialogue with Othello, of Lady Macbeth's with Macbeth, Cleopatra's with Antony and Volumnia's with Coriolanus. The roles would almost certainly have been taken by the apprentice of the lead actor, usually Burbage, who delivers the majority of the cues. Given that apprentices lodged with their masters, there would have been

11. Hypothetical reconstruction of the interior of an Elizabethan playhouse during a performance.

ample opportunity for personal instruction, which may be what made it possible for young men to play such demanding parts.

After the parts were learned, there may have been no more than a single rehearsal before the first performance. With six different plays to be put on every week, there was no time for more. Actors, then, would go into a show with a very limited sense of the whole. The notion of a collective rehearsal process that is itself a process of discovery for the actors is wholly modern and would have been incomprehensible to Shakespeare and his original ensemble. Given the number of parts an actor had to hold in his memory, the forgetting of lines was probably more frequent than in the modern theatre. The book-holder was on hand to prompt.

Backstage personnel included the property man, the tire-man who oversaw the costumes, call-boys, attendants and the musicians, who might play at various times from the main stage, the rooms above and within the tiring-house. Scriptwriters sometimes made a nuisance of themselves backstage. There was often tension between the acting companies and the freelance playwrights from whom they purchased scripts: it was a smart move on the part of Shakespeare and the Lord Chamberlain's Men to bring the writing process in-house.

Scenery was limited, though sometimes set-pieces were brought on (a bank of flowers, a bed, the mouth of hell). The trapdoor from below, the gallery stage above and the curtained discovery-space at the back allowed for an array of special effects: the rising of ghosts and apparitions, the descent of gods, dialogue between a character at a window and another at ground level, the revelation of a statue or a pair of lovers playing at chess. Ingenious use could be made of props, as with the ass's head in *A Midsummer Night's Dream*. In a theatre that does not clutter the stage with the material paraphernalia of everyday life, those objects that are deployed may take on powerful symbolic weight, as when Shylock bears his weighing scales in one hand and knife in the other, thus becoming a parody of the figure of Justice who traditionally bears a sword and a balance. Among the more significant items in the property cupboard of Shakespeare's company, there would have been a throne (the 'chair of state'), joint stools, books, bottles, coins, purses, letters (which are brought on stage, read or referred to on about eighty occasions in the complete works), maps, gloves, a set of stocks (in which Kent is put in *King Lear*), rings, rapiers, daggers, broadswords, staves, pistols, masks and vizards, heads and skulls, torches and tapers and lanterns which served to signal night scenes on the daylit stage, a buck's head, an ass's head, animal costumes. Live animals also put in appearances, most notably the dog Crab in *The Two Gentlemen of Verona* and possibly a young polar bear in *The Winter's Tale*.

The costumes were the most important visual dimension of the play. Playwrights were paid between £2 and £6 per script, whereas Alleyn was not averse to paying £20 for 'a black velvet cloak with sleeves embroidered all with silver and gold'. No matter the period of the play, actors always wore contemporary costume. The excitement for the audience came not from any impression of historical accuracy, but from the richness of the attire and perhaps the transgressive thrill of the knowledge that here were commoners like themselves strutting in the costumes of courtiers in effective defiance of the strict sumptuary laws whereby in real life people had to wear the clothes that befitted their social station.

To an even greater degree than props, costumes could carry symbolic importance. Racial characteristics could be suggested: a breastplate and helmet for a Roman soldier, a turban for a Turk, long robes for exotic characters such as Moors, a gabardine for a Jew. The figure of Time, as in *The Winter's Tale*, would be equipped with hourglass, scythe and wings; Rumour, who speaks the prologue of *2 Henry IV*, wore a costume adorned with a thousand tongues. The wardrobe in the tiring-house of the Globe would have contained much of the same stock as that of rival manager Philip Henslowe at the Rose: green gowns for outlaws and foresters, black for melancholy men such as Jaques and people in mourning such as the Countess in *All's Well that Ends Well* (at the beginning of *Hamlet*, the prince is still in mourning black when everyone else is in festive garb for the wedding of the new king), a gown and hood for a friar (or a feigned friar like the duke in *Measure for Measure*), blue coats and tawny to distinguish the followers of rival factions, a leather apron and ruler for a carpenter (as in the opening scene of *Julius Caesar* – and in *A Midsummer Night's Dream*, where this is the only sign that Peter Quince is a carpenter), a cockle hat with staff and a pair of sandals for a pilgrim or palmer (the disguise assumed by Helen in *All's Well*), bodices and kirtles with farthingales beneath for the boys who are to be dressed as girls. A gender switch such as that of Rosalind or Jessica seems to have taken between fifty and eighty lines of dialogue – Viola does not resume her 'maiden weeds', but remains in her boy's costume to the end of *Twelfth Night* because a change would have slowed down the action at just the moment it was speeding to a climax. Henslowe's inventory also included 'a robe for to go invisible': Oberon, Puck and Ariel must have had something similar.

As the costumes appealed to the eyes, so there was music for the ears. Comedies included many songs. Desdemona's willow song, perhaps a late addition to the text, is a rare and thus exceptionally poignant example from tragedy. Trumpets and tuckets sounded for ceremonial entrances, drums denoted an army on the march. Background music could create atmosphere, as at the beginning of *Twelfth Night*, during the lovers' dialogue near the end of *The Merchant of Venice*, when the statue seemingly comes to life in *The Winter's Tale*, and for the revival of Pericles and of Lear (in the Quarto text, but not the Folio). The haunting sound of the hautboy suggested a realm beyond the human, as when the god Hercules is imagined deserting Mark Antony. Dances symbolized the harmony of the end of a comedy – though in Shakespeare's world of mingled joy and sorrow, someone is usually left out of the circle.

The most important resource was, of course, the actors themselves. They needed many skills: in the words of one contemporary commentator, 'dancing, activity, music, song, elocution, ability of body, memory, skill of weapon, pregnancy of wit'. Their bodies were as significant as their voices. Hamlet tells the player to 'suit the action to the word, the word to the action': moments of strong emotion, known as 'passions', relied on a repertoire of dramatic gestures as well as a modulation of the voice. When Titus Andronicus has had his hand chopped off, he asks 'How can I grace my talk, / Wanting a hand to give it action?' A pen portrait of 'The Character of an Excellent Actor' by the dramatist John Webster is almost certainly based on his impression of Shakespeare's leading man, Richard Burbage: 'By a full and significant action of body, he charms our attention: sit in a full theatre, and you will think you see so many lines drawn from the circumference of so many ears, whiles the actor is the centre . . . .'

Though Burbage was admired above all others, praise was also heaped upon the apprentice players whose alto voices fitted them for the parts of women. A spectator at Oxford in 1610 records how the audience were reduced to tears by the pathos of Desdemona's death. The puritans who fumed about the biblical prohibition upon cross-dressing and the encouragement to sodomy constituted by the sight of an adult male kissing a teenage boy on stage were a small minority. Little is known, however, about the characteristics of the leading apprentices in Shakespeare's company. It may perhaps be inferred that one was a lot taller than the other, since Shakespeare often wrote for a pair of female friends, one tall and fair, the other short and dark (Helena and Hermia, Rosalind and Celia, Beatrice and Hero).

We know little about Shakespeare's own acting roles – an early allusion indicates that he often took royal parts, and a venerable tradition gives him old Adam in *As You Like It* and the ghost of old King Hamlet. Save for Burbage's lead roles and the generic part of the clown, all such castings are mere speculation. We do not even know for sure whether the original Falstaff was Will Kempe or another actor who specialized in comic roles, Thomas Pope.

Kempe left the company in early 1599. Tradition has it that he fell out with Shakespeare over the matter of excessive improvisation. He was replaced by Robert Armin, who was less of a clown and more of a cerebral wit: this explains the difference between such parts as Lancelet Gobbo and Dogberry, which were written for Kempe, and the more verbally sophisticated Feste and Lear's Fool, which were written for Armin.

One thing that is clear from surviving 'plots' or story-boards of plays from the period is that a degree of doubling was necessary. *2 Henry VI* has over sixty speaking parts, but more than half of the characters only appear in a single scene and most scenes have only six to eight speakers. At a stretch, the play could be performed by thirteen actors. When Thomas Platter saw *Julius Caesar* at the Globe in 1599, he noted that there were about fifteen. Why doesn't Paris go to the Capulet ball in *Romeo and Juliet*? Perhaps because he was doubled with Mercutio, who does. In *The Winter's Tale*, Mamillius might have come back as Perdita and Antigonus been doubled by Camillo, making the partnership with Paulina at the end a very neat touch. Titania and Oberon are often played by the same pair as Hippolyta and Theseus, suggesting a symbolic matching of the rulers of the worlds of night and day, but it is questionable whether there would have been time for the necessary costume changes. As so often, one is left in a realm of tantalizing speculation.

THE KING'S MAN

The new king, James I, who had held the Scottish throne as James VI since he had been an infant, immediately took the Lord Chamberlain's Men under his direct patronage. Henceforth they would be the King's Men, and for the rest of Shakespeare's career they were favoured with far more court performances than any of their rivals. There even seem to have been rumours early in the reign that Shakespeare and Burbage were being considered for knighthoods, an unprecedented honour for mere actors – and one that in the event was not accorded to a member of the profession for nearly three hundred years, when the title was bestowed upon Henry Irving, the leading Shakespearean actor of Queen Victoria's reign.

Shakespeare's productivity rate slowed in the Jacobean years, not because of age or some personal trauma, but because there were frequent outbreaks of plague, causing the theatres to be closed for long periods. The King's Men were forced to spend many months on the road. Between November 1603 and 1608, they were to be found at various towns in the south and Midlands, though Shakespeare probably did not tour with them by this time. He had bought a large house back home in Stratford and was accumulating other property. He may indeed have stopped acting soon after the new king took the throne. With the London theatres closed so much of the time and a large repertoire on the stocks, Shakespeare seems to have focused his energies on writing a few long and complex tragedies that could have been played on demand at court: *Othello*, *King Lear*, *Antony and Cleopatra*, *Coriolanus* and *Cymbeline* are among his longest and poetically grandest plays. *Macbeth* only survives in a shorter text, which shows signs of adaptation after Shakespeare's death. The bitterly satirical *Timon of Athens*, apparently a collaboration with Thomas Middleton that may have failed on the stage, also belongs to this period. In comedy, too, he wrote longer and morally darker works than in the Elizabethan period, pushing at the very bounds of the form in *Measure for Measure* and *All's Well that Ends Well*.

From 1608 onwards, when the King's Men began occupying the indoor Blackfriars playhouse (as a winter house, meaning that they only used the outdoor Globe in summer?), Shakespeare turned to a more romantic style. His company had a great success with a revived and altered version of an old pastoral play called *Mucedorus*. It even featured a bear. The younger dramatist John Fletcher, meanwhile, sometimes working in collaboration with Francis Beaumont, was pioneering a new style of tragicomedy, a mix of romance and royalism laced with intrigue and pastoral excursions. Shakespeare experimented with this idiom in *Cymbeline* and it was presumably with his blessing that Fletcher eventually took over as the King's Men's company dramatist. The two writers apparently collaborated on three plays in the years 1612–14: a lost romance called *Cardenio* (based on the love-madness of a character in Cervantes' *Don Quixote*), *Henry VIII* (originally staged with the title 'All is True'), and *The Two Noble Kinsmen*, a dramatization of Chaucer's 'Knight's Tale' These were written after Shakespeare's two final solo-authored plays, *The Winter's Tale*, a self-consciously old-fashioned work dramatizing the pastoral romance of his old enemy Robert Greene, and *The Tempest*, which at one and the same time drew together multiple theatrical traditions, diverse reading and contemporary interest in the fate of a ship that had been wrecked on the way to the New World.

The collaborations with Fletcher suggest that Shakespeare's career ended with a slow fade rather than the sudden retirement supposed by the nineteenth-century Romantic critics who read Prospero's epilogue to *The Tempest* as Shakespeare's personal farewell to his art. In the last few years of his life Shakespeare certainly spent more of his time in Stratford-upon-Avon, where he became further involved in property dealing and litigation. But his London life also continued. In 1613 he made his first major London property purchase: a freehold house in the Blackfriars district, close to his company's indoor theatre. *The Two Noble Kinsmen* may have been written as late as 1614, and Shakespeare was in London on business a little over a year before he died of an unknown cause at home in Stratford-upon-Avon in 1616, probably on his fifty-second birthday.

About half the sum of his works were published in his lifetime, in texts of variable quality. A few years after his death, his fellow-actors began putting together an authorized edition of his complete *Comedies, Histories and Tragedies*. It appeared in 1623, in large 'Folio' format. This collection of thirty-six plays gave Shakespeare his immortality. In the words of his fellow-dramatist Ben Jonson, who contributed two poems of praise at the start of the Folio, the body of his work made him 'a monument without a tomb':

And art alive still while thy book doth live
And we have wits to read and praise to give ...
He was not of an age, but for all time!

SHAKESPEARE'S WORKS: A CHRONOLOGY

1589–91	*? Arden of Faversham* (possible part authorship)
1589–92	*The Taming of the Shrew*
1589–92	*? Edward the Third* (possible part authorship)
1591	*The Second Part of Henry the Sixth*, originally called *The First Part of the Contention betwixt the Two Famous Houses of York and Lancaster* (element of co-authorship possible)
1591	*The Third Part of Henry the Sixth*, originally called *The True Tragedy of Richard Duke of York* (element of co-authorship probable)
1591–92	*The Two Gentlemen of Verona*
1591–92 perhaps revised 1594	*The Lamentable Tragedy of Titus Andronicus* (probably co-written with, or revising an earlier version by, George Peele)
1592	*The First Part of Henry the Sixth*, probably with Thomas Nashe and others
1592/94	*King Richard the Third*
1593	*Venus and Adonis* (poem)
1593–94	*The Rape of Lucrece* (poem)
1593–1608	*Sonnets* (154 poems, published 1609 with *A Lover's Complaint*, a poem of disputed authorship)
1592–94/ 1600–03	*Sir Thomas More* (a single scene for a play originally by Anthony Munday, with other revisions by Henry Chettle, Thomas Dekker and Thomas Heywood)
1594	*The Comedy of Errors*
1595	*Love's Labour's Lost*

1595–97	*Love's Labour's Won* (a lost play, unless the original title for another comedy)
1595–96	*A Midsummer Night's Dream*
1595–96	*The Tragedy of Romeo and Juliet*
1595–96	*King Richard the Second*
1595–97	*The Life and Death of King John* (possibly earlier)
1596–97	*The Merchant of Venice*
1596–97	*The First Part of Henry the Fourth*
1597–98	*The Second Part of Henry the Fourth*
1598	*Much Ado about Nothing*
1598–99	*The Passionate Pilgrim* (20 poems, some not by Shakespeare)
1599	*The Life of Henry the Fifth*
1599	'To the Queen' (epilogue for a court performance)
1599	*As You Like It*
1599	*The Tragedy of Julius Caesar*
1600–01	*The Tragedy of Hamlet, Prince of Denmark* (perhaps revising an earlier version)
1600–01	*The Merry Wives of Windsor* (perhaps revising version of 1597–99)
1601	'Let the Bird of Loudest Lay' (poem, known since 1807 as 'The Phoenix and Turtle' (turtle-dove))
1601	*Twelfth Night, or What You Will*
1601–02	*The Tragedy of Troilus and Cressida*
1604	*The Tragedy of Othello, the Moor of Venice*
1604	*Measure for Measure*
1605	*All's Well that Ends Well*
1605	*The Life of Timon of Athens*, with Thomas Middleton
1605–06	*The Tragedy of King Lear*
1605–08	? contribution to *The Four Plays in One* (lost, except for *A Yorkshire Tragedy*, mostly by Thomas Middleton)
1606	*The Tragedy of Macbeth* (surviving text has additional scenes by Thomas Middleton)
1606–07	*The Tragedy of Antony and Cleopatra*
1608	*The Tragedy of Coriolanus*

1608	*Pericles, Prince of Tyre*, with George Wilkins
1610	*The Tragedy of Cymbeline*
1611	*The Winter's Tale*
1611	*The Tempest*
1612–13	*Cardenio*, with John Fletcher (survives only in later adaptation called *Double Falsehood* by Lewis Theobald)
1613	*Henry VIII (All is True)*, with John Fletcher
1613–14	*The Two Noble Kinsmen*, with John Fletcher

THE HISTORY BEHIND
THE TRAGEDIES

Era/Date	Event	Location	Play
Greek myth	Trojan war	Troy	*Troilus and Cressida*
Greek myth	Theseus King of Athens	Athens	*The Two Noble Kinsmen*
c.tenth–ninth century BC?	Leir King of Britain (legendary)	Britain	*King Lear*
535–510 BC	Tarquin II King of Rome	Rome	*The Rape of Lucrece*
493 BC	Caius Martius captures Corioli	Italy	*Coriolanus*
431–404 BC	Peloponnesian war	Greece	*Timon of Athens*
17 Mar 45 BC	Battle of Munda: Caesar's victory over Pompey's sons	Munda, Spain	*Julius Caesar*
Oct 45 BC	Caesar returns to Rome for triumph	Rome	*Julius Caesar*
15 Mar 44 BC	Assassination of Caesar	Rome	*Julius Caesar*
27 Nov 43 BC	Formation of Second Triumvirate	Rome	*Julius Caesar*
Oct 42 BC	Battle of Philippi	Philippi, Macedonia	*Julius Caesar*
Winter 41–40 BC	Antony visits Cleopatra	Egypt	*Antony and Cleopatra*
Oct 40 BC	Pact of Brundisium; marriage of Antony and Octavia	Italy	*Antony and Cleopatra*
39 BC	Pact of Misenum between Pompey and the triumvirs	Campania, Italy	*Antony and Cleopatra*
39–38 BC	Ventidius defeats the Parthians in a series of engagements	Syria	*Antony and Cleopatra*

34 BC	Cleopatra and her children proclaimed rulers of the eastern Mediterranean	Alexandria	*Antony and Cleopatra*
2 Sep 31 BC	Battle of Actium	On the coast of western Greece	*Antony and Cleopatra*
Aug 30 BC	Death of Antony	Alexandria	*Antony and Cleopatra*
12 Aug 30 BC	Death of Cleopatra	Alexandria	*Antony and Cleopatra*
Early first century AD	Cunobelinus/ Cymbeline rules Britain (and dies before AD 43)	Britain	*Cymbeline*
During the reign of a fictional (late?) Roman emperor		Rome	*Titus Andronicus*
c.ninth–tenth century AD	Existence of legendary Amleth?	Denmark	*Hamlet*
15 Aug 1040	Death of Duncan I of Scotland	Bothnguane, Scotland	*Macbeth*
1053	Malcolm invades Scotland	Scotland	*Macbeth*
15 Aug 1057	Death of Macbeth	Lumphanan, Scotland	*Macbeth*
7 Oct 1571	Naval battle of Lepanto between Christians and Turks	The Mediterranean, off the coast of Greece	A context for *Othello*

FURTHER READING
AND VIEWING

CRITICAL APPROACHES

Adelman, Janet, *Suffocating Mothers: Fantasies of Maternal Origin in Shakespeare's Plays, Hamlet to The Tempest* (1992). Psychoanalytical approach.

Bradley, A. C., *Shakespearean Tragedy* (1904). Immensely influential.

Colie, Rosalie L., *Shakespeare's Living Art* (1974). Excellent on the idea of melancholy.

Frye, Roland Mushat, *The Renaissance Hamlet: Issues and Responses 1600* (1984). Invaluable historical placing.

Granville-Barker, Harley, *Hamlet* in his *Prefaces to Shakespeare*, Vol. 1 (1946). Very satisfying reading by a great man of the theatre.

Greenblatt, Stephen, *Hamlet in Purgatory* (2001). Powerful reading of context of religious controversy.

Jones, Ernest, *Hamlet and Oedipus* (1949). Extended Freudian reading.

Knight, G. Wilson, 'The Embassy of Death', in his *The Wheel of Fire* (1930, repr. 2001). Very strong on imagery.

Mercer, Peter, *Hamlet and the Acting of Revenge* (1987). Worth comparing with Prosser.

O'Toole, Fintan, *Shakespeare is Hard, but so is Life* (2002), originally published as *No More Heroes* (1995). Highly sensible introductory account, with strong emphasis on politics; dispels the myth of the 'tragic flaw'.

Prosser, Eleanor, *Hamlet and Revenge* (1967). Worth comparing with Mercer.

Rosenberg, Marvin, *The Masks of Hamlet* (1992). Scene by scene account, using actors' and directors' interpretations down the ages.

Wilson, J. Dover, *What Happens in Hamlet* (1935). Thorough investigation of key problems.

THE PLAY IN PERFORMANCE

Brooke, Michael, '*Hamlet* on Screen', www.screenonline.org.uk/tv/id/566312/index.html. Valuable overview. Registered schools, colleges, universities and libraries have access to video clips, including extracts from the 1913 silent version, Olivier's 1948 film and the 1964 production at Elsinore.

Dawson, Anthony B., *Hamlet*, Shakespeare in Performance (1996). Excellent roundup.

Hapgood, Robert, ed., *Hamlet, Prince of Denmark*, Shakespeare in Production (1999). Good accounts of wide range of productions.

Howard, Tony, *Women as Hamlet: Performance and Interpretation in Theatre, Film and Fiction* (2007). Fascinating, and of even further-reaching interest than its title suggests.

Lavender, Andy, *Hamlet in Pieces: Shakespeare Reworked by Peter Brook, Robert Lepage, Robert Wilson* (2001). Lively accounts of experimental versions.

Maher, Mary Z., *Modern Hamlets and Their Soliloquies* (2003). Based on interviews with actors, including David Warner, Ben Kingsley and Kevin Kline.

Players of Shakespeare 1, 2, 3 (1985–93). Each of these three volumes includes excellent interviews with actors who have played major roles in *Hamlet*.

Royal Shakespeare Company, 'Exploring Shakespeare: Hamlet', www.rsc.org.uk/learning/hamletandmacbeth/keyidea/hamletkeyidea.htm. Rehearsal footage, actor and director interviews, commentary on Michael Boyd's 2004 production.

For a more detailed Shakespeare bibliography and selections from a wide range of critical accounts of the play, with linking commentary, visit the edition website, www.rscshakespeare.co.uk.

AVAILABLE ON DVD

Hamlet, directed by Hay Plumb (1913, DVD 2004). The longest Shakespeare film from the age of silent film.

Hamlet, directed by Laurence Olivier (1948). Highly influential.

Hamlet, directed by Grigori Kozintsev (1964). Powerful Russian version.

Richard Burton's Hamlet, directed by Bill Colleran (1964). Film of American stage production.

Hamlet at Elsinore, directed by Philip Saville (1964). Film of BBC television production that played at Elsinore; not currently available, but extracts may be seen via screenonline website (see p. 240, Brooke).

Hamlet, directed by Tony Richardson (1969). Film of London Roundhouse stage production starring Nicol Williamson.

Hamlet, BBC Television Shakespeare, directed by Rodney Bennett (1980). Starring Derek Jacobi.

Hamlet, directed by Franco Zeffirelli (1990). Starring Mel Gibson.

Hamlet, directed by Kenneth Branagh (1996). Uncut text.

Hamlet, directed by Michael Almereyda (2000). Underrated version transposed to contemporary New York.

The Tragedy of Hamlet, directed by Peter Brook (BBC4 television, tx. 6 March 2002, DVD 2006). Starring Adrian Lester; superbly lucid version, in heavily cut text, with a documentary 'Brook by Brook'.

REFERENCES

1 Anthony B. Dawson, *Shakespeare in Performance: Hamlet* (1995), p. 25.
2 Printed by J. P. Collier, *Annals of the Stage*, 1831, Vol. 1, in Gamini Salgado, *Eyewitnesses of Shakespeare: First Hand Accounts of Performances 1590–1890* (1975), pp. 38–9.
3 John Downes, *Roscius Anglicanus* (1708, repr. 1969), p. 21.
4 Richard Steele, in an originally unsigned review of *Hamlet* in *The Tatler, with Notes and a General Index: Complete in One Volume* (1835), p. 154.
5 Colley Cibber, *An Apology for the Life of Mr Colley Cibber* (repr. 1889), p. 61.
6 Henry Mackenzie, *The Mirror* (Edinburgh), No. 99, 17 April 1780.
7 Walter Scott, 'Life of John Philip Kemble', *Quarterly Review*, 34 (1826), p. 214.
8 Georg Lichtenberg, *Lichtenberg's Visits to England*, translated and annotated by Margaret L. Mare and W. H. Quarrell (1969), p. 10.
9 Mary Russell Mitford, *The Life of Mary Russell Mitford* (1870), Vol. 2, p. 336.
10 Theodore Martin, 'An Eye-Witness of John Kemble', *Nineteenth Century* (1880), p. 292.
11 Robert Hapgood, *Shakespeare in Production: Hamlet* (1999), p. 27.
12 James Henry Hackett, *Notes and Comments upon Certain Plays and Actors of Shakespeare* (early nineteenth century, printed 1968), p. 140.
13 William Charles Macready, *The Diaries of William Charles Macready 1833–1851*, ed. William Toynbee (1912), p. 242.
14 *New York Herald*, 28 November 1864.
15 J. Ranken Towse, 'Henry Irving', *Century Magazine*, 27 March 1884, p. 666.
16 Charles Edward Russell, *Julia Marlowe* (1926), p. 39.
17 *Academy*, 18 September 1897.
18 Eden Phillpotts, 'Irving as Hamlet', in *We Saw Him Act* (1939), p. 122.
19 George Bernard Shaw, *Shaw on Shakespeare*, ed. Edwin Wilson (1969), p. 91.
20 Shaw, *Shaw on Shakespeare*, p. 87.
21 *Daily News*, 13 September 1897.
22 James Agate, *Brief Chronicles* (1943), p. 247.
23 John Gielgud, *Notes from the Gods* (1994), p. 98.
24 Laurence Olivier, *On Acting* (1986), pp. 60–1.
25 Olivier, *On Acting*, p. 62.
26 Ivor Brown, quoted in Claire Cochrane, *Shakespeare and the Birmingham Repertory Theatre 1913–29* (1993), p. 119.
27 *Sunday Times*, 30 August 1925.
28 Gielgud, *Notes from the Gods*, p. 102.
29 Hapgood, *Shakespeare in Production*, p. 65.
30 Quoted in Richard Findlater, *The Player Kings* (1921), p. 201.
31 Dawson, *Shakespeare in Performance*, p. 116.
32 Hapgood, *Shakespeare in Production*, p. 69.
33 Andy Lavender, *Hamlet in Pieces: Shakespeare Reworked by Peter Brook, Robert Lepage, Robert Wilson* (2001), p. 232.

34 Sarah Bernhardt, *Harper's Bazaar*, 15 December 1900, quoted in Hapgood, *Shakespeare in Production*, p. 47.

35 Voltaire, 'Essai sur la poésie épique' (1733), *Oeuvres Complètes* (1877–83), Vol. 8, pp. 317–18.

36 Jonathan Bate, 'Which Hamlet?', note in *Hamlet*, RSC Programme, 2004.

37 Philip Franks, 'Hamlet', in Russell Jackson and Robert Smallwood, eds, *Players of Shakespeare 3* (1993).

38 Mary Z. Maher, *Modern Hamlets and Their Soliloquies* (2003), p. 177.

39 Maher, *Modern Hamlets*, p. 179.

40 Peter Hall, 'Hamlet', in *Theatre at Work: Playwrights and Productions in the Modern British Theatre*, ed. Charles Marowitz and Simon Trussler (1967).

41 Georgina Brown, *Mail on Sunday*, 6 May 2001.

42 John Gross, *Sunday Telegraph*, 6 May 2001.

43 Susannah Clapp, *Observer*, 6 May 2001.

44 Nicholas de Jongh, *Evening Standard*, 3 May 2001.

45 Matthew Warchus, *Hamlet and The Spanish Tragedy*, RSC Education Pack (1997).

46 Lyn Gardner, interview with Matthew Warchus, *Guardian*, 'Ban the Bard', 8 May 1997.

47 Michael Billington, *Guardian*, 10 May 1997.

48 Andrew Billen, *Observer*, 11 May 1997.

49 Robert Butler, *Independent*, 11 May 1997.

50 Michael Pennington, 'Hamlet', in *Players of Shakespeare*, ed. Philip Brockbank (1985).

51 Irving Wardle, *The Times*, 3 July 1980.

52 Michael Billington, *Guardian*, 3 July 1980.

53 Greenblatt, 'Who's There?', note in *Hamlet*, RSC Programme, 2004.

54 Robert Butler, *Independent*, 11 May 1997.

55 Dawson, *Shakespeare in Performance*, p. 69.

56 Maher, *Modern Hamlets*, p. 166.

57 Ronald Bryden, *New Statesman*, 27 August 1965.

58 Stanley Wells, *Shakespeare: A Dramatic Life* (1994), p. 236.

59 Pennington, in Brockbank, *Players of Shakespeare*, p. 177.

60 Irving Wardle, *The Times*, 3 July 1980.

61 Paul Taylor, *Independent*, 29 July 2004.

62 *Hamlet*, RSC Online Playguide, 2005.

63 Greg Hicks, *Hamlet*, RSC Online Playguide, 2005.

64 Michael Boyd, *Hamlet*, RSC Online Playguide, 2005.

65 Meg Fraser, *Hamlet*, RSC Online Playguide, 2005.

66 Michael Coveney, *Observer*, 20 December 1992.

67 Bob Crowley, designer, in interview with Andy Lavender, *The Times*, 16 December 1992.

68 Nicholas de Jongh, *Evening Standard*, 3 May 2001.

69 Irving Wardle, *The Times*, 27 April 1989.

70 Michael Schmidt, *Daily Telegraph*, 28 April 1989.

71 *Guardian*, 28 December 1989.

72 John Peter, *Sunday Times*, 30 April 1989.

73 Frances Barber, 'Ophelia in *Hamlet*', in *Players of Shakespeare 2*, ed. Russell Jackson and Robert Smallwood (1988), p. 94.

74 Meg Fraser, *Hamlet*, RSC Online Playguide, 2005.

75 Dawson, *Shakespeare in Performance*, p. 65.

76 Tony Church, 'Polonius in *Hamlet*', in Brockbank, *Players of Shakespeare*.

ACKNOWLEDGEMENTS AND PICTURE CREDITS

Preparation of '*Hamlet* in Performance' was assisted by a generous grant from the CAPITAL Centre (Creativity and Performance in Teaching and Learning) of the University of Warwick for research in the RSC archive at the Shakespeare Birthplace Trust. The Arts and Humanities Research Council (AHRC) funded a term's research leave that enabled Jonathan Bate to work on 'The Director's Cut'.

Picture research by Helen Robson and Jan Sewell. Grateful acknowledgement is made to the Shakespeare Birthplace Trust for assistance with picture research (special thanks to Helen Hargest) and reproduction fees.

Images of RSC productions are supplied by the Shakespeare Centre Library and Archive, Stratford-upon-Avon. This Library, maintained by the Shakespeare Birthplace Trust, holds the most important collection of Shakespeare material in the UK, including the Royal Shakespeare Company's official archives. It is open to the public free of charge.

For more information see www.shakespeare.org.uk.

1. 'Rapier and Dagger' in private collection © Bardbiz Limited
2. 'They change rapiers' in private collection © Bardbiz Limited
3. London's Drury Lane Theatre, Forbes Robertson (1913) Reproduced by permission of the Shakespeare Birthplace Trust
4. Sarah Bernhardt (1899) Reproduced by permission of the Shakespeare Birthplace Trust
5. Directed by Peter Hall (1965) Reg Wilson © Royal Shakespeare Company

6. Directed by Buzz Goodbody (1975) Joe Cocks Studio Collection © Shakespeare Birthplace Trust

7. Directed by Ron Daniels (1989) Joe Cocks Studio Collection © Shakespeare Birthplace Trust

8. Directed by Michael Boyd (2004) Manuel Harlan © Royal Shakespeare Company

9. Directed by Ron Daniels (1989) Joe Cocks Studio Collection © Shakespeare Birthplace Trust

10. Directed by Michael Boyd (2004) Manuel Harlan © Royal Shakespeare Company

11. Reconstructed Elizabethan Playhouse © Charcoalblue

"Thanks to Bate and Rasmussen, we now have a rendering of the complete works that, in a rare publishing achievement, would also give complete satisfaction to the author himself."
- Robert McCrum, The Observer

Also Available:

www.rscshakespeare.co.uk